The Enterprise Business Analyst

DEVELOPING CREATIVE SOLUTIONS TO COMPLEX BUSINESS PROBLEMS

The Enterprise Business Analyst

DEVELOPING CREATIVE SOLUTIONS TO COMPLEX BUSINESS PROBLEMS

KATHLEEN B. HASS, PMP

ſſſ
MANAGEMENT CONCEPTS

MANAGEMENTCONCEPTS

8230 Leesburg Pike, Suite 800
Vienna, VA 22182
(703) 790-9595
Fax: (703) 790-1371
www.managementconcepts.com

Some of the material in this book has been extracted or adapted with permission from:

- *The Art and Power of Facilitation: Running Powerful Meetings* by Alice Zavala, PMP, and Kathleen B. Hass, PMP. Copyright © 2008 by Management Concepts, Inc.
- *Business Analysis Center of Excellence: The Cornerstone of Business Transformation* by Kathleen Hass, PMP, with Richard Avery and Terry Longo. Copyright © 2007 by Management Concepts, Inc.
- *Business Analyst Proficiency: How Capable Do I Need to Be?* Copyright © 2010 by Kathleen Hass and Associates, Inc.
- *From Analyst to Leader: Elevating the Role of the Business Analyst* by Kathleen B. Hass, PMP. Copyright © 2008 by Management Concepts, Inc.
- *From Strategy To Action: Enterprise Portfolio Management* by Kathleen B. Hass, PMP. Copyright © 2008 by Management Concepts, Inc.
- *Managing Complex Projects: A New Model* by Kathleen B. Hass, PMP. Copyright © 2009 by Management Concepts, Inc.
- *Planting the Seeds to Grow a Mature BA Practice,* Copyright © 2010 by Kathleen Hass and Associates, Inc.
- *Professionalizing Business Analysis: Breaking the Cycle of Challenged Projects* by Kathleen B. Hass, PMP. Copyright © 2008 by Management Concepts, Inc.

Printed in the United States of America

Library of Congress Control Number: 2011936401

ISBN 978-1-56726-349-7

10   9   8   7   6   5   4   3   2   1

About the Author

Kathleen (Kitty) B. Hass is a senior practice consultant specializing in strategic planning and execution, enterprise business analysis, and complex project management. She is a prominent presenter at industry conferences and has authored and coauthored eight books on project management and business analysis, including the Business Analysis Essential Library series and *Managing Complex Projects: A New Model*, which was awarded the David I. Cleland Project Management Literature Award by the Project Management Institute in 2009.

Kitty has more than 25 years of experience in project portfolio management, business process reengineering, IT applications development and technology deployment, training and mentoring, and requirements management. She has managed large, complex projects in the airline, telecommunications, retail, and manufacturing industries and for the federal government.

Kitty's consulting experience includes engagements with multiple federal agencies, including USDA, USGS, NARA, and an agency within the intelligence community, as well as industry engagements at Colorado Springs Utilities, Toyota Financial Services, Toyota Motor Sales, the Salt Lake Organizing Committee for the 2002 Olympic Winter Games, New Zealand Ministry of Education, Sun Life Financial, Maco Mutual, Manheim, West Bend Insurance.

Kitty is member of the Board of Directors for the International Institute of Business Analysis (IIBA) and has served as IIBA® Chapter Council Chair and a member of the IIBA Business Analysis Body of Knowledge committee. She holds a BA in business administration, summa cum laude, from Western Connecticut University.

To my wonderful Irish parents, who helped me believe in myself. May God rest their souls.

To my wonderful, supportive, and loving siblings:

Jim, Sally, Debbie, and Bebe. You continue to inspire me.

Contents

Preface

I think the 21st century will be the century of complexity.

—Stephen W. Hawking

I t was a perfect storm. As we entered the second decade of the 21st century, we found ourselves struggling to thrive, and sometimes just to *survive*. All over the world, people faced environmental and economic turbulence, financial calamity, a stubborn recession that seemed to resist recovery, intractable societal troubles, high unemployment, and uncompromising complexity. The fiercely competitive global business ecosystem was changing so rapidly that we were confronted with complicated situations we had never seen before.

It is no coincidence that the business analysis profession is taking hold in the 21st century. Business analysis is all about understanding the needs of organizations, helping them remain competitive, identifying creative solutions to complex business problems, bringing about innovation, and constantly adding value for the customer and revenue to the bottom line. My fear is that business analysis will remain a tactical, project-focused role for too long, and organizations around the world will not leverage the often underestimated and undervalued creative talent that is bottled up in our business analysts.

CREATIVE LEADERSHIP

We know that creative leaders are top performers, but how are they different? It is becoming obvious that we need creative leaders from all areas of the organization, not just one or two individuals at the top who are leading the way. Where is the cadre of creative leaders going to come from? Could business analysts become the creative leaders we need to spark innovation? To be sure, they work with teams and individuals at all levels of their organizations. Our 21st-century challenge is this: to arm business analysts with the knowledge, skill, credibility, and confidence needed to awaken creativity throughout their organizations. We can then calm the storm, at least as it affects our businesses, and look ahead to a dramatic increase in the number of innovative changes set in motion through expertly facilitated creative sessions.

THE BUSINESS ANALYST AS CREATIVE LEADER

What should business analysts be doing to hone their creative aptitude and to foster creativity in their organizations? Business analysts participate in the development of creative leaders across their organizations by deepening partnerships with their stakeholders, especially employees and customers. As they focus on relationships, business needs, operational agility, and innovation at every turn—the hallmark of business analysis—they can instill a universal understanding that everyone is creative. To accept the challenge, business analysts need to learn to be courageous, prepared, and willing to make deep changes to their organizations' business model.

SHARED LEADERSHIP

Project leadership is no longer just about the project manager or even just about the project manager and the business analyst. Combining disciplines leads to success, and complex projects should be led by a highly seasoned, multitalented team consisting of strategic thinkers and creativity enthusiasts. The complex project leadership team ought to comprise the best resources available, including experienced and creative project managers, business analysts, solution architects and developers, and business visionaries. This leadership team collaboratively makes managerial and technical decisions about how to capitalize on the complexities they face. As project success improves, we will all benefit.

WHO WILL BENEFIT FROM READING THIS BOOK?

This book presents a new model for all members of project leadership teams in general, and business analysts specifically, to learn how to capitalize on complexity. It delves deep into the behaviors of business analysts in their functions as expert facilitators and creative leaders and offers guidance not just on managing complexity, but also on leveraging it as a competitive advantage. In addition to business analysts, this book is an important resource for project, program, and portfolio managers; solution architects; business process owners and managers; functional managers; and senior IT technologists.

HOW THIS BOOK IS ORGANIZED

The introduction begins with a look at the current state of the global marketplace. The demands of technology and the global economy have made the business environment more complicated and challenging than ever, ramping up the demand for creative leaders. We then consider the current and future roles of the business analyst and take an early look at how we can unleash the creative potential of business analysts.

PART I: INSIGHTS INTO THE PROFESSION OF BUSINESS ANALYSIS

Part I presents an overview of the business analysis profession as we traverse the second decade of the 21ˢᵗ century. Chapter 1, The Heart of the Matter—An Examination of the Profession of Business Analysis, defines the full reach of the business analysis profession and the role of business analysts as they struggle to find their place in these tumultuous and confusing times.

Chapter 2, The Business Analyst's Role from Strategy Development to Strategy Execution, explores the important and emerging role of business analysis in contemporary business practices by presenting an overview of the business analyst's specific duties, from strategic planning activities through more tactical project-focused tasks, including shepherding requirements throughout the life of a project.

Chapter 3, The Adaptive Business Analyst, examines the striking and at times subtle changes in the business analyst role and activities as projects become more and more complex.

PART II: UNLOCKING THE SECRETS OF CREATIVE LEADERSHIP

In Part II, we explore the mystery of creativity, the secrets to igniting innovation in organizations, and how the business analyst can fill the gap in creative leadership in the business world. In Chapter 4, Creative Leadership: What's All the Fuss About?, we explore leadership models for the 21ˢᵗ century, including the emerging shared leadership model that can help organizations deal successfully with complexity and uncertainty. We present the case for the business analyst becoming a critical member of complex project leadership teams, focusing on the business analyst's role as change agent, visionary, and credible leader.

Chapter 5, Fostering Team Creativity: The Business Analyst's Sweet Spot, presents the case for developing teams and fostering team creativity, using both time-tested and contemporary practices. We explore creative problem-solving and decision-making and present multiple techniques to incite creativity in team sessions.

Chapter 6, Igniting Creativity in Complex Distributed Teams, discusses the complexities associated with large, diverse teams. We present several strategies to consider when managing diverse teams and suggest ways to cultivate creativity and innovation in multisite teams.

Chapter 7, Creativity-Inducing Facilitation, presents an array of tools and techniques to ignite creativity at all levels of the organization.

Chapter 8, Creatively Eliciting and Evolving Breakthrough Requirements, presents best practices for planning and managing requirements elicitation sessions and for visualizing requirements to ensure understanding.

PART III: STRATEGIES TO FOSTER INNOVATION

In Part III, we explore the complex world of smart products and the complexity-management strategies available to us when leading innovation teams. Chapter 9, Developing Products for Competitive Advantage, explores the nature of innovative products, which often rely on software as the discriminator. We discuss best practices for innovative product development, recognizing the complexity of IT-intensive product development.

Chapter 10, Strategies to Foster Innovation, presents the case for the business analyst to become a major player in helping companies become innovation-driven organizations.

Chapter 11, Communication Strategies to Enable Innovation, explores strategic communication strategies to arm the business analyst and other project team leaders with the tools needed to secure management's support and approval.

PART IV: INNOVATION-DRIVEN BUSINESS PRACTICES

In Part IV, we examine ways in which business analysts and organizations can further develop business analysis capability and maturity. In Chapter 12, How Capable Do Business Analysts Need to Be to Ignite Creativity? we provide guidance to business analysts preparing an approach to their own professional development, which can help create enterprise- and innovation-driven analysts.

In Chapter 13, Building a Mature, Innovation-Driven Business Analysis Practice, we describe the elements needed to build a mature BA practice that focuses on innovation. Within such a practice, business requirements are managed, business needs are met, strategy is executed, and business and technology are optimized such that technology becomes a competitive advantage.

Chapter 14, Innovation-Driven Management, examines the elements of an innovation-driven portfolio management practice that leads to competitive advantage.

In Chapter 15, The Business Analysis Center of Excellence: The Cornerstone of Business Transformation and Innovation, we propose implementation of an innovation-driven enterprise center of excellence that works collaboratively to leverage the best practices of both business analysis and complex project management disciplines.

Kathleen (Kitty) Hass
September 2011

Introduction

I n the first decade of the 21st century, as the profession of business analysis was just coming of age, the global economic crisis served as a wake-up call. In his introduction to the 2010 Global CEO Study, Samuel J. Palmisano, chairman, president, and chief executive officer of IBM Corporation, said that the biggest challenge CEOs are facing is the network of complexities brought about by the Internet and the global economy. CEOs in the study said their organizations are not equipped to effectively manage this uncompromising complexity because they do not have the creative leaders they need.

> *What we heard . . . is that events, threats and opportunities aren't just coming at us faster or with less predictability; they are converging and influencing each other to create entirely unique situations. These firsts-of-their-kind developments require unprecedented degrees of creativity—which has become a more important leadership quality than attributes like management discipline, rigor or operational acumen.*[1]

What does this alarming level of complexity and the need for extraordinarily creative leaders have to do with the emerging discipline of business analysis? If indeed we are faced with a competitive and economic environment unlike anything that has come before, and if enterprises today are not equipped to cope effectively with this complexity in the global environment, and if business analysis is all about understanding the needs of organizations to remain competitive, then it seems as if the gale-force global economic winds are causing two new business disciplines to converge: *business analysis* and *complex project management*. And there is a new leadership role that might well be filled by the *enterprise business analyst*, a leader focused on business/technology optimization through the development of innovative solutions. The business analyst's leadership is a strategic resource that, if used appropriately, can unleash in organizations around the globe the innovation and creativity needed to meet 21st century challenges.

THE LOOMING STORM

In the face of rising complexity and multifaceted and multilayered problems, the pressure to perform is greater than ever. Those who acquire and master business analysis capabilities will more effectively react to and preempt changes in the marketplace, capitalize on complexity, and flow value through the enterprise to the customer, thus remaining competitive. Today, we struggle to operate in a web of organizational relationships and interconnected systems. The emergence of the global economic and information network and the transition from labor-based to information-based organizations is marginalizing our traditional hierarchical structures, often replacing them with virtual sets of connections and partnerships. Businesses are rejecting traditional management organizations to create complex communities comprising alliances with strategic suppliers, networks of customers, and partnerships with key political groups, regulatory entities, and even competitors. Business processes and supporting technology have become more interconnected, interdependent, and interrelated than ever before.

We are in the middle of a transformation that is creating turmoil and disorder while companies are struggling to leverage the dynamics of the new economy: new business models, unprecedented change, unparalleled complexity, rapid innovation, and new leadership capabilities to convert strategic business needs into innovative products and services.

NEW BUSINESS MODELS

Noted futurists Don Tapscott and Anthony Williams, authors of the book Wikinomics, predict the rise of "mass collaboration" as the new business model that will replace the current corporate model. While this may not be the case, the conventional wisdom about how best to organize business must be rethought and reexamined. "We have both a need and an opportunity to devise a new form of economic organization, and a new science of management, that can deal with the breakneck realities of 21st century change," Tapscott and Williams write. Our 21st century business models must be "more like the marketplace and less like corporations of the past. [Business] will need to be flexible, agile, able to quickly adjust to market developments, and ruthless in reallocating resources to new opportunities."[2]

In the face of the radical changes that are needed, we are falling behind: 63 percent of IT professionals say the United States has lost its position as a global IT innovation leader. Among the top reasons cited for the decline:

➤ Offshoring of jobs

➤ Failure of the U.S. educational system to prepare students in science, technology, engineering, math, creativity, problem solving, and critical and systems thinking

➤ Lack of a cohesive national policy in technology areas (mobile payments, smart electricity grids, transportation systems, green computing)

➤ Dearth of technology leadership at the executive level.[3]

UNPRECEDENTED CHANGE

According to the *Wall Street Journal*, "We are in an economic climate where decades-old corporations like Lehman Brothers and Bear Sterns can disappear overnight, while new ones like Google and Twitter can spring up from nowhere."[4]

In the midst of this chaos, organizations are addressing the pressures of whirlwind change, global competition, time-to-market compression, rapidly changing technologies, corporate inertia, and yes, uncompromising complexity. Business systems and consumer products are significantly more complex than in the past, and for many reasons the projects that implement them are also exceedingly complex. To reap the rewards of significant, large-scale business/technology innovations designed to not only keep organizations in the game but make them a major player, we must find new ways to not just harness but to capitalize on complexity.

UNPARALLELED COMPLEXITY

In IBM studies conducted at the turn of the 21st century, CEOs consistently said that coping with unrelenting change was their most pressing challenge. While change management is still a major problem, the conversations with CEOs in the 2010 IBM study indicated that complexity was their primary challenge. CEOs reported that they operate in a world that is substantially more volatile, uncertain, and complex than ever before. Many shared the view that incremental changes are no longer sufficient in a world that is operating in fundamentally different ways and at Internet speed. The 2010 IBM study revealed that organizations are faced with an extraordinary combination of pressures to deliver increased revenue in traditional terms (through added profits, avoided costs, lower taxes, higher productivity, less employee turnover, less risk exposure) and to constantly generate brand-new revenue channels and sources of customer value to continue to thrive. They cannot rely on simply offering more of the same.[5]

Not only are we facing systemic complexity, the very nature of change itself is changing. According to consultant Jonathan Wilson, "It is happening not just more quickly, but faster than ever. It is happening in new ways with more turbulence, less predictability. The key cause of the changing of change in business is the acceleration of the flow of information and the exponential increase in the number of connections within and between organizations."[6]

RAPID INNOVATION

Competitive advantage is now coupled with an organization's ability to rapidly innovate and to change products and systems quickly as the marketplace changes. Information technology (IT) has finally come into its own and is now viewed as a critical component of innovation. Business change initiatives must not only deliver high-quality products faster, better, and cheaper (traditionally the responsibility of the project manager), they are also under intense scrutiny to positively impact the bottom line (increasingly, the joint responsibility of the project sponsor and the business analyst).

Clay Christensen's book *The Innovator's Dilemma* documents many examples of decades-old companies failing because they missed "game-changing transformation in industry after industry—computers (mainframes to PCs), telephony (landline to mobile), photography (film to digital), stock markets (floor to online)—not because of 'bad' management, but because they followed the dictates of 'good management.'"[7] The strategy consultant Gary Hamel tells us that big companies fail "not necessarily because they didn't see the coming innovations, but because they failed to adequately invest in those innovations." Hamel contends that companies that control large pools of capital need to act more like venture capitalists. And workers at all levels will need to really feel a drive toward creativity and innovation.[8] One obvious example of a company that is doing this is Google. To foster innovation, Google engineers spend 20 percent of their time working on projects other than their current assignments.

NEW LEADERSHIP CAPABILITIES

In their quest to build the organizational capabilities needed to invest in innovation projects, organizations have discovered that the core competency of business analysis must be elevated in importance. Most organizations have invested handsomely in IT systems to help operate the business and capture business intelligence about the marketplace. Over the last two decades, organizations have also embraced the practice of professional project management. However, businesses are just now beginning to understand the importance of the leadership capabilities needed to convert strategic business needs into innovative products and services, to operate with speed and agility, and to try more disruptive approaches than ever before.

THE ENTERPRISE BUSINESS ANALYST

According to a Forrester Research study,[9] business analysts in the first decade of the 21st century were mostly tactical and were either IT or business focused. The IT-oriented business analysts strove to improve operations through changes in technology and were mostly generalists, though specialist roles were emerging, e.g., process analysts and data analysts. At the same time, the business-oriented business analysts worked to improve operations through changes to policy and process, using techniques such as Six Sigma and business process improvement. These analysts were mostly functionally focused, improving departmental operations such as finance, marketing, or human resources.

The Forrester study also revealed that the industry will begin to groom and field more strategic business analysts, driving business analysis practice maturity from a focus on tactical efforts to more strategic endeavors. Emerging strategic enterprise-level business analyst roles include enterprise analysts, business architects, and business/technology analysts. (These roles are detailed in Chapter 1.) The enterprise analyst, the business architect, and the business/technology analyst are the future creative leaders CEOs are making every effort to find. The hallmark of these strategic analysts is not just understanding the business need but fulfilling it, not through incremental change, but through game-changing innovation and creativity.

UNLEASHING THE CREATIVE POTENTIAL OF THE BUSINESS ANALYST

Since there appears to be an insatiable demand for innovative products, services, business systems, and supporting applications, executives across the spectrum are adopting the practice of business analysis to increase the value innovative initiatives bring to customers and to the business. As we begin to understand that the root cause of far too many failed and challenged projects is our inability to manage complexity (see Figure I-1), we conclude that the talents, competencies, and heroics of project managers and technologists alone cannot drive innovation in these demanding times.

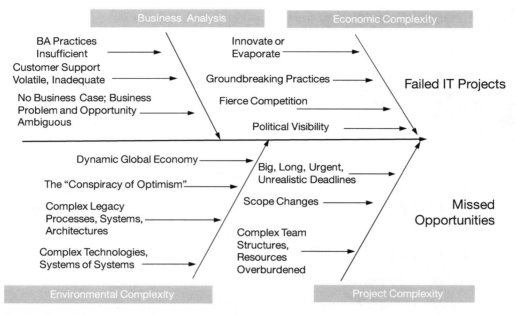

FIGURE I-1. Why Businesses Cannot Manage Complexity

© 2011 By Kathleen B. Hass and Associates, Inc.

THE PROFESSIONAL BUSINESS ANALYST

For business needs and goals to be converted into innovative solutions that truly bring wealth to the enterprise, a stronger partnership must be built between the business, its partners, technologists, and the ultimate customer. That partnership is built by employing the practices of professional business analysis before and during the development of innovative solutions.

The CEOs of better-performing companies manage complexity on behalf of their organizations, customers, and partners. These CEOs have long recognized the need for innovation. But somehow they failed to acquire or groom the creative leaders needed to ignite creativity to negotiate the new economy. Organizations that successfully unleash the potential of innovation-focused strategic business analysts are learning how to not just *manage* complexity, but also to *capitalize* on complexity.

CAPITALIZING ON COMPLEXITY

According to the 2010 IBM report, winning CEOs and their teams are focusing on three transformational courses of action to capitalize on complexity.

The effects of rising complexity call for CEOs and their teams to lead with bold creativity, connect with customers in imaginative ways and design their operations for speed and flexibility to position their organizations for twenty-first century success.... To capitalize on complexity, CEOs....

Embody creative leadership. CEOs now realize that creativity trumps other leadership characteristics. Creative leaders are comfortable with ambiguity and experimentation. To connect with and inspire a new generation, they lead and interact in entirely new ways....

Reinvent customer relationships. Customers have never had so much information or so many options. CEOs are making "getting connected" to customers their highest priority to better predict and provide customers with what they really want....

Build operational dexterity. CEOs are mastering complexity in countless ways. They are redesigning operating strategies for ultimate speed and flexibility. They embed... complexity [that creates value] in elegantly simple products, services and customer interactions.[10]

STANDOUT ORGANIZATIONS

An organization that embraces the roles of strategic business analysts (business architects, enterprise business analysts, strategy analysts, and business/technology analysts) to fill the void in creative leadership will produce the advances needed to succeed and become a *standout organization,* one that consistently delivers solid financial results even in economic downturns, has a revenue growth five or six times higher than its peers, and plans to get at least 20 percent of revenues from new sources. The IBM CEO study revealed that standout organizations have learned how to consistently mitigate complexity and convert it to opportunity by:

➤ Navigating complexity superbly by tolerating change and adapting to it

➤ Upsetting the status quo

➤ Having confidence in their capabilities to prosper from complexity

➤ Making decisions quickly, testing them in the market, and then making required course corrections

➤ Pursuing iterative, ongoing strategy, requirements, and solution development

➤ Reinventing their business analysis model often to adapt to lessons learned

➤ Seeding creativity across their organizations.[11]

BUILDING A CORPS OF CREATIVE LEADERS

Creativity is the premier skill requirement for the innovation-focused leader. Creativity is defined as the ability to generate innovative ideas and concepts and then to produce something original and useful. The process involves original thinking and then creating—generating something new. In creative thinking, there is not just one right answer.

According to creativity experts, "to be creative involves *divergent thinking* (generating many unique ideas) and then *convergent thinking* (combining those ideas into the best result)."[12] But even creativity is not enough; our competitive climate calls for us to be *purposefully disruptive*, to continually reinvent our business model and our products and to foster bold, breakthrough thinking.

THE CREATIVE PROCESS

The creative process calls for us to keep going when surrounded by uncertainty and ambiguity by doing lots of experimentation, prototyping possible solutions, engaging in out-of-the-box thinking, testing ideas through trial and error, and keeping options open until the last responsible moment. Top creative performers exhibit "unusual visual perspective . . . an ability to synthesize diverse elements into meaningful products."[13]

The CEOs who participated in the IBM study stressed the relationship between integrity and creativity, the need for global thinking, and a strong focus on customers.[14] It is important for organizations striving to mature the role of the strategic business analyst into that of a strategic innovator to identify strategic thinkers early and groom them as quickly as possible to unleash their creativity. Figure I-2 shows several of the functions of creative business analysts.

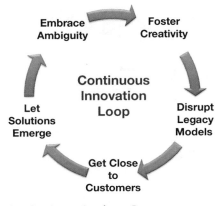

FIGURE I-2. What Creative Business Analysts Do

Business analysts must possess special attributes to become innovation leaders and to be able to defy complexity with creativity. They must be action and outcome oriented, as well as focused and courageous. You will know them when you see them:

➤ Sharing the project leadership role with the project manager

➤ Creating and leading innovative requirements-integration teams

➤ Influencing, swaying, and persuading groups and individuals

➤ Embracing uncertainty and ambiguity

➤ Taking risks that disrupt legacy models

➤ Rejecting traditional management styles

➤ Getting close to customers; bringing customers into the process

➤ Using cost-benefits trade-offs based on customer needs.

ORGANIZATIONAL CREATIVITY

So what does creativity look like in organizations? Creativity in the context of standout organizations is about *creative leadership*—that is, the ability to shed long-held beliefs and come up with original and at times radical concepts and execution. It requires bold, breakthrough thinking. It isn't about having one or two lone creative leaders at the top, but rather about creating a plethora of creative leaders by igniting the collective creativity of the organization from the bottom up.[15]

Based on their 50 years of collective experience working with creative leaders worldwide, Navi Radjou, Jaideep Prabhu, Prasad Kaipa, and Simone Ahuja have developed some questions business analysts should address to help their organizations identify creative leaders who can cope with increasing complexity. We present these here to get your creative juices going.

➤ What cultural, political, organizational, and technological barriers should your organization overcome if it has to develop a cadre of creative leaders?

➤ What structures, reward systems, processes, metrics, and goals do you have in place to support creative leaders?

➤ How do you encourage risk taking and learning from failure? How do you measure it?

➤ Do you simply adopt best practices learned from industry leaders, or do you shape "next practices" that will make your organization the leader in the future?

➤ How effective are you in partnering with customers, suppliers, employees, and even your competition to improvise "good enough" solutions?[16]

PUTTING IT ALL TOGETHER: WHAT DOES THIS MEAN TO THE BUSINESS ANALYST?

Because the 21st century is rife with complexity, we need to learn how to leverage it—use it to our advantage. As the business analyst transitions from a tactical project-focused resource to an innovation-focused strategic asset, our organizations will begin to capitalize on the complexity that often leaves us baffled, perplexed, and challenged. It is no surprise that two new important disciplines are coming to life in the 21st century and spawning new roles: the complex project manager (CPM) and the enterprise business analyst (EBA). As these disciplines mature, CPMs and EBAs will form collaborative partnerships in their quest to defy complexity with creativity. This book focuses on the new creativity-focused enterprise business analyst.

NOTES

1. IBM Corporation, "Capitalizing on Complexity: Insights from the Global Chief Executive Officer Study," 2010. Online at http://public.dhe.ibm.com/common/ssi/ecm/en/gbe03297usen/GBE03297USEN.PDF (accessed May 2011): 4.

2. Alan Murray, "The End of Management," *The Wall Street Journal Essential Guide to Management* (New York: HarperCollins, 2010). Online at http://www.honestconversation.com/resources/About-Us/The-End-of-Management---WSJ.com.pdf (accessed May 2011): 4.

3. InformationWeek Analytics, "Research: Innovation Mandate," August 2010. Online at http://www.informationweek.com/news/global-cio/227600039 (accessed May 2011).

4. Murray, 4.

5. IBM Corporation, 9, 13, 37, and 51.

6. Jonathan Wilson, "No Plans for the Future," *Measuring Business Excellence* 3, no. 3 (1999). Online at http://www.trojanmice.com/articles/noplans.htm (accessed July 2010).

7. E.G. Insight Blog, "Listening with an Ear For Innovation," which quotes Clay Christensen in *The Innovator's Dilemma: The Revolutionary Book that Will Change the Way You Do Business* (New York: HarperCollins, 2003). Online at http://www.eginsight.com/news/2010/08/listening-with-an-ear-for-innovation (accessed May 2011).

8. Murray, 4.

9. Carey Schwaber, Rob Karel, and Forrester Research, Inc., "The New Business Analyst," April 8, 2008. Online at http://www.forrester.com/rb/Research/new_business_analyst/q/id/43178/t/2 (accessed April 2011).

10. IBM Corporation, 9, 13, 37, and 51.

11. IBM Corporation.

12. Po Bronson and Ashley Merryman, "The Creativity Crisis," *Newsweek* (July 19, 2010): 45. Online at http://www.newsweek.com/2010/07/10/the-creativity-crisis.html (accessed April 2011).

13. Ibid.

14. IBM Corporation, 9.

15. Navi Radjou, Jaideep Prabhu, Prasad Kaipa, and Simone Ahuja, "How To Ignite Creative Leadership In Your Organization," *Harvard Business Review* Blogs (May 19, 2010). Online at http://blogs.hbr.org/cs/2010/05/how_to_ignite_creative_leaders.html (accessed July 2010).

16. Ibid.

Insights into the Profession of Business Analysis

n the first part of this book, we examine the foundational elements of the business analysis profession. The creative business analyst/leader will base his or her practice on these elements.

- ➤ In Chapter 1, we first look into the building blocks of the business analysis profession that have taken hold around the world, as well as the nature of the business analyst role.

- ➤ In Chapter 2, we examine the subtle and not-so-subtle ways the business analyst's activities change as she transitions from strategic activities to more tactical project-focused activities throughout the life of a project.

- ➤ In Chapter 3, we scrutinize the emerging understanding of business and project complexity and look at how the business analyst adapts her leadership style and methods as projects become more complex.

CHAPTER 1

The Heart of the Matter—An Examination of the Profession of Business Analysis

Let's begin by examining the entire scope of the business analysis profession and the business analyst (BA) role. The emergence of business analysis practices began in the 1980s when businesses turned their attention to improving software requirements and streamlining processes. By the early 21st century, a number of large companies that already had substantial business analysis practices called for common standards. This led to the creation of the International Institute of Business Analysis (IIBA) in 2003 (www.theiiba.org). IIBA is the fast-growing, independent, nonprofit professional association serving the field of business analysis. It is dedicated to advancing the professionalism of the occupation.

IIBA members comprise individuals with various titles who fill a diverse set of roles: requirements engineers, business systems analysts, quality analysts, requirements analysts, project managers, technical architects, business architects, developers, consultants—really anyone involved in analysis for systems, business, or process improvement designed to add value to an organization.

A WORD TO THE WISE

Join IIBA and your local IIBA chapter to help advance the profession. Both the international organization and local chapters offer a wealth of professional development activities to help you become a professional business analyst.

DEFINING BUSINESS ANALYSIS

IIBA has developed a standard definition and role delineation for business analysis, underscoring its emergence as a formal occupation. Since this book is about business analysis leadership, we will consistently emphasize the strategic, creative leadership role of the business analyst. As you read the definition of business analysis, note the reference to defining organizational goals and determining courses of action to achieve the goals, both very strategic in nature. IIBA defines business analysis as:

> *The set of tasks and techniques used to work as a liaison among stakeholders in order to understand the structure, policies and operations of an organization, and recommend solutions that enable the organization to achieve its goals.*

> *Business analysis involves understanding how organizations function to accomplish their purposes, and defining the capabilities an organization requires to provide products and services to external stakeholders. It includes the definition of organization goals, how those goals connect to specific objectives, determining the course of action that an organization has to undertake to achieve those goals and objectives, and defining how the various organizational units and stakeholders within and outside that organization interact.*[1]

CODIFYING BUSINESS ANALYSIS

IIBA has codified the profession in its *Guide to the Business Analysis Body of Knowledge® (BABOK® Guide).*[2] The IIBA website describes the *BABOK® Guide* as:

> *The collection of knowledge within the profession of Business Analysis and reflects current generally accepted practices. As with other professions, the body of knowledge is defined and enhanced by the Business Analysis professionals who apply it in their daily work role. The BABOK® Guide describes Business Analysis areas of knowledge, their associated activities and the tasks and skills necessary to be effective in their execution. The BABOK® Guide is a reference for professional knowledge for Business Analysis and provides the basis for the Certified Business Analysis Professional™ (CBAP®) Certification.*[3]

Figure 1-1 lists knowledge areas and associated activities covered in the *BABOK® Guide.*

Knowledge Areas	Purpose
Business Analysis Planning and Monitoring	Determine what we need to do
Enterprise Analysis	Understand the business problem and the scope of possible solutions
Elicitation	Find out what the real needs of our stakeholders are
Requirements Analysis	Describe the characteristics and qualities of the solution that meets stakeholder needs
Solutions Assessment and Validation	Determine whether a particular solution is right for our stakeholders
Requirements Management and Communications	Ensure that stakeholders agree on what needs to be delivered

FIGURE 1-1. *BABOK® Guide* Knowledge Areas

In particular, the enterprise analysis activities present the business analyst with the chance, indeed the responsibility, to create and innovate. Per the *BABOK® Guide*:

> *Enterprise Analysis describes the business analysis activities necessary to identify a business need, problem, or opportunity, define the nature of a solution that meets that need, and justify the investment necessary to deliver that solution . . . . It describes the business analysis activities that take place for organizations to:*

➤ Analyze the business situation in order to fully understand business problems and opportunities

➤ Assess the capabilities of the enterprise in order to understand the change needed to meet business needs and achieve strategic goals

➤ Determine the most feasible business solution approach

➤ Define the solution scope and develop the business case for the proposed solution

➤ Define and document business requirements.[4]

A WORD TO THE WISE

Join a study group sponsored by your local IIBA chapter. Certification instills in your current and future employers confidence in your business analysis knowledge and skills.

CERTIFYING BUSINESS ANALYSTS

IIBA has also developed a Business Analyst Certification Program unique to the profession of business analysis. Establishing a certification for business analysis has helped standardize and professionalize the practice of business analysis. Certification creates common expectations for organizations of the knowledge, skills, and competencies certified business analysts must acquire.

As of this writing, there are two certification levels. Both designations require candidates to make a robust commitment to professional development and to adhere to the code of conduct for business analysts. The two certification levels are described below.

CERTIFIED BUSINESS ANALYSIS PROFESSIONAL™ (CBAP®)

This designation is awarded to candidates who have successfully demonstrated their business analysis expertise. This certification is awarded to business analysts who have documented their work experience in business analysis through the CBAP application process and have passed the IIBA CBAP examination. An individual must have accumulated five years of relevant work experience within ten years before he or she can apply to become a Certified Business Analysis Professional. CBAPs are experts in identifying the business needs of an enterprise to determine the best solutions, a role that is increasingly seen as a vital component of any standout organization. More and more companies are recognizing the CBAP designation and the value and expertise that these professionals bring to bear.

CERTIFICATION OF COMPETENCY IN BUSINESS ANALYSIS™ (CCBA™)

This intermediate-level certification is for professionals who wish to expand their career options and obtain recognition for their ongoing investment in their professional development. This certification was launched in 2010, with the first candidates writing the CCBA exam in 2011. The certification benefits organizations that need to signal to their stakeholders that their business analysts have gained significant knowledge of best practices and standards in the field. The certification process itself also offers employers the opportunity to assess staff competencies and recognize employees' professional achievement and commitment to excellence. Candidates can apply for the CCBA designation after they have accumulated about two and a half years of business analysis experience within the past seven years.

All certified business analysts gain proficiency in areas of knowledge outlined in the *BABOK® Guide*. However, professionals with the intermediate CCBA certification are expected to apply their skills to smaller-scope and less complex tasks than those with the more rigorous CBAP designation. Details on how to obtain either designation can be found in the certification section of the IIBA website (www.theiiba.org).

THE BUSINESS ANALYST COMPETENCY MODEL

IIBA has developed the world's most comprehensive Business Analysis Competency Model for assessing the ability of business analysts to successfully fulfill the role. It covers knowledge, skills, and behaviors and describes the qualities that can make a business analyst successful. Per the IIBA, "The Competency Model is different from the *BABOK® Guide* in that while the guide outlines the work a business analyst performs and details the knowledge required to perform that work, the model provides a method for identifying what behaviors make a BA successful in performing the activities outlined in the *BABOK®*."[5]

BUILDING A MATURE BUSINESS ANALYSIS PRACTICE

The following elements are essential in building a mature BA practice:

➤ An acknowledgement of the value of business analysis as a critical business practice

➤ A competent BA workforce

➤ Effective business analysis methods, tools, and support

➤ A BA center of excellence that establishes and maintains the practice.

Figure 1-2 depicts how the elements fit into an overall framework.

FIGURE 1-2.   The Framework of a Mature BA Practice

© 2011 By Kathleen B. Hass and Associates, Inc.

THE BUSINESS ANALYST ROLE: BOTH TACTICAL AND STRATEGIC

Given that business analysis is a relatively new profession, varied opinions and interpretations exist of the purpose and importance of business analysis. Some organizations restrict the practice to the process of requirements management: gathering requirements from the customer; structuring requirements by classes or categories; evaluating requirements for selected qualities; modeling requirements to further represent their relationships; decomposing requirements into more detail; finalizing requirements in the form of documents, models, diagrams, matrices, and tables; and then managing subsequent changes to the requirements. Others broaden the definition to include very different but related fields such as financial analysis, quality assurance, organizational development, solution testing, training, and documenting business policies and procedures. Indeed, in many organizations individuals fulfill multiple project roles concurrently, while being dubbed the project or systems manager. These roles may include the responsibilities of project manager, technical lead, *and* requirements manager.

As the profession matures, the business world is realizing that it needs business analysts who operate at multiple levels. While companies need innovation experts to break new ground, they also need more tactically focused business analysts who concentrate on business operations continuity and incremental improvements to products, business processes, and applications.

Less seasoned business analysts typically work at the operations level, while very senior business analysts are more strategically focused. Not everyone can be creative enough to become a strategic enterprise business analyst charged with converting opportunities into innovative products and services. However, for organizations to remain healthy and to stand out among their peers, they need business analysts operating at four levels, each with its own business focus, as shown in Figure 1-3.[6]

Business Operations Enhanced	Business Objectives Met	Business Strategy Executed	New Business Strategy Forged
Operations/Support Focus	Project Focus	Enterprise Focus	Competitive Focus
PROJECTS	**PROJECTS**	**PROJECTS**	**PROJECTS**
Low-complexity projects that continually enhance business processes, products, and/or technology	Moderately complex new development projects that improve business processes, products, and/or technology	Highly complex programs and portfolios that improve multiple business processes, products, and/or technology	Innovation projects that improve competitive advantage and translate strategy into breakthrough processes and technology
OUTCOMES	**OUTCOMES**	**OUTCOMES**	**OUTCOMES**
Value of operational business process and systems is continually enhanced	Business requirements and project scope are managed to ensure new solutions meet business objectives	The enterprise is investing in the most valuable initiatives and is realizing the business benefits forecasted in the business case	New strategies, optimized business/technology, and improved competitive position
TYPE OF LEADER	**TYPE OF LEADER**	**TYPE OF LEADER**	**TYPE OF LEADER**
Generalists, business/system specialists, product managers	Business domain experts, IT system experts	Enterprise change experts, business architects	Strategists, business/technology optimization experts, innovation and cultural change experts, research and development
Entry-level and senior BAs	Entry-level and senior BAs	Senior and enterprise BAs	Enterprise and business/technology optimization BAs

Continuous Advancement of Competence, Credibility, and Influence

FIGURE 1-3. BA Workforce Capability Model

THE OPERATIONS-/SUPPORT-FOCUSED BUSINESS ANALYST

Level 1 includes both generalist analysts and business system analysts. These business analysts are tactically focused, ensuring business operations are maintained and continually improved. They typically spend about 30 percent of their time doing business analysis activities for low-complexity projects designed to maintain and continually improve business processes and technology. In their remaining time, they may fulfill other roles, including project manager, developer, engineer, subject matter expert (SME), domain expert, and tester. As legacy processes and systems age, these business analysts are becoming more and more valuable, since they are likely the best (and often only) SMEs who fully understand the legacy operational processes and technology. As application modernization efforts emerge, these BAs are invaluable, working closely with business architects to document the current state of the business supported by the applications undergoing modernization. Operations- or support-focused BAs may be entry-level, intermediate, or senior-level analysts.

A WORD TO THE WISE

Regardless of the focus of your work assignments, strive to remove yourself from transactional, tactical thinking and look at the entire system you are supporting, including customers and users, products and services, business processes, business rules, data, application systems, and technologies. Prioritize your work based on its value to the customer and the wealth it will bring to the organization. And make every effort to bring about innovation, not just conduct business as usual.

THE PROJECT-FOCUSED BUSINESS ANALYST

Level 2 analysts include both IT- and business-oriented analysts who work on moderately complex projects designed to develop new/changed products, services, business processes, and IT systems to meet business objectives. Similar to operations analysts, project-focused analysts may be entry level, intermediate, and senior level. Typically, these BAs come in two types:

➤ IT-oriented analysts who improve business results through changes to technology. These are mostly generalists; specialists include experience analysts, business rules analysts, business process analysts, and data analysts.

➤ Business-oriented analysts who improve operations through changes to policy and procedures. Business-oriented analysts are mostly specialized, functionally focused on finance, human resources, marketing, manufacturing, among other business areas. In decentralized organizations, these analysts are dedicated to a major business area, improving the processes and the corresponding technologies that are used to run the operations. In more centralized organizations, these business analysts are organized as a pool of talent whose efforts can be transferred seamlessly to the areas of the enterprise that are in most need of business analysis support.

THE ENTERPRISE-FOCUSED BUSINESS ANALYST

At this level, the business analyst is focused on strategy execution. Level 3 includes enterprise analysts and business architects who are operating across the enterprise. Business architects make the enterprise visible and keep the business and IT architecture in sync. Enterprise analysts ensure that the business analysis activities are dedicated to the most valuable initiatives and that the business analysis assets (such as models, documents, matrices, and diagrams) are considered corporate property, are secured and managed as part of the enterprise architecture, and are therefore reusable. Enterprise analysts focus on the analysis needed to prepare a solid business case for innovative initiatives that will transform the enterprise into a highly competitive, standout organization. Partnering with complex-project managers, these analysts work on highly complex enterprise-wide projects. It is at this level that the creative skills of the business analyst begin to give birth to innovation. Enterprise-focused BAs are typically very senior-level, seasoned analysts.

THE COMPETITIVE-FOCUSED BUSINESS/TECHNOLOGY ANALYST

Business analysts with a competitive focus usually function as enterprise analysts, strategists, or business/technology analysts. These BAs are recognized business domain and technology visionaries who serve as innovation experts, organizational change specialists, and cross-domain experts. They are concerned with nothing less than the future viability of the organization. They convert business opportunities to innovative business solutions, turning new products or services and even new business processes into sources of competitive advantage, and they translate strategy into breakthrough process and technology. Their focus is outside the enterprise; they look at what is happening in the industry, formulate the future vision and strategy, and design innovative new approaches to doing business to ensure the enterprise remains competitive or even leaps ahead of the competition.

BUSINESS ANALYSIS IN PRACTICE

The goal of an effective business analysis practice that serves the organization at all four levels is threefold (see Figure 1-4):

Chart the Course	Stay the Course	The Finish Line and Beyond
• Business architecture • Opportunity analysis • Problem analysis • Solution feasibility analysis • Business case development • Solution assessment and validation	• Planning • Elicitation • Definition • Analysis • Specification • Validation • Change management • Communication	• Organizational readiness • Organizational change management • Business artifacts: business policies, procedures, rules, training, retooling, restructuring • Benefits measurement and management
Enterprise Analysis	**Requirements Management**	**Organizational Change**

FIGURE 1-4. The Goals of Business Analysis

1. ***Implement rigorous enterprise analysis practices.*** The strategic business analyst ensures his organization is investing in the most valuable projects and is building innovative solutions to business problems and opportunities.

2. ***Implement effective requirements management practices.*** This is the role most often associated with the business analyst: eliciting, documenting, and managing changes to requirements.

3. ***Conduct meticulous organizational change management practices.*** This is the area project teams most often forget.

RIGOROUS ENTERPRISE ANALYSIS PRACTICES

Enterprise analysis activities are consistently shortchanged, underfunded, and underutilized. But these practices are paramount if an organization is to remain competitive and become a standout organization. Enterprise analysis activities include but are not limited to the following:

➤ Building the current- and future-state business architecture

➤ Conducting rigorous opportunity analysis and problem analysis with a small expert team to ensure understanding of the business need

➤ Conducting feasibility analysis with a small expert team to identify the most feasible solution to propose

➤ Developing a business case with a small expert team to propose a new project to build the solution

➤ Continually validating the assumptions and forecasts made in the business case throughout the project

➤ Conducting solution assessment and validation throughout the project

➤ Measuring the business benefits of the deployed solution compared with the forecasts in the business case.

EFFECTIVE REQUIREMENTS MANAGEMENT PRACTICES

Requirements management activities are the typical, tactically focused endeavours in which business analysts engage on a daily basis. They include but are not limited to the following:

➤ Planning the requirements approach and activities

➤ Eliciting requirements using multiple elicitation techniques and validating elicitation results

➤ Defining and specifying requirements using multiple techniques (e.g., text, models, tables, matrices)

➤ Analyzing requirements to ensure they are accurate, complete, and testable

➤ Validating that the requirements meet the business need throughout the project

➤ Managing changes to requirements; welcoming changes that add business value; reducing the cost of change through iterative development

➤ Communicating requirements using custom messages for each stakeholder.

THOROUGH CHANGE MANAGEMENT PRACTICES

Change management activities that are vital for a successful transformation effort are often overlooked, but more and more, organizations are looking to their business analysts to help manage the cultural and organizational changes needed to successfully deploy a significant change. These change management practices include but are not limited to the following:

➤ Ensuring the organization is ready to operate the new business solution efficiently and effectively

➤ Managing the organizational change required to ensure the new business solution is operated efficiently and effectively

➤ Developing the necessary business artifacts: business policies, procedures, rules, training, retooling, restructuring

➤ Implementing an effective benefits measurement and management system for the new solution.

A BUSINESS ANALYSIS PRACTICE MATURITY MODEL

In 2010, my business partner, Lori Lindbergh, and I researched the current state of business analysis practices using a proprietary business analysis practice maturity model (see Figure 1-5).[7] The purpose of this

Technology Used as a
Competitive Advantage

Business Needs Met/
Strategy Executed

4

Business/Technology
Innovation

Business Requirements
Managed

3

Business
Alignment

2

BA
Framework

BA Value
Acknowledged

1

BA
Awareness

Competitive Focus

Customer relationship mgt.

Opportunities converted into innovative business solutions

Strategy translated into breakthrough process and technology

Cultural change **mgt.**

Strategy development standards:
- Visioning and strategic planning
- Innovation and research and development

BACOE manages innovation and research and development

Innovation training

BA career path leading to strategic **BAs**

CBAP®:
- Business/technology analysts

Enterprise Focus

Customer satisfaction

Business architecture

Organizational change mgt.

Benefits metrics

BABOK® standards:
- Enterprise analysis
- Solution assessment and validation

Integrated BA/PM/ QA/SDLC COE: portfolio mgt., standards, resources, contractors

Business alignment training

BA career path to VP of **BAs**

CBAP®:
- Business architects
- Enterprise analysts
- Product managers

Project Focus

Customer involvement

Project metrics

Project change **mgt.**

BABOK® standards:
- BA planning/ monitoring
- Elicitation
- Requirements **mgt.**/ comm.
- Requirements analysis

BACOE manages BA framework

BA framework training

BA career track

Certified **BAs** (CBAP®):
- IT oriented
- Business oriented

Informal BA practices

BA community of practice

Increasing awareness of the value of BA

Continuous Improvement of BA Practices

FIGURE 1-5. A Business Analysis Practice Maturity Model

study was to evaluate and benchmark the current state of business analysis practices in organizations and contribute to the advancement of the body of knowledge and research in the field of business analysis. To date, limited research has been conducted on business analysis practices at the organizational level and their linkage to improved project and business outcomes. By gaining a better understanding of BA practices, organizations can more effectively evaluate their current state and establish an effective road map for the advancement of BA practices through prioritized, sequential improvements.

The findings from this study are encouraging.[8] They indicate that organizations have begun to recognize business analysis as a critical business management practice. Business analysis centers of excellence are emerging, with defined business analysis processes and standards, training programs, career paths, and professional development programs. Four key findings from the study are outlined below.

FINDING #1: BUSINESS ANALYSIS PRACTICES ARE MOSTLY TACTICAL, BUT AN ENTERPRISE FOCUS IS EMERGING

Most organizations' BA practices focus on managing requirements at the project level to meet the immediate business need. An enterprise—that is, more strategic—business analysis practice is emerging, with a focus on creativity and innovation, but this is not yet commonly accepted practice. Often, enterprise-focused activities are not yet thought of as part of the business analysis disciplines.

It is interesting to note that the maturity of BA practices appears to be consistent across industries. All of the organizations have begun to implement BA practices and are approaching level 2 maturity. Level 2 organizations mainly focus their BA efforts at the project level to ensure business requirements are managed. The emphasis is on

➤ BA planning and monitoring

➤ Requirements elicitation

➤ Requirements management and communication

➤ Requirements analysis.

Most organizations are continuing to build maturity and consistency in these practice areas and have begun to implement an enterprise focus to ensure business needs are met and strategies are executed through rigorous enterprise analysis and solution assessment and validation.

FINDING #2: COMPLEXITY MATTERS

Organizations with more complex projects reported more challenges in meeting delivery commitments for full scope, schedule, budget, or some combination of these. Significant correlations were found between scope and budget challenges and projects with multiple complexity dimensions. Organizations are beginning to acknowledge that mature BA practices and a highly competent BA workforce will help them better manage the complexity dimensions that impact project success.

FINDING #3: MATURE BUSINESS ANALYSIS PRACTICES DELIVER MORE SUCCESSFUL PROJECTS AND BUSINESS BENEFITS

More mature BA practices were significantly correlated with improved budget, schedule, and scope performance. The findings suggest that the maturity of BA practices in the participating organizations may be inadequate to manage highly complex projects.

FINDING #4: PROFICIENT BUSINESS ANALYSTS LEAD TO PROJECT SUCCESS

Organizations need a competent, valued BA workforce that takes a deliberate approach to business analysis using effective planning, stakeholder management, change management, and flexible business analysis approaches. Organizations with more projects on track for scope, schedule, and/or budget were significantly more likely to:

➤ Have more mature BA training programs with a focus on building BA competency, BA professional development programs, and BA career advancement opportunities

➤ Have a stronger focus on customer involvement and satisfaction

➤ Use a more systematic approach for dealing with change.

COLLABORATIVE LEADERSHIP

> *Simply put, a project manager increases their chance of getting an 'unqualified success' by over 400% by using elite analysts with specific competencies at the start of requirements discovery.*
>
> —IAG BUSINESS ANALYSIS BENCHMARK

Every significant business transformation project, especially those with a major technology component, whether it is developed in house or outsourced, or whether it is a commercial-off-the-shelf (COTS) purchase, a custom development, or a complex systems integration, needs exceptional business analysis. On high-performing teams, business analysts align themselves with professional project managers, architects, the best developers, and business visionaries to define business needs and determine the most appropriate, cost-effective, and innovative solution.

COMPLEX PROJECT TEAMS: SHARED LEADERSHIP

As this core leadership team forms, a project performance partnership emerges that rivals the world's great teams (e.g., U.S. Navy SEALS, special operations teams, professional sports teams, heart transplant teams, or firefighter and paramedic teams). What do high-performing teams have in common? They all have a well-understood mission and clear roles and responsibilities. They are highly trained and practiced to hone their skills. They are small, so they can be nimble and coordinated—but they are mighty in their execution. They call upon subteams and subject matter experts to assist when needed. They all have a coach or sponsor they can enlist when they come upon a barrier to success. Organizations need to develop similar high-performing teams for critical business change initiatives.

A WORD TO THE WISE

Do everything you can to build strong relationships with the key stakeholders you work with—especially the project manager. Work to make yourself indispensible, a valued colleague, a credible expert, a central member of the project team.

At the center of the team is the dynamic twosome: the project manager and the business analyst. One has her eye on the management of the project, while the other focuses on management of the business requirements, business benefits, and customer value. The wise project manager welcomes this teaming trend, understanding that "it takes a team" to lead complex projects, and that inadequate information relating to requirements leads to poor estimates and makes time and cost management virtually impossible.

Project managers rely on business analysts to help provide more-detailed project objectives; business needs analysis; clear, structured, useable requirements; solution innovation and trade-off analysis; requirement feasibility and risk analysis; and cost-benefit analysis. Obviously, this differs from the traditional systems analyst focus—leaping over business requirements and focusing on writing system specifications. Without a business analyst acting as a key liaison between the business, product development, and IT departments, requirements will be poorly defined, resulting in a disconnect between what is built and what the business needs.

THE BUSINESS ANALYST'S LEADERSHIP

The business analyst serves as the liaison between the customer groups, the business community, and the technical solution providers throughout the project life cycle. As projects become large, cross-functional, global, and complex, business analysis skills are indispensable.

The business analyst leads the requirements elicitation effort, and the proposed solution must be one that breaks new ground before it is considered ready to be designed and implemented. Since requirements play a vital role in engineering IT systems, and 60 to 70 percent of IT project failures are tied directly to poor requirements management, it is not surprising that the business analyst role is becoming more significant. Collaborating with the project manager, the business visionary (the business representative who understands the business vision and strategy), and lead developers, the business analyst manages the entire requirements life cycle—from understanding the business strategy to ensuring that the delivered solution meets the need and adds value to the bottom line. In divergence with the past, the business analyst has a critical role throughout the project, not simply during the requirements phase. The business analyst possesses a vast array of knowledge and skills to do the job. In addition, the business analyst is directly or indirectly involved in creating and maintaining numerous important deliverables, such as the business case.

ENTERPRISE ANALYSIS AND PORTFOLIO MANAGEMENT

Management works diligently to fund and manage a portfolio of valuable projects—*the right projects.* Subsequently, the focus is on flawless project execution to maximize the value delivered to the organization—in other words, *doing projects right.* The business analyst plays a vital role in both endeavors. All too often, project success is elusive. Projects are late, are over budget, or may never even be delivered. Sometimes work is incomplete, does not meet requirements or expectations, and does not deliver the benefits or returns on investment expected by the organization. Because a disappointing (and costly) project delivery record cannot be tolerated, businesses must build the wherewithal to break the cycle. Executives must assemble an array of key leadership capabilities to improve the performance of change initiatives. These include:

➤ Effectual portfolio management to ensure the highest value projects are funded

➤ Agile and lean project management and systems engineering processes, tools, and techniques

➤ Appropriate executive decision-making at key control gates

➤ Exceptional project leadership and high-performing teams

➤ Collaboration and respect between the business and IT communities

➤ Professional business analysis processes that ensure executive teams invest in the most valuable projects and that solution teams have a clear understanding of the customer's overall business and information needs.

LEADERS OF CHANGE

As the complex project management discipline matures into a strategic business practice, so will business analysts evolve into strategic leaders of change and innovation. Organizations embarking upon initiatives requiring far-reaching innovation and cutting-edge technology are beginning to focus on business analysis as well as project management, business architecture, and development prowess. Those working on IT initiatives are realizing that technical skills may be relatively easy to outsource, but they cannot abdicate control of their business requirements and solution innovation. In virtually every organization, the elevated leadership role of the business analyst is beginning to shape the future of business transformation.

Where can we get exceptional business analysts who can bridge the chasm between the business and technical communities? Frequently, we assume that expertise in the technical area of a project makes a qualified business analyst. To support important change initiatives, technically adept engineers are often asked to serve as business analysts as well as perform their technical role. In this case, business analysis is treated as a subset of the technical discipline. (Sometimes individuals assume a trio of leadership roles on projects: technical lead, project manager, and business analyst.) But time and again, difficulties arise on projects—not from lack of technical expertise, but from teams' inability to gather, understand, analyze, and manage business requirements. Projects are often initiated, and design and construction of a solution is underway, before the solution team members have a clear understanding of what the business really needs. Once requirements are captured at a high level and the project plan is being executed, technical activities tend to demand the majority of attention. Under these conditions, requirements and project management suffer, and the initiative is positioned to become a runaway project. This approach to projects has contributed significantly to the prevalence of challenged and failed projects.

Tolerance is low for technical failure and high for inadequate and ever-evolving requirements. All too often, projects suffer from requirements creep caused by "let's start developing and see how it turns out" syndrome. While this approach may be appropriate in some situations, it often falls short for complex business initiatives. Simply put, without a well-understood and documented requirements baseline, it is virtually impossible to meet project objectives. It has been said that if an organization has the resources and budget to invest in only a single life cycle area to improve project performance, that area should be requirements definition and management.

THE BUSINESS ANALYST'S KEY KNOWLEDGE, SKILLS, AND COMPETENCIES

It is increasingly clear that while technical expertise is necessary, it is insufficient for successfully managing the large, enterprise-wide, complex, mission-critical, innovative projects that are the norm today. Just as a business leader must be multiskilled and strategically focused, business analysts must possess an extensive array of leadership skills as they rise to a senior strategic position in the enterprise. And as IT's contribution moves beyond improving efficiency to boosting business effectiveness, the business analyst becomes the central figure on the project team. She must be "bilingual," speaking both business and technical languages, or even "trilingual," also speaking for the customer.

A WORD TO THE WISE

Make your own professional development plan a living, breathing document. Seek out a mentor from among the leaders in your organization. Read everything you can find on your industry, the technology that supports your company, and the business analysis profession. Become expert at promoting yourself, innovation, and your project.

Expectations are high and growing for the business analyst. To perform in this pivotal role, the business analyst must possess a broad range of knowledge, skills, and competencies. A look through the more than 5,000 job postings for business analysts on monster.com turned up this lofty job description:

> *The main purpose of the role will be to design and specify innovative solutions which meet the business requirements allowing the business benefit to be attained; and to facilitate divisional communication and awareness of the standards and quality expectations within the System Analyst teams.*[9]

Staffing surveys reveal an increasing demand for senior individuals who can perform the ever-widening range of business analysis functions. Since business analysts walk in customer, business, and technology worlds, they arrive from various fields. Some come from the ranks of engineering and programmer/analyst positions, while others have conventional business expertise supplemented by some IT training. To successfully fill the business analyst role, one must master a unique combination of technical, analytical, business, and leadership skills (see Figure 1-6).

Depending on the business analyst's level of responsibility and placement in the organization, duties may include the following:

➤ Identify and understand the business problem and the impact of the proposed solution on the organization's operations

➤ Document the complex areas of project and product scope, objectives, added value, or benefit expectations, using an integrated set of analysis and modeling techniques

➤ Translate business objectives into requirements using powerful analysis and modeling tools

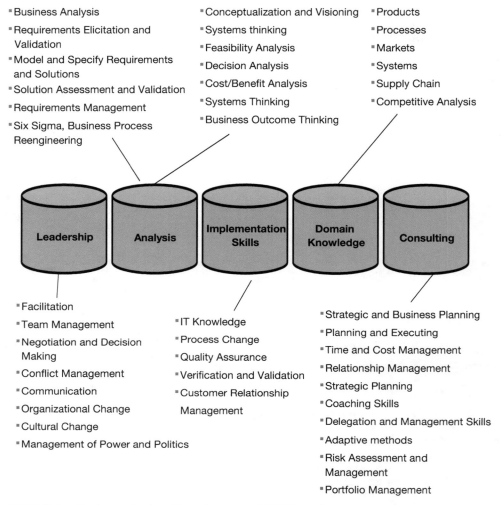

- Business Analysis
- Requirements Elicitation and Validation
- Model and Specify Requirements and Solutions
- Solution Assessment and Validation
- Requirements Management
- Six Sigma, Business Process Reengineering

- Conceptualization and Visioning
- Systems thinking
- Feasibility Analysis
- Decision Analysis
- Cost/Benefit Analysis
- Systems Thinking
- Business Outcome Thinking

- Products
- Processes
- Markets
- Systems
- Supply Chain
- Competitive Analysis

Leadership | **Analysis** | **Implementation Skills** | **Domain Knowledge** | **Consulting**

- Facilitation
- Team Management
- Negotiation and Decision Making
- Conflict Management
- Communication
- Organizational Change
- Cultural Change
- Management of Power and Politics

- IT Knowledge
- Process Change
- Quality Assurance
- Verification and Validation
- Customer Relationship Management

- Strategic and Business Planning
- Planning and Executing
- Time and Cost Management
- Relationship Management
- Strategic Planning
- Coaching Skills
- Delegation and Management Skills
- Adaptive methods
- Risk Assessment and Management
- Portfolio Management

FIGURE 1-6. Business Analyst Knowledge and Skill Requirements

© 2011 By Kathleen B. Hass and Associates, Inc.

➤ Drive collaboration on solution alternatives until the most innovative solution comes into view

➤ Evaluate customer business needs, thus contributing to strategic planning of information systems and technology directions

➤ Assist in determining the strategic direction of the organization

➤ Liaise with major customers during preliminary installation and testing of new products and services

➤ Bring about creativity and innovation through superior business analysis.

BUILDING A CAPABLE BUSINESS ANALYST WORKFORCE

Your organization needs to ensure it has appropriately skilled BAs who have the capabilities needed to successfully deliver complex new business solutions that meet 21st-century business needs. But it's not just about competency (what you think you can do or your score on a multiple-choice knowledge assessment); it's *all* about *capability*—examining your competency level against your current and future work assignments and the performance and project outcomes you achieve within your organizational context.

Individual business analyst capability assessments provide the information needed for individual business analysts to baseline their competencies and prepare their own professional development plans. Business analyst workforce assessments provide valuable information for management to draft an overall business analyst professional development plan for their organization. This plan forms a basis for workforce adjustments or realignment, training requirements, professional development activities, and specific mentoring and coaching needs. Organizations are increasingly using assessments to grow their business analyst competencies and to mature their business analysis practices.

POSITIONING THE BUSINESS ANALYST IN AN ORGANIZATION

As organizations struggle to implement contemporary business analysis practices, they are also wrestling with tough decisions about how best to incorporate the new role of the business analyst into the organization. Does it make sense to have business analysts centralized, reporting to a neutral organization like finance, IT, or an enterprise project management office (PMO) or center of excellence (COE), or should they report to individual business units? Should business analysts and project managers report to the same functional manager?

ORGANIZATIONAL PLACEMENT

While there is no one right answer to the organizational placement of business analysts, there are some general guidelines. For mid-level business analysts (those who manage day-to-day operational issues and also coordinate IT application system maintenance and enhancement projects), we see both the decentralized model, where the business analysts are placed in the business units, and the centralized model, where they reside in IT. Both models have challenges that must be understood and managed.

➤ When mid-level business analysts are placed in IT, an unintended consequence may emerge: the business may not take ownership of its technology needs, and the business analyst might begin to speak for the business, as opposed to bringing others into the decision-making process. In this case, IT management needs to reach out to the business units to conduct working sessions and ensure the appropriate business SMEs are fully engaged in decisions about IT support, maintenance, and enhancement work.

➤ When mid-level business analysts are placed in a business unit, it is difficult for them to feel like a team, and it is hard to manage consistency, standards, improvement of the business analysis process, and advancement of the business analysis profession within the organization. In addition, these business analysts tend to be more removed from IT and may not possess a deep understanding of the IT domain. In this instance, IT should foster communities of practice, where the business analysts can get together as a team for mentoring and training, to discuss lessons learned, and to improve methods and tools.

THE ENTERPRISE ANALYST

It is important for senior-level business analysts to be a part of an enterprise-wide project management office (PMO) or center of excellence (COE), a group that focuses on strategy and raising the value of project portfolios. This makes sense, since strategic projects have high stakes and are cross-functional, enterprise-wide, complex, and high risk. Placement in some sort of enterprise-wide office allows business analysts to:

➤ Provide pre-project support: identify new business opportunities, conduct feasibility studies, conduct alternative analysis for the most creative solution, and then develop the business case for new projects, which will then be submitted to management for project selection and prioritization

➤ Serve as the business analyst (or lead of a business analyst team, for a large program with supporting projects) for strategic, high-risk, complex projects, ensuring that requirements are fully understood and constantly validating that the solution will meet the business need during the entire solution development life cycle

➤ Continually validate that the business case remains viable, trade-offs and risk mitigations are not compromising innovation, and the project investment is sound.

THE ROLE OF BUSINESS ANALYSTS

IT organizations are debating the role of business analysts. Should business analysts be line managers? Should they be fully dedicated to business analysis?

Should they have other responsibilities "as assigned"? Organizations typically have several levels of business analysts; for smaller, low-risk projects, a business analyst will likely work on more than one project concurrently. Business analysts are not typically line managers. However, a pool of business analysts may report to a manager who is a senior business analyst. For large, strategic, high-risk, complex projects, a senior business analyst should be dedicated full time to the project, with no other responsibilities (as should a senior project manager). Organizations are learning that business analysis is a profession, and one needs to be able to master the knowledge, skills, and practices to become a superior business analyst and a strategic asset to the enterprise.

What is the business analyst's role in critical initiatives that do not have a significant IT component? Business analysts get involved and play a leadership role in many nontechnical projects. Examples include developing the business architecture, business process reengineering, competitive analysis and benchmark studies, pre-project enterprise analysis, business case development, facilities enhancements, and organizational restructuring and relocating.

PUTTING IT ALL TOGETHER: WHAT DOES THIS MEAN TO THE BUSINESS ANALYST?

The business analyst is a vital 21st-century asset. In this chapter, we have characterized the new profession of business analysis as it is emerging in the early decades of this century. We see the role of the business analyst as both tactical and strategic. As businesses struggle to invent new products and services to remain competitive in the global, technology-based economy, the leadership role of the business analyst will become more valued, in fact vital.

NOTES

1. International Institute of Business Analysis, *A Guide to the Business Analysis Body of Knowledge®* (*BABOK® Guide*), Version 2.0 (Toronto: International Institute of Business Analysis, 2009): 3.

2. *BABOK® Guide*.

3. International Institute of Business Analysis, "Guide to the Business Analysis Body of Knowledge (BABOK)," 2011. Online at http://www.theiiba.org/AM/Template.cfm?Section=Body_of_Knowledge&Template=/CM/HTMLDisplay.cfm&ContentID=8030 (accessed June 2011).

4. *BABOK® Guide*, 81.

5. International Institute of Business Analysis, "IIBA Business Analysis Competency Model, Version 2," June 2010. Online at http://www.theiiba.org/AM/Template.cfm?Section=Business_Analysis_Competency_Model&Template=/CM/HTMLDisplay.cfm&ContentID=6960 (accessed July 2010).

6. Kathleen B. Hass, "Planting the Seeds to Grow a Mature Business Analysis Practice," 2009. Online at http://www.kathleenhass.com/Whitepapers-docs/BA%20Practice%20Maturity%20White%20Paper-2.pdf (accessed June 2011).

7. Ibid., 15.

8. Kathleen B. Hass and Lori Lindbergh, "The State of BA Practices in Organizations," 2011. Online at www.kathleenhass.com and www.loriusllc.com (accessed June 2011).

9. Monster, "Business Analyst Jobs – Job Search Beta," 2010. Online at http://jobsearch.monster.com/search/Business-Analyst_5 (accessed July 2011).

CHAPTER 2

The Business Analyst's Strategic Role

The business analyst is a key participant in strategic activities, working to inform decision makers to ensure that the organization invests in the most valuable projects as well as tactical project-focused activities once a project is funded. In this chapter, we first discuss the business analyst's role in strategic planning and enterprise analysis. We then present the business analyst's role in activities intended to define and manage business requirements and to continuously validate that the solution will meet business needs: planning, elicitation, requirements analysis, specification, documentation, solution assessment and validation, change management, solution delivery, cultural change management, and solution maintenance and enhancement. Figure 2-1 illustrates the BA's roles and responsibilities on projects.

STRATEGIC PLANNING

Strategic planning is not typically thought of as a project phase. It is, however, the first set of activities in a business project's life. During strategic planning, the leadership team examines the current state of an enterprise and determines the desired future state by describing a set of broad goals.

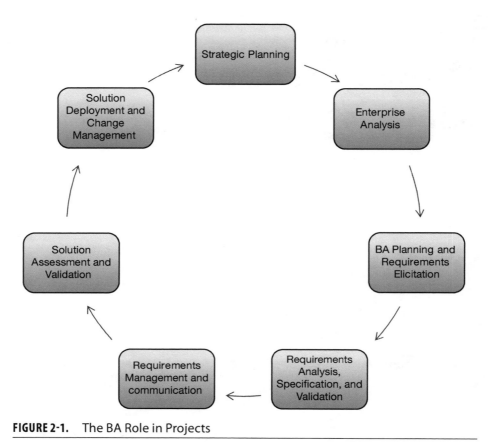

FIGURE 2-1. The BA Role in Projects

© 2011 by Kathleen B. Hass and Associates, Inc.

The business architect, an emerging position, is charged with developing a complete set of documentation that depicts the current state of the business so that everyone has a consistent, accurate understanding of the business. The business architect also documents the future state of the business—how it will look when the strategy has been achieved—so that everyone has a common understanding of the future state of the business. Enterprise analysts (often called strategy analysts, portfolio managers, business planners, or business/technology analysts, among other titles) then identify gaps in capabilities needed to achieve the future state and conduct enterprise analysis, converting the future strategy to measurable objectives to close the gaps.

A STRATEGY-EXECUTION FRAMEWORK

Many organizations struggle or even fail to execute their strategy, even when it is well formed. The reason most often given for this failure is that executives do not think they have a framework for strategy execution. That framework is called portfolio management. The decisions made during the strategic planning and goal-setting process drive portfolio management, the critical business practice embedded between strategic planning and project execution in which projects are selected, prioritized, and funded, thus converting strategic goals into actionable objectives, scope, and approach.

CAREER ADVICE
Business Enterprise Analysts

Less than one-fifth of companies have effective portfolio management practices. Enterprise analysts are needed to prepare high-quality business cases to provide management with sound decision-support information.

A Word to the Wise

Business architects and enterprise business analysts are emerging to fill the gap in enterprise analysis and creative leadership.

- Muster the courage to jump into high-level strategic roles.
- If your project does not have a business case, gather a small expert team and guide them through the steps to create one.
- Present the business case to the sponsor for review/approval.
- Update the business case throughout the project to validate that continued investment in the project is warranted. If not, propose a course correction to the project manager and the sponsor.

As enterprise analysts become more common in organizations, they will be called upon to conduct feasibility analysis, competitive analysis, opportunity analysis, problem analysis, financial analysis, and benchmark studies and to devise innovative recommendations to provide the senior team with the information needed to forge the optimal future vision and to convert innovative ideas into a business case, which serves as a new project proposal in the portfolio management process.

In today's world, the strategic plan is considered a living, breathing road map that changes and evolves with changes in the dynamic and often chaotic marketplace. As the strategies change, the portfolio of programs and projects must also change. Therefore, organizations need to be able to make changes to their project portfolio quickly and effectively.

THE CORPORATE SCORECARD

Scores of broad, important goals are likely to be developed during the strategic planning cycle. Strategic goals are then converted into an organized, actionable, measurable set of portfolios to attain the intended results. There needs to be a simple approach to tracking progress toward achieving the strategy. To monitor the journey, executive teams are building corporate scorecards as an outgrowth of their strategic plans. Increasing the wealth of stakeholders is the ultimate goal of for-profit organizations; as a result, financial goals often rank highest. However, nonfinancial decision criteria are also needed; these represent investments in the future health of the enterprise. A specific model, called the balanced scorecard, provides an effective tool to frame strategic goals.[1] In this model, goals are partitioned into four dimensions: financial, customer, internal operations, and learning and innovation, as described below.

> *Financial goals* are the quantitative goals that address the business's finance and accounting outcomes. Example: "Earn 6 percent on sales, 18 percent on investments, and 12 percent on assets this year."

➤ The primary measure of *customer goals* is customer satisfaction. Example: "Earn a customer satisfaction rating of 95 percent or better this year."

➤ *Internal operations goals* relate to process and operational performance and the effectiveness of core competencies. Measures are typically internal, comparing performance with industry benchmarks. Example: "Achieve inventory turns of 8.0 or better this year."

➤ *Learning and innovation goals* address new product development, organizational learning and skill development, and application of technology and productivity tools. Example: "Increase revenue by 50 percent through new products and services."

Mission results drive agencies in the public sector and nonprofit organizations, so strategic goals take on a slightly different slant. Measures are established to answer the following questions.

➤ *Customer:* "How do our customers view our effectiveness?"

➤ *Financial:* "Are our solutions the most cost-effective ones?"

➤ *Internal processes:* "Are our business processes effective and efficient?"

➤ *Innovation and improvement:* "How do we continue to improve and create value for our customers?"

ITERATIVE PLANNING CYCLES

Today the stakes are so high and the environment is so volatile that attention must be rigorously focused on evolving the organization's strategy, goals, and resulting change initiatives. Just as the strategic plan is a living document, strategic goals and objectives also are dynamic, so the planning process includes iterative planning cycles to monitor progress and make course corrections along the way. The bar for adding business value is raised for every planning cycle. As always, the executive management team is ultimately accountable for setting the right strategies for the success of the organization. However, they need accurate information, analysis of business problems and opportunities, creative ideas, and innovative approaches provided by seasoned business analysts who are experts in the relevant lines of business and in the technology that not only supports but optimizes the business results.

ENTERPRISE ANALYSIS

Enterprise analysis should not be thought of as a phase, but as a series of activities that are performed iteratively throughout the life of a project. In more mature organizations, a significant amount of enterprise analysis occurs to support strategy development. After the business architect depicts the future view of the business, the enterprise analyst conceptualizes creative new business solutions to seize new opportunities and therefore execute strategy. At this point, the business analyst demonstrates the leadership and creativity needed for the organization to remain competitive through the enterprise analysis activities described below. In practice, enterprise analysis is too often short changed—or worse omitted altogether.

ENTERPRISE ANALYSIS ACTIVITIES

The core enterprise analysis activities center on (1) identifying new business opportunities or solutions to business problems; (2) conducting studies, gathering information, brainstorming, innovating, and creating to determine the most feasible solution alternatives; and (3) developing a business case or project proposal document to recommend a new project to management, which will then decide whether to select, prioritize, and fund the change initiative. If the initiative is selected, a new project is formed and the planning and requirements activities of the project begin.

CAREER ADVICE
Business Enterprise Analysts

All too often, enterprise analysis activities are misunderstood, undervalued, not budgeted for, and skipped altogether. Absent *real* enterprise analysis, organizations are:

- Unable to ensure they are invested in the most valuable projects.
- Unsure of the value of their project portfolio.
- Missing valid business objectives that describe the expected value to the customer and project revenue anticipated from the organization's funded projects.

A Word to the Wise

Work with the line of business executives, the most influential managers, and senior project managers to inform them about the strategic value of enterprise analysis activities culminating in a sound business case. Bring together a small expert team and guide them through the enterprise analysis activities.

Enterprise analysis activities are carried on by the business analyst throughout the project to continually validate that the business need is understood, it has not changed, and the emerging solution will meet the need. The enterprise analysis activities even continue after the project has been completed and the enterprise has experienced, measured, and analyzed the benefits of the initiative.

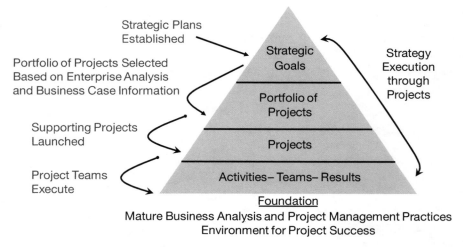

FIGURE 2-2. Organizational Strategic Alignment

An organization's ability to achieve goals through projects depends on its ability to select the most valuable projects and then execute them flawlessly. Organizational strategic alignment is achieved when strategic plans and goals are converted into a portfolio of programs and supporting projects. Strategic project leaders and project teams execute the project plans to meet objectives and deliver project outcomes, thus adding value to the enterprise (see Figure 2-2).

ENTERPRISE ANALYSIS IN PRACTICE

Business architects and enterprise business analysts play a significant role in translating business strategies into innovative new business change initiatives through enterprise analysis activities: analyzing the enterprise and the competitive environment and experimenting and brainstorming to identify the most creative solution. During these early discovery and definition activities, requirements are determined and documented at a very high level. Initial requirements definition originates early, when the product concept is first envisioned. The business architect documents the current and future states of the enterprise. Then the enterprise analyst works with a small team of experts to conduct creative sessions to identify the most feasible, innovative, lucrative approach and to document the results for all to see. The requirements for new business opportunities, the alternatives considered, and the approach to be proposed are captured in some kind of initiating document, called the business case, project charter, or statement of work. All requirements should be traceable to these original sources.

The array of enterprise analysis activities, which are guided by the business analyst and are described in Chapter 5 of the *BABOK® Guide*,[2] are listed below for your convenience. Organizations use some or all of these techniques, depending on the maturity of their business analysis practices. These activities appear to be sequential, but they are usually conducted concurrently and iteratively.

➤ ***Creating and maintaining the business architecture.*** The business architecture is the set of artifacts that comprise the attributes and characteristics of the business. It is a compilation of interrelated elements that depict information about the business: its operations, organizational structures and physical locations, the boundary of business processes, business rules, policies and procedures, and the lines of business used to flow value through to customers.

➤ ***Conducting feasibility, benchmark, and competitive analysis studies.*** A feasibility study is an evaluation conducted to determine if a business opportunity idea is achievable within cost, schedule, or other limitations. A benchmark study is a review of what best-of-breed organizations (often competitors) are doing to achieve their level of superior performance, so that the organization can try to replicate them. This study may also involve a comparison of performance between a new proposed product versus an existing product, system, or system component.

➤ A competitive analysis study is an evaluation of the competition in the marketplace, including past, current, and projected performance, to help the organization establish future plans to remain competitive.

➤ *Identifying new business opportunities.* As an outgrowth of strategic planning, the enterprise analyst reviews the results of feasibility, benchmark, and competitive analysis studies and the future business architecture to identify potential solution options for achieving strategic goals. The enterprise business analyst works with an expert team to identify new business opportunities and conduct trade-off analysis to determine the most viable option. The goal is to select a solution that will provide the most positive (valuable) outcome the fastest and that poses the least risk to the enterprise.

➤ *Scoping and defining new business opportunities.* Once the team has chosen the best alternative for achieving business goals, the solution must be defined to the level of detail the portfolio planning team considers necessary for deciding whether to invest in the change initiative. This is a challenging task for the business analyst because the organization does not want to make a significant investment in an idea that may not survive the project selection and prioritization process. So the business analyst works again with a team of subject matter experts to compile just enough information to determine if the proposed solution is viable.

➤ *Preparing the business case.* A business case should be developed for all significant change initiatives and capital projects, including major IT projects. Business unit managers may take the lead in developing business cases for projects that benefit their departments. However, many projects cross business units, and the talents of a senior business analyst facilitate the difficult decisions that must be made to satisfy the often competing demands of all areas impacted by the change. The business analyst brings key experts together to gain agreement on the initiative. Accurately predicting the costs and benefits of major initiatives is a critical skill that requires the combined disciplines of business analysis, project management, and IT expertise to estimate the costs of software development and technology acquisition, as well as business prowess to predict the business costs and value.

➤ ***Conducting the initial risk assessment.*** Once the business case is developed, the business analyst facilitates a risk management session using the same set of experts. The BA and the experts identify and analyze key risks, develop risk responses, estimate the cost of the risk responses, and determine an overall risk rating for the project. This information is essential for the project selection and prioritization effort. Obviously, the organization strives to invest in projects that have the lowest risk and the highest probability of success.

➤ ***Presenting new business opportunities to the portfolio management team*** for a decision on whether to fund the initiative as new programs and supporting projects.

PLANNING AND REQUIREMENTS ELICITATION

During the early project phases, the business need is analyzed and documented in as much detail as is needed to move into design and construction. The initial activities are planning and requirements elicitation. It is imperative to involve all stakeholders—including customers, users, business managers, architects, and developers—in these early activities.

BUSINESS ANALYSIS PLANNING ACTIVITIES

Ideally, the business analyst leads the business analysis planning activities in collaboration with a small core team consisting of the project manager, business visionary, and lead technologists. This team is charged with understanding the business opportunity, defining the scope of the effort at a more detailed level, determining the project approach (plan-based vs. adaptive), planning the business analysis activities to be completed and artifacts to be created, establishing a communication approach, defining a change-management method for requirements, conducting a stakeholder analysis, and ensuring a strong start to requirements elicitation.[3]

CAREER ADVICE
Planning

All too often, business analysts jump into requirements-gathering activities without adequate preparation. The result: inadequate time, budget, and resources to do a thorough job.

A Word to the Wise

Work closely with the project manager and business representatives to plan the approach to business analysis activities, tasks, resources needed, and artifacts to be produced.

With the PM, negotiate the commitment of the required business and technical SMEs and ensure their management commits individuals with the talent and knowledge to help create an innovative approach to the solution.

ELICITATION PREPARATION ACTIVITIES

The prudent business analyst spends a considerable amount of time preparing for the task at hand. Elicitation groundwork activities include:

➤ Gleaning a perspective of the needs and environment of customers, users, and stakeholders

➤ Reviewing (or creating if nonexistent) the business case, project charter, and statement of work (or similar scope definition document)

➤ Understanding the business vision, drivers, goals, objectives, and expected value to the customer and business benefits for the new/changed solution

➤ Assembling and educating a requirements team comprising key business and technical stakeholders

➤ Further understanding and documenting the scope of the project

➤ Deciding which elicitation activities will be performed, selecting the documents and models to be produced, and developing the requirements management plan

➤ Defining/refining the checklist of requirements activities, deliverables, and schedule

➤ Planning for change throughout the project.

ELICITATION GOALS

Requirements are conditions or capabilities that a solution must fulfill to support the essential activities of the enterprise. Requirements are derived from business goals and objectives. A critical success factor in the value of the solution after deployment is the extent to which it supports business requirements and helps the organization achieve its business objectives, so we must *get requirements right*. Requirements elicitation goals include:

➤ Identifying the customers, users, and stakeholders to determine who should be involved in the requirements gathering process.

➤ Understanding the business goals and objectives and thus identifying the essential user tasks that support the organizational goals. Successful solutions will support the business requirements and facilitate achievement of organizational goals.

➤ Identifying and beginning to document requirements for a target product, service, or system that will meet the needs of the users, customers, and stakeholders.

Many believe that requirements elicitation is the most critical and the most difficult aspect of a project.[4] But most business analysts rate themselves as very proficient in elicitation, which indicates that they may be underestimating the importance of elicitation activities. To be successful in requirements elicitation, the business analyst must establish a collaborative partnership between customers, users, and the project team. The business analyst should not just be a note taker when working with these groups; she is called upon to encourage creativity, innovation, and exploration. Business analysts can improve their skills in conducting elicitation discussions by seeking out training in creativity and innovation, group facilitation and decision-making, conflict resolution, negotiation, and elicitation techniques and can build on the training through experience and working with a coach or mentor.

ELICITATION ACTIVITIES

Requirements are always unclear at the beginning of a project. It is through the process of progressive elaboration that requirements evolve into maturity—hence, the iterative nature of requirements gathering, documenting, and validating. This requirements discovery process involves conducting a variety of requirements-gathering sessions.

CAREER ADVICE
Brainstorming

Of all the elicitation tools in the BA toolbox, brainstorming is perhaps the most used and the most useful. It is during brainstorming sessions that the team identifies all of the ideas that it will consider. This is the most creative part of elicitation.

A Word to the Wise

Become expert at facilitating brainstorming sessions. All too often, business analysts do not challenge SMEs to reach for unfamiliar or uncommon approaches and truly innovative solutions. Some brainstorming sessions even *reduce* the team's creative output.

ELICITATION TECHNIQUES

There is a vast array of requirements elicitation techniques. Select the techniques that are well suited to your stakeholder group to ensure success. Note that it may be necessary to educate your stakeholders on the techniques you plan to use prior to the actual events. Requirements-gathering techniques include:

➤ *Requirements elicitation workshops.* Requirements workshops link business users with solution developers and are an efficient way to gather information about business needs from a diverse group of stakeholders. The advantage of bringing stakeholders together to define requirements is that when conflicting and inconsistent requirements surface, they can be immediately resolved. Requirements are gathered quickly and collaboratively in a workshop session. A byproduct of these requirements workshops is that relationships begin to be built and ideally, a high-performing team begins to emerge.

The business analyst plays a critical role in facilitating the workshop to ensure a successful outcome, which is a difficult endeavor. Requirements workshops require a considerable amount of planning and preparation to be successful. When a business analyst is new to an organization, it is helpful to bring in an outside facilitator so that the business analyst can observe the facilitation approach and focus on the discussion. Business analysts often use the brainstorming technique, which is designed to solicit as many innovative ideas as possible, to foster creative thinking.

➤ *Interviews.* BAs conduct interviews with individuals and small groups to find out what business functions must be supported by the new solution.

➤ *Surveys.* Surveys can be used to collect a large amount of information from an array of stakeholders efficiently and quickly. Surveys can be used to collect initial information or to test the information you have already gathered.

Valid surveys are difficult to design and administer. To mitigate the risk of gathering inaccurate information from the survey, consult with a subject matter expert to help with the survey design and information compilation.

➤ *Review of existing system and business documents.* Conduct a review of all existing documentation about the business system, including policies, procedures, regulations, and process descriptions. Looking at market data about the business process under review can also be helpful.

➤ *Observation.* It is helpful to observe users conducting their day-to-day operational functions. This may help validate information gathered through workshops and interviews, resolve problems with requirements, and uncover missing requirements.

➤ *Note-taking and feedback loops.* Hold feedback sessions with customers, users, and stakeholders to continually validate the accuracy and completeness of the requirements.

ELICITATION DELIVERABLES

The key output of requirements elicitation is a very early iteration of documented business requirements that have been reviewed and approved by key business and technical stakeholders. Other artifacts of the process may include notes, documentation of issues or risks, diagrams, or other information captured during the elicitation sessions.

REQUIREMENTS ANALYSIS AND SPECIFICATION

Requirements are first stated in simple terms during the elicitation activities and are then analyzed, decomposed, and refined for clarity and accuracy. Requirements analysis is the process of structuring requirements information into various categories, evaluating requirements for selected qualities, representing requirements in different forms, deriving detailed requirements from high-level requirements, and negotiating priorities. While the focus of requirements elicitation is on understanding customer, user, and business requirements for the new solution, the focus of analysis shifts to understanding the solution itself and exploring the details of the problem domain. According to Scott Ambler, renowned software development guru, analysis represents the middle ground between requirements and design, the process by which your mindset shifts from what needs to be built to how it will be built.[5] And Karl Wiegers defines analysis as:

> *The process of classifying requirements information into various categories, evaluating requirements for desirable qualities, representing requirements in different forms, deriving detailed requirements from high-level requirements, negotiating priorities, and so on.*[6]

REQUIREMENTS ANALYSIS ACTIVITIES

Requirements analysis involves organizing and prioritizing requirements, specifying and modeling requirements, capturing assumptions and constraints, and verifying and validating requirements.[7] Requirements analysis includes the activities to determine required function and performance characteristics, the context of implementation, stakeholder constraints and measures of effectiveness, and validation criteria. Through the analysis process, requirements are decomposed and captured in a combination of textual and graphical formats. During requirements analysis, the business analyst should continually ask: "As this approach innovative enough, or simply business as usual?"

REQUIREMENTS ANALYSIS TECHNIQUES

Analysis techniques are many. Indeed, it is often difficult for the business analyst to decide which techniques to use. A rule of thumb: use the techniques that encourage collaboration and innovation. Also, use the techniques that make the requirements visible. Finally, keep the process as simple as possible. Often-used techniques include the following:

➤ *Context diagramming,* to ensure that the scope of the change initiative and the boundaries of the project are fully understood by all stakeholders.

➤ *Studying* requirements feasibility to determine if the requirement is viable technically, operationally, and economically.

➤ *Trading off* requirements to determine the most feasible requirement alternatives.

➤ *Assessing requirement risks and constraints* and modifying requirements to mitigate identified risks.

➤ *Modeling* requirements to provide a visual depiction of relationships and dependencies: data models, process models, organization models, interface, and context models.

➤ *Prototyping* interfaces and solution subcomponents to provide a visual depiction of the proposed solution.

➤ *Analyzing business rules* to determine what decisions have been made regarding business operations.

➤ *Decomposing* requirements to capture business needs in enough detail for the solution development team's use.

➤ *Clarifying and restating* requirements in multiple ways to ensure they describe the real needs of the customers.

➤ *Deriving* additional requirements as more is learned about the business need through the analysis activities.

➤ *Prioritizing* requirements to reflect the fact that not all requirements are of equal value to the business. Prioritization is necessary to ensure the most valuable features and functions are delivered to the business first.

➤ *Defining terms* in a glossary or data dictionary in natural (nontechnical) language to ensure that stakeholders have a common understanding of them.

➤ *Creating test cases* at a high level to ensure each requirement is testable.

➤ *Allocating* requirements to subsystems to ensure they are satisfied by components of the system.

REQUIREMENTS SPECIFICATION ACTIVITIES

Requirement specifications are elaborated from and linked to the structured requirements using a combination of textual statements, models, graphs, and matrices, resulting in a repository of requirements with a complete attribute set identifying specific characteristics of each requirement such as: owner, priority, status, author, and the like. Requirements must be sufficiently detailed, as they will be included in a solution specification document to be used by the development team. Through the process of progressive elaboration, the requirements team often finds requirements that are not defined in sufficient detail. These requirements must be made more specific to prevent uncontrolled changes to requirements.

Specification activities include identifying all the precise attributes of each requirement. This process ensures an understanding of the relative importance of each of the quality attributes.

REQUIREMENTS SPECIFICATION TECHNIQUES

Attributes are used for a variety of purposes, including structuring, grouping, explaining, selecting, and validating requirements. Attributes allow the requirements team to associate information with individual or related groups of requirements and often facilitate the requirements analysis process by filtering and sorting. In addition, attributes enable the association of descriptive information with each requirement. Attributes may be user defined or system defined.

CAREER ADVICE
Visualization

All too often, the project manager simply expects the BA to create a requirements document and perhaps use cases or user stories and then quietly go away. Unless requirements are visual, they are subject to interpretation and invalid assumptions.

- Text is important when describing very technical information.
- Models, graphs, and rich pictures are a necessity for demonstrating relationships, sequence, and dependencies and to promote a common understanding.

A Word to the Wise

Requirements alone are not complex; it is the relationships among requirements that create complexity.

- Select a few models that you will always use to define requirements.
- Become expert at facilitating modeling sessions.
- Limit dependencies among requirements to reduce complexity.
- Form a requirements integration team to manage requirement dependencies.
- Use a requirements management tool to link and integrate requirements artifacts to maintain integrating throughout the project.

Typical attributes attached to requirements may include:

➤ *A unique identifier* that does not change. The identifier is not to be reused if the requirement is moved, changed, or deleted.

➤ *Acceptance criteria.* These describe the nature of the test that would demonstrate to customers, end users, and stakeholders that the requirement has been met. Acceptance criteria are usually captured by asking end users, "What kind of assessment would satisfy you that this requirement has been met?"

➤ *Author* of the requirement—the person who wrote it.

➤ *Complexity indicator,* which communicates how difficult the requirement will be to implement.

➤ *Ownership*—the individual or group that needs the requirement to be met.

➤ *Performance,* which addresses how the requirement must be met.

➤ *Priority* of the requirement—a rating of its relative importance at a given point in time.

➤ *Source* of the requirement, which identifies who requested it. Every requirement should originate from a source that has the authority to specify requirements.

➤ *Stability,* an indicator of how mature the requirement is. This is used to determine whether the requirement is firm enough to begin work on it.

➤ *Status* of the requirement, which denotes whether it is proposed, accepted, verified with the users, or implemented.

➤ *Urgency,* which refers to how soon the requirement is needed.

REQUIREMENTS ANALYSIS AND SPECIFICATION DELIVERABLES

The modeled and documented, validated, structured requirements are an output of the requirements analysis and specification process. The requirements must clearly demonstrate the business value to be delivered and must be traced back to specific business objectives outlined in the business case. It is helpful if the requirements are structured to mirror the solution design; this facilitates traceability from requirement to design and construction of the solution.

REQUIREMENTS DOCUMENTATION

Requirements must be documented in clear, concise, and natural language, since requirements documentation is used by virtually everyone associated with the project. Certain types of requirements, such as regulatory mandates, safety standards, environmental tolerances, and security requirements, may need to be expressed formally, using scientific or technical language. This is acceptable, as long as the requirements are mapped back to the business objectives (which should be easier to understand). However, in most cases the language used to document business requirements should be as simple and straightforward as possible. Characteristics of good requirements include:

➤ *Feasibility.* The requirements must be technically, economically, and operationally possible.

➤ *Necessity.* The requirements must represent the real needs of the organization.

➤ *Prioritization.* The requirements must be prioritized according to the value of the function or feature to the organization.

➤ *Unambiguousness.* The requirements must be clear so that they will be interpreted consistently across stakeholder groups.

➤ *Completeness.* The requirements must represent all of the functions and features that are needed to meet the business objectives.

➤ *Verifiability.* The requirements must be testable.

➤ *Consistency.* The requirements must be in harmony with one another and must not contradict each other.

➤ *Correctness.* The requirements must accurately represent business functions and adhere to business rules.

➤ *Modifiability.* The requirements must be flexible so that they can be adapted to changing business needs.

➤ *Traceability.* The requirements must be structured so that they can be traced to hardware, software, test cases, training manuals, and documentation artifacts throughout the product development life cycle.

➤ *Usability after development.* The requirements must be sufficiently detailed so as to support maintenance and enhancement of the product after deployment.

TEXTUAL VS. GRAPHICAL REQUIREMENTS DOCUMENTATION

A diagram can express structure and relationships more clearly than text, whereas for precise definition of concepts, clearly articulated language is preferred to diagrams. Therefore, both textual and graphical representations are essential for a complete set of requirements. Transforming requirements represented graphically into textual form can make them more understandable to nontechnical members of the team.

CATEGORIZING REQUIREMENTS

Requirements are categorized into types depending on their source and applicability. Understanding requirement types helps in analyzing, structuring, and prioritizing requirements and enables the technical team to conduct trade-off analysis, estimate the system cost and schedule, and better assess the level of requirement changes to be expected. Finally, reviewing the list of requirement types can help the business analyst identifying areas that may require further investigation.

Typically, requirements are broadly characterized as *functional* or *non-functional* (aka *supplemental*). Functional requirements are capabilities the system will be able to perform in terms of behaviors or operations. They are specific system actions or responses. A functional requirement is best expressed as a verb or verb phrase. Functional requirements are written so as not to unnecessarily constrain the solution, thus providing a firm foundation for the system architects.

Nonfunctional requirements stipulate a physical or performance characteristic and serve as constraints on system capabilities. Constraints pose restrictions on the acceptable solution options. Technical constraints may include the requirement to use a predetermined language or database or specific hardware. Constraints may also specify restrictions such as resource utilization, message size and timing, software size, or the maximum number of and size of files, records, and data elements. Technical constraints also include any enterprise architecture standards that must be followed. Business constraints include budget limitations, restrictions on the people who can do the work, and the skill sets available. Business rules define the constraints on business processes that must be followed.

REQUIREMENTS VALIDATION

Documentation activities involve translating the collective requirements into written requirements specifications and models in terms that are understood by all stakeholders. The process of validating requirements typically requires substantial time and effort, as each stakeholder may have different expertise, perspectives, and expectations.

Requirements validation is the process of evaluating requirements documents, models, and attributes to determine whether they satisfy the business needs and are complete to the point that the technical team can commence work on solution design and development. The set of requirements is compared to the original initiating documents (e.g., the business case, project charter, or statement of work) to ensure completeness. If a requirement cannot be traced to a business adjective, it may not be valid.

Beyond establishing completeness, validation activities include evaluating requirements from a technical standpoint to ensure that design risks associated with the requirements are minimized before further investment is made in system development.

CAREER ADVICE
Requirements Validation

Requirements validation occurs throughout the project, not just in the early elicitation and analysis stages.

A Word to the Wise

Requirements *emerge*; many iterative sessions are needed to fully understand and capture requirements.

- Seek ways to continually validate requirements, assess the solution as it comes into view, and validate that the solution will satisfy the business need.
- Insert many solution assessment and validation sessions into your business analysis plan.

REQUIREMENTS VALIDATION ACTIVITIES

The objective of requirements validation is to ensure that all business and technical stakeholders have reviewed the requirements, identified errors and omissions, and made corrections so that the solution team can proceed with solution design, construction, and testing. Requirements are also used by the project manager to prepare time and cost estimates for the project.

REQUIREMENTS VALIDATION TECHNIQUES

Validation techniques include defining acceptance criteria and conducting document reviews, product demonstrations, prototyping, and finally user acceptance testing to ensure the criteria have been satisfied.

➤ *Prototyping.* The best representation of the solution is the solution itself. Therefore, the most useful technique for validating that analysis is complete is *prototyping*, which provides a visual model of the solution or a component of the solution.

➤ *Test-driven requirements.* If requirements are particularly difficult to define, it is sometimes necessary to start by designing the test that will verify that the requirement has been met, and *then* back into the actual requirement.

➤ *Business scenarios* (aka usage-based scenarios) are often used to ensure an understanding of business requirements.

➤ *Acceptance criteria.* Developing acceptance criteria, performance metrics, and business benefit measures is another good way to ensure requirements are complete and acceptable to the business.

> ➤ *Structured walkthroughs* of the solution with key customers and users is an effective way to validate that the requirements are accurate, complete, and unambiguous.

REQUIREMENTS MANAGEMENT

A major requirement review occurs once firm, basic requirements are complete enough to transition to the more detailed work of defining system specifications, and designing and constructing the solution design. This involves presenting requirements for review and approval at a formal session. At this point, the project manager updates the project schedule, cost, and scope estimates and the business analyst updates the business case to provide the salient information needed to determine whether continued investment in the project is warranted. Upon securing approval to proceed, the business analyst transitions into requirements management activities.

Once the requirements are defined, approved, and baselined, changes to these firm, basic, approved requirements must be managed throughout the solution development life cycle. Requirements management involves tracking and coordinating requirements allocation, status, and change activities throughout the rest of the business solutions life cycle. Spreadsheets and traceability tools that help validate that all requirements have been satisfied by solution components are the most common requirements management tools. The business analyst and project manager work collaboratively to define and manage the project and product scope. Requirements management activities include:

> ➤ *Allocating* requirements (also referred to as partitioning) to different subsystems or subcomponents of the system. Top-level requirements

are allocated to components defined in the system architecture, such as hardware, software, manual procedures, and training.

➤ *Tracing* requirements throughout system design and development to track where in the system each requirement is satisfied. As requirements are converted to design documentation, the sets of requirements documentation, models, specifications, and designs must be rigorously linked to ensure that the relevant business needs are satisfied.

➤ *Managing changes* and enhancements to the system. Managing requirements involves being able to add, delete, and modify requirements during all phases of the system development life cycle.

➤ *Validating and verifying* requirements. The business analyst continues to facilitate the validation and verification of requirements throughout the development life cycle. The purpose of verification and validation is to ensure that the system satisfies the requirements as well as the specifications and conditions imposed on it by those requirements. Validating requirements provides evidence that the solution satisfies the business requirements and is done through user involvement in testing, demonstration, and inspection techniques. The final validation step is the user acceptance testing, led and facilitated by the business analyst. Verifying requirements provides evidence that the solution satisfies the technical specifications and is done through testing, inspection, demonstration, analysis, or some combination of these.

MANAGING CHANGES TO REQUIREMENTS

Managing changes to requirements is a difficult endeavor. How the business analyst manages change depends on the complexity of the project,

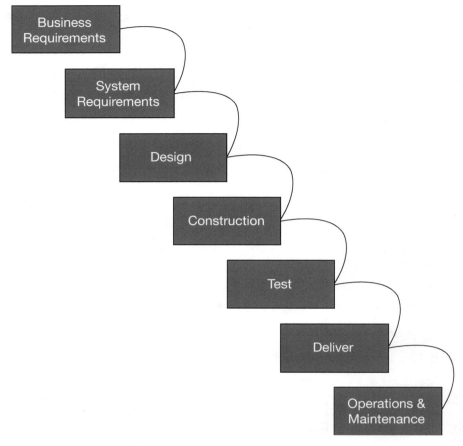

FIGURE 2-3. The Waterfall Model

the time-to-market urgency for the solution, the volatility of the business climate, and the level of understanding of the requirements. We will examine the nature of change control for projects of varying complexity.* In Chapter 3, we fully examine changes to the role of the business analyst for varying levels of project complexity.

----

* This section on managing changes to requirements is adapted with permission from "Change: Manage It, Prevent It, or Welcome It?," a *PMI® Community Post* by Kathleen B. Hass (June 25, 2010). Project Management Institute, *PMI® Community Post*, Project Management Institute, Inc., 2010. Copyright and all rights reserved. Material from this publication has been reproduced with the permission of PMI.

MANAGING REQUIREMENTS ON PROJECTS OF LOW TO MODERATE COMPLEXITY

For short-duration projects with stable requirements and few dependencies, the waterfall model depicted in Figure 2-3 is highly effective for managing requirements. This linear ordering of activities presumes requirements are complete before design and construction begin. It assumes that events affecting the project are predictable, tools and activities are well-understood, and once a phase is complete, it will not be revisited.

CAREER ADVICE
Welcome Change!

Requirements will change—there is no doubt about it. Our requirements practices are not effective enough to gather all requirements early and then fiercely control changes. And the world is changing all around us, so we must embrace change.

A Word to the Wise

Two very effective approaches:

- Welcome changes that add value to the customer and wealth to the organization.
- Reduce the cost of change through iterative development and by limiting dependencies among requirements and solution components.

The strengths of this approach are that it lays out the steps for development and stresses the importance of requirements. The limitations are that projects rarely follow the sequential flow, and it is difficult to state all requirements up front. Therefore, once design and construction begin, change management systems are needed to:

➤ Identify the business need and value of a proposed change

➤ Analyze the feasibility of change within cost and time constraints

➤ Recommend acceptance, deferral, or rejection of the change based on the business need

➤ Seek approval

➤ Implement approved changes.

If no organizational change management process exists, or if the project will deviate from the standard process, it is the job of the project leadership team to develop a change management plan that includes the elements listed above. If the project deliverable is urgently needed, the team should strive to minimize scope and prevent change. Tools typically used to successfully control changes are low-tech tables and spreadsheets.

MANAGING REQUIREMENTS ON HIGHLY COMPLEX PROJECTS AND PROGRAMS

Since complex projects are by their very nature less predictable, it is important for the project team to build options into the approach. This often involves rapid prototyping—a fast build of a solution component to prove an idea is feasible—which is typically used for high-risk components, requirements understanding, or proof of concept. The spiral model, an iterative waterfall approach, is often used. Another option is the evolutionary development model, which implements the solution incrementally based on experience and lessons learned from the results of prior releases. Functions are prioritized based on business value, and once high-risk areas are resolved, the highest value components are delivered first.

This "keep our options open" approach requires a change management system that welcomes changes that add value and strives to reduce the cost of change. It is only necessary to control changes on the current increment, since little time has been invested in defining the scope of increments to be developed in the future. Iterative development requires a flexible approach to change management. The project team strives to welcome and manage change, not to prevent it. Tools used to track changes for complex projects are sophisticated configuration management systems.

MANAGING REQUIREMENTS ON MEGAPROJECTS

For megaprojects, a "conspiracy of optimism" takes hold, which drives us to estimate costs significantly lower than they will really be. We are optimists; if we knew the real costs of a megaproject at the outset, they would likely kill the project. So we forge ahead, due to political and commercial pressures. For example, the Boston Big Dig is modern America's most ambitious urban-infrastructure project, spanning the terms of six presidents and seven governors. The cost of the project, which features many never-before-done engineering and construction marvels, rose from $2.6 billion to $14.8 billion over its duration.[8]

Implementing an effective change management system for megaprojects is difficult. Teams of people, a political management plan, a highly complicated change control process, and sophisticated tools are needed to traverse the litany of inevitable changes.

MANAGING TRANSITIONAL REQUIREMENTS

Planning for the organizational change that is brought about by the delivery of a major new product or business solution is often partially or even completely overlooked by project teams that are focused solely on system development and implementation of the IT application. While the technical members of the project team plan and support the implementation of the new product or system into the IT production environment, the business analyst's role in solution delivery involves working with the management of the business unit to bring about the benefits expected of the new solution. To that end, the business analyst performs several assessments, which will help her understand organizational change management requirements.

➤ *Readiness assessment.* Assessing the organizational readiness for change and planning and supporting a cultural change program.

➤ *Skill assessment.* Assessing the current state of the knowledge and skills resident within the business, determining the knowledge and skills needed to optimize the new business solution, and planning for and supporting training, retooling, and staff acquisition to fill in skill gaps.

➤ *Organizational assessment.* Assessing the current state of the organizational structure within the business domain, determining the organizational structure needed to optimize the new business solution, and planning for and supporting organizational restructuring.

➤ *Communication assessment.* Developing and implementing a robust communication campaign to support the organizational change initiative.

➤ *Management support assessment.* Determining, enlisting, and supporting management's role in the championing the change.

MANAGING CULTURAL CHANGES

Many cultural and physical barriers to adoption of a major change initiative exist. The business leadership may have too many conflicting and demanding priorities. The physical facilities needed to support the new product or business solution may not be well understood. The users— the actual operators of the new process or system—may not have the knowledge and skills needed to optimally use the new technology. The go-to-market commercial practices may need to be overhauled. It may be difficult to secure active involvement from the organization's senior leadership because they may not believe that it is their role to model and teach the new practices.

Overcoming barriers to cultural change may involve major shifts to the organization's legacy vision and skills. There are many strategies the business analyst can employ for making change work, including the following:

➤ Working with the leadership team to create a climate where change can succeed

➤ Enlisting formal and informal leaders within the organization to drive the change

➤ Ensuring there is clear ownership and accountability within the business unit(s) for the quality of the new business process and IT systems

➤ Focusing on and communicating improvements early in the deployment

➤ Providing role modeling, mentoring, and coaching to reinforce new business practices

➤ Implementing reward and recognition systems that are aligned with the new business practices

➤ Reacting to critical incidents with the new business solution quickly

➤ Recognizing and addressing stress and resistance associated with culture change

➤ Employing strategies to sustain culture change, including:

  › Coaching and mentoring programs

  › Permanently linking rewards to the use of new business practices

> ❯ Placing equal emphasis on all aspects of the business system, including customer satisfaction, profit, employee satisfaction, continuous learning, process efficiency, and driving value through the organization to the customer.[9]

MAINTAINING AND ENHANCING THE SOLUTION

The business analyst's contribution to the success of the project does not end when the business solution is delivered and operational. The business analyst is responsible for tracking and reporting the actual business costs and benefits that have been realized as a result of the new solution.

CAREER ADVICE
Benefits Management

To close the loop in the portfolio management process, the actual costs and benefits need to be measured and compared to those forecasted in the business case.

A Word to the Wise

It is the responsibility of the business analyst to:

- Measure the actual costs and benefits that were/are being realized via the new or changed solution.
- Report the results to the executive sponsor and the portfolio management team.

If the forecasted benefits were not realized, the BA conducts root cause analysis to determine what went wrong (e.g., the cost and time estimates were too optimistic, the project was not executed optimally, or the solution is not operating efficiently and is more costly to maintain than anticipated). The results of the root cause analysis are included in the benefits report with recommendations for improvement to avoid similar situations in the future.

The business analyst also maintains key responsibilities during the operations and maintenance (O&M) phase of the business solution life cycle. O&M is the phase in which the system is operated and maintained for the benefit of the business. The business analyst provides maintenance services to prevent and correct defects in the business solution. These defects could be problems with the IT system (e.g., inaccurate data, application defects, or technical infrastructure inadequacies) or issues within the business process (e.g., procedure inefficiencies, information gaps, or skill gaps).

Documentation produced and reviewed by the business analyst includes process efficiency measures, customer satisfaction indicators, system validation procedures, system validation reports, maintenance reports, annual operational reports, and the deactivation plan and procedures. The business analyst also plays a major role in managing enhancements to the system and in determining when the system should be replaced and therefore deactivated. (Enhancements are defined as changes to increase the value provided by the system to the business.) Clearly, if requested enhancements cost more to implement than the value provided to the business, they are not cost-effective. It is the business analyst who continues to examine the value proposed functions and features will bring about, comparing it with the cost to develop and operate the new system components.

PUTTING IT ALL TOGETHER: WHAT DOES THIS MEAN TO THE BUSINESS ANALYST?

The business analyst is integral throughout the project. Many organizations are of the erroneous opinion that the business analyst simply needs to elicit and document requirements. After this, she is no longer needed, so she can then move on to another project. The truth is that developing business requirements is an iterative process. Requirements emerge as more is learned about the business, the solution, and the evolving business needs. Therefore, it is imperative that the business analyst remain an essential member of the complex project leadership team throughout the project. Indeed, the business analyst plays a critical role even after the project is closed, adding value to the solution and measuring the actual business benefits achieved.

NOTES

1.   Robert S. Kaplan and David P. Norton, *The Balanced Scorecard: Translating Strategy into Action* (Boston: Harvard Business School Press, 1996).

2.   International Institute of Business Analysis, *A Guide to the Business Analysis Body of Knowledge* (*BABOK® Guide*), Version 2.0 (Toronto: International Institute of Business Analysis, 2009): 81–98.

3.   Ibid., 17–52.

4.   Karl Wiegers, *Software Requirements: Practical Techniques for Gathering and Managing Requirements throughout the Product Development Cycle,* 2nd ed. (Redmond, WA: Microsoft Press, 2003): 45.

5.   Scott Ambler, "Agile Analysis," 2010. Online at http://www.agilemodeling.com/essays/agileAnalysis.htm (accessed July 2010).

6.   Wiegers, 483.

7.   *BABOK® Guide,* 99–120.

8.   Nicole Gelinas, "Lessons of Boston's Big Dig," *City Journal* (Autumn 2007). Online at http://www.city-journal.org/html/17_4_big_dig.html (accessed July 2010).

9.   Rita Chao Hadden, *Leading Culture Change in Your Software Organization: Delivering Results Early* (Vienna, VA: Management Concepts, 2003).

CHAPTER 3
The Adaptive Business Analyst

To understate the obvious, business analysis is a difficult and risky business. Ideally, we would like to get a clear and thorough picture of the business need before we obtain customer sign-off on the requirements, begin developing the solution, and then set up procedures that limit requirements changes following sign-off. However, regardless of the care taken in requirements engineering, requirements are going to change for several reasons:

➤ The business environment is dynamic. In today's economy, fundamental business forces are rapidly changing the value of system features. What might now be a good set of requirements may not be so in a few months or a year.

➤ Everything in IT systems depends on the requirements. We are finally acknowledging that complete and accurate requirements are seldom able to be elicited, analyzed, documented and frozen before the solution is designed and constructed. This means the baseline plan created early in the project is always subject to change. Estimation is difficult for projects involving software development because they are basically unique endeavors, much like research and development projects.

➤ The nature of IT systems and software is intangible, and the real value is difficult to predict.

In acknowledgement of the difficulty of defining and managing business requirements, it is imperative that we discuss three additional concepts relating to *how* to implement the business analysis techniques we've discussed: *agile development*, the *iterative* nature of requirements generation and system development (especially for software-intensive systems), and the element of *scalability*.

CAREER ADVICE
Agile Methods

There are many different agile methodologies, all embracing the iterative approach to requirements and solution development.

A Word to the Wise

Familiarize yourself with the agile methodologies that are prevalent or emerging in your organization.

- Seek assignment on a project using agile methods.
- Remember to always keep your eye on the business case, working to ensure the business benefits are being met. It may be up to the business analyst to determine when "enough is enough"— the business case has been fulfilled, return on additional releases will be marginalized, and it is time to close the project and transfer resources to more valuable endeavors.

AGILITY

Over the past few years, there's been a rapidly growing interest in agile (aka lightweight) methodologies. Alternately described as an approach to rid IT development of burdensome bureaucracy or a license to hack, agile methodologies have generated interest throughout the world.[1] The emphasis in agile methods differs substantially from traditional, heavyweight engineering methods. The most notable divergence is that they are less document-oriented, usually resulting in less documentation for a given requirement. Moreover, agile methods often spotlight source code as a key part of requirements documentation. Additionally, there are two more fundamental distinctions:

➤ *Agile methods are adaptive rather than predictive.* Engineering methods plan out a large part of the solution in great detail and then manage changes throughout the project. Agile methods attempt to adapt and thrive on change.

➤ *Agile methods are people oriented rather than process oriented.* The goal of engineering methods is to define a process that is repeatable and independent of the development team. Agile methods focus on the skill of the development team, trying to make the process more tightly support the team in its work.

AGILE REQUIREMENTS ANALYSIS

The world of agile analysis challenges business analysts to become the communication mentors and coaches of project teams. To do this, one of the tenets of agile development must be followed: that of active stakeholder participation throughout the project life cycle. The focus of activities changes from finding out what customers want to helping customers determine what they need to meet business objectives.

An obvious enabler of active stakeholder participation is collocation of the business and development team. However, the business community cannot always free critical resources to work with the development team on a full-time basis. In addition, project teams are often located many hundreds or even thousands of miles from their internal and external customers. In this case, the business analyst will need to conduct interviews and workshops with the business community in its own environment, with key members of the development team present to hear the voice of the customer. These sessions may be face-to-face or remote, using web meetings and video teleconferencing.

What is agile analysis? According to IBM agile and lean methodologist Scott Ambler, the business analyst follows the agile methods outlined above, while incorporating these traits into the analysis:

➤ *Richness of communication*. Face-to-face meetings and teleconferencing are valued over documentation and email.

➤ *Highly iterative activities*. Analysis and design activities are dependent on each other and in practice are matured in an iterative manner. Indeed, since estimating is part of analysis, it is impossible to estimate the cost of a solution without knowing the solution design.

➤ *Constant feedback*. Agile analysis is highly incremental, so that components of the solution can be implemented for customer feedback before committing to further investment in development. Hence, estimation and prioritization of requirements in increments is a must. This approach facilitates trade-off analysis and critical decision-making on the part of the customer.

➤ *Just enough is good enough to proceed*. Agile analysis follows the premise that good is good enough. It is the art of applying just the right amount of rigor—no more and no less.[2]

Ambler presents this definition of agile analysis:

> *Agile analysis is a highly iterative and incremental process where developers and project stakeholders actively work together to understand the domain, to identify what needs to be built, to estimate that functionality, to prioritize the functionality, and in the process, optionally producing artifacts that are just barely good enough.*[3]

USING AGILE METHODS

So, when is it appropriate to use agile methods? Current thinking suggests that these methods should be used when the following conditions are present; the absence of one or more of these circumstances will likely put the agile approach at risk.[4]

➤ *Transitioning to more rigor*. When you have been following the code and fix method, using agile methods will apply some discipline to the process. The agile approach has the advantage of being easier to implement than a more rigorous method. Much of the advantage of agile methods stems from their light weight. Simpler processes are more likely to be followed when little or no process has been employed in the past.

➤ *Small core team*. The development team must be small, collocated, high performing, dedicated full time, highly skilled, and empowered to make most project decisions.

➤ *Unknown requirements*. Agile approaches are appropriate when requirements are uncertain or volatile. Logic dictates that if requirements are unstable, you cannot have a stable design or rigidly adhere to a planned process.

➤ *Highly invested stakeholders*. It is important for the customer to understand that when requirements change, following a predictive process is risky. In addition, the customer must be willing to be involved during the entire development process.

➤ *Incremental development*. Agile methods work well when you are working iteratively and building the solution incrementally.[5]

The improved performance resulting from agile methods can be dramatic:

➤ Business value is delivered faster and often more reliably.

➤ Customers are able to see visible progress.

➤ Frequent feedback allows for continuous improvement and fine-tuning.

➤ Acceptance of change is built into the project—change that adds value is encouraged with each increment.

➤ Value-based prioritization ensures the most important features are built first.

ITERATION

Although other chapters of this book may suggest that the steps of business analysis are sequential, they are unquestionably performed iteratively. Iterating is the best defense when attempting to control an unpredictable process. Incremental, evolutionary, staged, or spiral methodologies are all iterative in nature.

Throughout the requirements phase, the business analyst should facilitate real dialogue that allows requirements to evolve and permits innovative solutions to emerge. Requirements emerge throughout the project (see Figure 3-1).

The business analyst needs to build in candid feedback mechanisms at frequent intervals to show the real status of requirements and solution design. The genius of this approach is that it allows the team to improve requirements and the solution design after each iteration. During the requirements phase, the solution architects work on early iterations of the solution design and prototypes. As the business analyst conducts requirements trade-off analyses, the architect does the same with solution options. Thus, prototyping is the first step in iterative development.

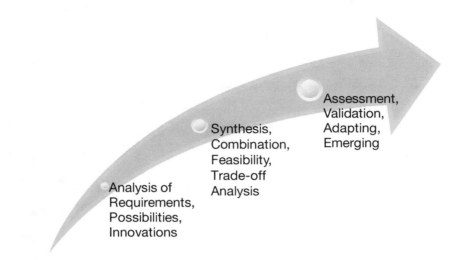

FIGURE 3-1. Emerging Requirements

These early prototypes are followed by incremental working versions of the final system containing a subset of the required features. These working subsystems possess limited functionality but are otherwise true to system requirements.

The value of iterative development is found in regular customer reviews and feedback following each iteration. The best validation that requirements have been met is a tested, integrated system. Documents and models often contain undetected defects. When users actually work with a system, flaws become evident, whether caused by a system defect or a misunderstood requirement.

For the project manager, a new approach to planning is essential. Rolling wave planning is the order of the day, where short-term plans cover a single iteration and are quite detailed, while later iterations are planned at only a high level. Iterative development provides a firm foundation in each increment that becomes the basis of later waves of plans.

SCALABILITY

Whether a team uses a light or heavy methodology, it performs all the activities discussed thus far. They are likely to be executed in a broad sense at project initiation and progressively elaborated as the project traverses its life cycle. For small, straightforward projects that are easily understood, a minimal amount of requirements documentation and models is appropriate. Indeed, the rule is the smaller the team, the less formal the documentation. However, for significant, complex, high-risk projects, a full set of approved requirements documentation is in order. For low- to moderate-risk projects, the rigor should be scaled appropriately, applying more formality and structure in the higher-risk areas of the project.

THE RECIPE FOR PROJECT SUCCESS

Whatever the nature of the project, a business analyst can't go wrong if she remembers to structure the project by following the recipe for success, which is adapted from the Standish Group's famous recipe: [6]

Their message is clear: *size matters*. When structuring a project or major project phases, the project manager and business analyst should strive to follow these guidelines to reduce project risk.

Ingredients:	Minimization, communications, standardization
Mix with:	Full-time core team members: business analyst, project manager, business visionary, and architects and developers, coached by an involved project sponsor
Bake:	No longer than six months, no more than six people, at no more than $750,000. To achieve success more than 80% of the time, the current conventional wisdom is for even smaller projects: no longer than 3 months, no more than four people, no more than $500,000.

UNAVOIDABLE CHALLENGES

Any discussion of the business analyst role is incomplete without addressing the pitfalls of filling this difficult and vital function. The business analyst's responsibilities are many—she is expected to scope the system, translate business needs for architects and developers, translate technical issues for business representatives, model and document requirements, act as communication broker, serve as political mentor, test and validate the solution (and in general, represent customers, users, and stakeholders)—but the position may be invested with too much power.[7] In many organizations, the addition of credible and influential business analysts has greatly improved the elicitation and documentation of requirements. However, there are common problems with the role. It pays the business analyst to take heed and avoid these pitfalls:

➤ *Lack of knowledge and skills.* Business analysts often lack the necessary management skills because it is common for IT to thrust strong technologists into managerial positions.

➤ *Barrier vs. bridge*. Business analysts sometimes assume too much influence over project decisions. Some business analysts may stand between the technical and business communities instead of serving as a facilitator and enabler by bringing them together at the table. In such cases, the business analyst acts as a communication barrier, not a bridge.

➤ *Lagging business and technical acumen*. Business analysts quickly become generalists in both the business and technical arenas. Maintaining credibility with both communities requires staying current with both technology advances and business trends.

➤ *Analysis paralysis*. Business analysts are often tempted to overanalyze, stretching out the analysis period rather than iterating. Overanalysis sometimes leads the business analyst to make promises based on theoretical models that may not work in practice. Several iterations, with feedback from both the business and technical communities, are worth more than a single, all-encompassing analysis.

USING DIFFERENT MANAGEMENT APPROACHES

Does the business analyst role change, either significantly or subtly, in different project management approaches? If so, how? All projects have a cycle, a sequence of stages through which the project passes. Typical cycles are made up of a series of periods and phases, each with a defined output that guides research, development, construction, and acquisition of goods and services.[8]

Project cycle models are not interchangeable; *one size does not fit all*. As projects have become more complex, project cycles have evolved to address the various levels of complexity. It is important to understand the complexity of your project and to apply the approach that is best suited to manage or reduce that complexity. In addition, the business analyst needs to have a keen understanding of how to operate optimally within each cycle model.

Project cycles can be categorized into three broad types:

➤ *Linear*: used when the business problem, opportunity, and solution are clear, no major changes are expected, and the effort is considered to be routine. A linear cycle is typically used for maintenance, enhancement, and continuous process improvement projects. It is also used for development projects when requirements are well understood and stable, as in shrink-wrap software development projects.

➤ *Adaptive*: used when the business problem, opportunity, and solution are unclear and the schedule is aggressive. An adaptive cycle is typically used for new technology development, new product development, or complex business process reengineering projects.

➤ *Extreme*: used when the business objectives are unclear and the solution is undefined. An extreme cycle is typically used for research and development, new technology, and new product development projects.[9]

CAREER ADVICE
Choosing the Right Project Approach

Diagnosing project complexity is an essential first step when determining the appropriate management approach, plan-driven versus adaptive.

A Word to the Wise

Work collaboratively with the project manager and other key project leaders to diagnose the complexity of the project before deciding the project approach.

Figure 3-2 shows the distinct differences between linear and adaptive methods.

Linear Methods	Adaptive Methods
• Industrial-age thinking • Plan based • Distinct life cycle phases • Tasks completed in orderly sequence • Assumes predictability • Lays out development steps • Stresses the importance of requirements	• Many rapid planning and development cycles • Produces small batches of tailored products on a tight schedule • Constant evaluation of the evolving product • Constant evaluation of the value of functions in backlog

FIGURE 3-2. Linear vs. Adaptive Methods

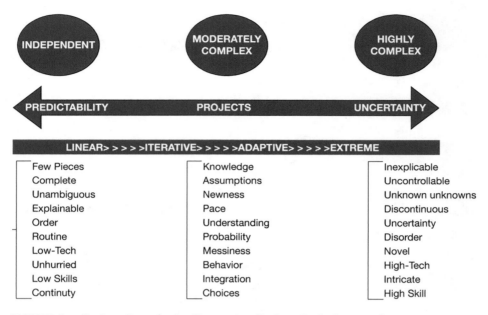

FIGURE 3-3. Project Complexity Mapped to Project Cycle Approaches

© 2011 By Kathleen B. Hass and Associates, Inc.

As we move along the complexity continuum from simpler to highly complex projects, we also move along the spectrum of project cycle types. A linear approach works for a simple project whereas adaptive and extreme approaches are used to manage the uncertainties of increasingly complex efforts (see Figure 3-3).

THE BEST BUSINESS ANALYSIS PRACTICES FOR LOW-COMPLEXITY PROJECTS

The traditional role of the business analyst as discussed in Chapter 2 does not need to change much for a business analyst to successfully execute activities on low-complexity projects. However, to optimize the business analyst role, it is wise to adopt some of the principles of agile and iterative development:

> ➤ Prototype for requirements understanding, to reduce risk, and to prove a concept

➤ Keep the business analyst as a member of the core project leadership team throughout the project

➤ Continuously validate, evolve, and improve requirements throughout the project.

CAREER ADVICE
Linear Methods

Sometimes it is appropriate to use some agile techniques even when using the waterfall model on low-complexity projects..

A Word to the Wise

Work collaboratively with the project manager and other key project leaders to determine which agile techniques might add value to the project.

THE BEST BUSINESS ANALYSIS PRACTICES FOR MODERATELY COMPLEX PROJECTS

There's no question about it: agile methods expedite the new product development process, especially for products that are software intensive. Agile is a streamlined methodology, based on having only essential people work in tight-knit teams for quick and efficient results. As we've seen, one very important member of the team is the business analyst; if companies hope to achieve strategic goals, they need someone who is focused on the business value expected from the project outcomes. The business analyst provides guidance during a project, before funds are invested, and after the solution is delivered. She continually focuses on the evolving business requirements and serves as the steward of the business benefits.[10]

On all projects, business analysts serve by conducting enterprise analysis and developing the business case, in which they analyze the best approach to a particular project, forecast quantifiable benefits, and create a release plan. Once a project is approved and funded, the business analyst continues to oversee and elaborate the business requirements for each release, and makes sure the releases are prioritized according to business value.

Through leadership and collaboration, the project manager and business analyst guide the agile team, ensuring that it is both efficiently and effectively run and that it adds significant long-term benefits for the company. The business analyst plays close attention to the original business case, recommending the project be terminated when the ROI has been realized.

ELICITING FIRM, BASIC BUSINESS REQUIREMENTS

A business analyst's main priorities when she is first attached to a specific project are to elicit firm, basic business requirements (what we used to call high-level requirements, which outline the breadth of requirements and which we do not expect to change), to collaboratively determine the most feasible solution, and then to categorize releases into valuable features or functions. Then each feature is initially described in enough detail to determine its cost versus its benefits, thus developing an ROI for each release.

Knowing what it will take to deliver each individual component of the solution as well as what the return will be to the organization, the development team can then build components or features based on business value, delivering the highest-value features first. As the project moves through the release schedule, the business analyst elaborates the requirements in enough detail to meet the development team's needs and continually validates that the emerging solution meets the changing business needs.

TRACKING BUSINESS VALUE

As an agile project progresses through its life cycle of requirements, design, construction, testing, and deployment for each iteration, the team continually learns new information. It becomes clearer how many resources will be needed to perform detailed design, construction, and tests for each release, how much risk there is to the project, and how the risk needs to be managed. Accordingly, it is important to go back and check original assumptions about business value and costs to develop and operate the new solution to see if they are still true, or if the original business case has been compromised. Also, the business analyst continually validates that the emerging solution meets the business needs.

CAREER ADVICE
Agile Methods

If the project team has not worked in an agile environment, it is best that the team not only attend training but use an experienced facilitator when establishing project plans.

A Word to the Wise

Work collaboratively with the project manager and other key project leaders to ensure you have the training and support needed for your team. Agile methods will require significant changes to how your team works with your customers and business partners. Be sure all of the project leaders are able to accommodate your needs.

Working with the project manager and the core team of developers and customers, the business analyst updates the business case after each release. For example, the business analyst may discover that a project is going to take 12 months instead of 6 and will cost $10 million instead of $8 million. The portfolio management team needs to be informed of this new information so that they can decide if the project is still a good investment and if it should continue. The business analyst can then make an appropriate recommendation, such as continuation with some sort of course correction, like a scaling down of the requirements.

Because agile projects often involve upgrading information systems, it can be easy for the technical developers to focus on what technology can do rather than on how technology can best serve the specific goals of the company. Throughout the constant adjustments made during the development process, the business analyst keeps the focus on the business requirements, the costs and risks involved, and the value the emerging solution will ultimately return to the organization.

If the project ROI is met early and the value of future releases is marginalized, it is up to the business analyst to bring this to the attention of the project team and project sponsor, recommending that the project be brought to a close and the team members be reassigned to higher-value projects that are waiting to be resourced.

VALIDATING OPERATIONAL COMPONENTS AFTER EVERY RELEASE

The business analyst's role of liaison between the project manager, the QA/testers, the developers (engineers who may not understand the intricacies of the business process), and customers (business people who may not know what exactly to request technologically) is an important one. By being involved during the development process, business analysts can validate that new components are actually meeting business needs. They also take information to other groups outside the agile team to further corroborate that the changes have the support of other stakeholders.

The business analyst confirms that these stakeholders will benefit from the revised requirements or at least not have conflicting requirements that need to be addressed.

ANALYZING AND ASSESSING OPERATIONAL COMPONENTS

In conjunction with the cost of the development of a new business solution, the operational component needs to be analyzed and assessed before the solution is implemented. If it is a major new business system, perhaps there will be a need for some reorganization, retooling, retraining, or acquisition of new staff. Working with management, the business analyst helps to ensure the organization is prepared for the impact of the changes and can support the release plan. That way, when the complete solution is delivered, it can be operated efficiently and effectively.

COMPARING ACTUAL COSTS TO ACTUAL BENEFITS

Once the new system is in place, the actual costs of development or acquisition, deployment, and cost to operate should be compared to the system's actual benefits to the company. This final analysis shows the organization whether it has received its forecasted return on project investment. If the performance metrics show that the project was a success, wonderful! If not, the business analyst investigates to find out what went wrong. Was the project a bad investment because the risk was too high? Was the project executed poorly and so ended up costing a lot more than expected? Was the organization not prepared for the new way of operating the business, so operating costs were much higher than predicted? This type of post project evaluation is crucial to improving future project decisions because it allows a company to learn from its mistakes.

"LIGHTENING" THE REQUIREMENTS

Agile requirements are typically "lighter" than those developed for linear project models. Requirements are visually documented whenever possible. The wise business analyst uses modeling to manage complexity. Less formal user stories (a high-level description of solution behavior) may suffice, as opposed to use cases. Agile user stories are typically:

➤ *Independent.* Avoid dependencies with other stories; this reduces the complexity and the cost of changes because changes only impact one story.

➤ *Negotiable.* Encourage discussion of stories.

➤ *Valuable.* Stories provide real business benefits to the users, customers, and stakeholders.

➤ *Estimable.* Stories are detailed enough for the team to estimate time and cost.

➤ *Sized appropriately.* Stories are small enough to be completed in one iteration; larger stories are acceptable if in backlog.

➤ *Testable.* Clear acceptance criteria are stated in customer terms.[11]

MANAGING CHANGES TO REQUIREMENTS

Managing changes to requirements using iterative development is less complex because iterative development eliminates the many-to-many relationships that are often found in complex system builds. This frees the team to welcome changes that add value to iterations that are in backlog, since detailed requirements and design have not yet occurred.

DEVELOPING ADVANCED SKILLS

Advanced skill development is required for business analysts who are working on agile projects. They need to develop new or higher-level leadership skills, including facilitation, coaching, collaborative decision-making, team development, and team building. The analyst will also need to learn a new terminology as well as new skills for documenting requirements and for managing them. The analyst also needs to have a good understanding of software architecture and be proficient in decoupling the breadth of the solution from the depth of the solution into feature-driven requirements.

THE BEST BUSINESS ANALYSIS PRACTICES FOR HIGHLY COMPLEX PROJECTS, PROGRAMS, AND MEGAPROJECTS

Welcome a certain amount of complexity and churn because it creates a chemical reaction that jars creative thinking.

—COLLEEN YOUNG

Projects sometimes fail because project leadership is inappropriately matched to project characteristics. For highly complex projects, the project manager and business analyst are in critical leadership positions. Once it is clear that a project is highly complex, organizations need to assign their most senior resources to fill project leadership roles—project managers and business analysts who understand how to not just manage complexity, but capitalize on it.

Highly complex projects offer the greatest opportunities for creativity. But the business analyst must understand the nature of complexity to foster innovation and creativity. *Complexity* is one of those words that is difficult to define. Some say *complexity* is the opposite of *simplicity*; others say *complicated* is the opposite of *simple*, while *complex* is the opposite of *independent*. A complex structure is said to use interwoven components that introduce mutual dependencies and produce more than the sum of their parts. In today's business systems, this is the difference between a collection of legacy systems kluged together through inconsistent data interfaces and an architected set of integrated business processes and applications.

A complex system can also be described as one in which many different components interact in multiple ways.[12] In the context of a design that is difficult to understand or implement, complexity is the quality of being intricate and compounded.[13] When project managers characterize a project as complex, they usually mean the project is "challenging to manage because of size, complicated interactions, or uncertainties. Often, anxiety goes hand in hand with complexity."[14]

Since complex projects are by their very nature unpredictable, it is imperative that the project team keep its options open as long as possible, building those options into the project approach. This adaptive approach requires that considerable time be dedicated to researching and studying the business problem or opportunity; conducting competitive, technological, and benchmark studies; defining dependencies and interrelationships; and identifying potential options to meet the business need or solve the business problem. In addition, the team experiments with alternative solutions and analyzes the economic, technical, operational, cultural, and legal feasibility of each until it becomes clear which solution option has the highest probability of success. When the opportunity is unclear and the solution is unknown, traditional linear approaches simply will not work.

MAKING DESIGN DECISIONS AT THE LAST RESPONSIBLE MOMENT

On highly complex projects, it is important to separate design from construction. The key is to use expert resources and allow them to spend enough time experimenting before they make design decisions; the construction activities will thereby become much more predictable. Linear methods will likely be appropriate during the construction phase of the project.

Models for adaptive project management are still emerging. We suggest two that are designed to provide iterative learning experiences, adapt and evolve as more is learned, allow analysis and experimentation to determine solution design viability, and delay decision-making as long as possible (that is, until the last responsible moment, the point at which further delays will put the project at risk): the adaptive evolutionary prototyping model and the eXtreme project management model. There are significant differences between the adaptive and eXtreme approaches (see Figure 3-4).

Adaptive Evolutionary Prototyping Model

The keep-our-options-open approach often involves rapid prototyping—a fast build of a solution component to prove that an idea is feasible—which

Adaptive Methods	eXtreme Methods

• Many rapid planning and development cycles
• Produce small batches of tailored products on a tight schedule
• Constant evaluation of evolving product
• Constant evaluation of the value of functions in backlog
	• Keep your options opens
	  – Build options into the approach
	• Discover, experiment, create, innovate
	  – Analyze problem/opportunity
	  – Conduct competitive, technical, and benchmark studies
	  – Brainstorm to identify all possible solutions
	  – Analyze feasibility of each option
	  – Design and test multiple solutions

FIGURE 3-4. Adaptive vs. Extreme Methods

is typically used for high-risk components, requirements understanding, or proof of a concept.

Evolutionary prototyping is quite effective for multiple iterations of requirements elicitation, analysis, and solution design. Iteration is the best defense against uncertainty because with each iteration, the technical and business experts examine the prototype and glean more information and certainty about functions that are built into the next iteration.

The strength of prototyping is that customers work closely with the project team, providing feedback on each iteration (see Figure 3-5). If requirements are unclear and highly volatile, prototyping helps bring the business need into view.

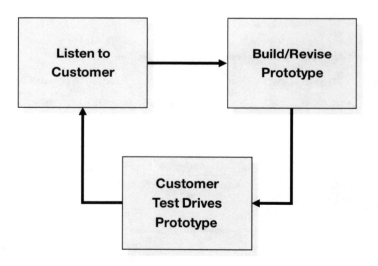

Rapid Prototype = Throwaway Prototype

Evolutionary Prototype = Evolve to End Product

FIGURE 3-5.   Adaptive Evolutionary Prototype Model

eXtreme Project Management Model

> *An extreme project is a complex, high-speed, self-correcting venture during which people interact in search of a desirable result under conditions of high uncertainty, high change, and high stress.*
>
> —Doug DeCarlo

The eXtreme project management model was developed by Doug DeCarlo and is fully defined in his book, *eXtreme Project Management: Using Leadership, Principles, and Tools to Deliver Value in the Face of Volatility*.[15] The model is designed to be used when a great deal of change is expected during a project, speed is of the essence, and uncertainty and ambiguity exist. Pharmaceutical research for a groundbreaking drug, new product development for a pioneering invention, and major business transformation efforts are examples of extreme projects.

eXtreme project management is sometimes also called radical project management or adaptive project management. Some equate it to agile project management. The eXtreme project management approach consists of a number of short, experimental iterations designed to determine project goals and identify the most viable solution. As in the agile model, eXtreme project management requires that the customer be involved every step of the way until the solution emerges—a practice that involves many iterations. Like the iterative spiral model, the eXtreme model terminates after the solution is found (or when the sponsor is unwilling to fund any more research); the project team then transitions to one of the other appropriate models.

DeCarlo depicts eXtreme project management as a squiggly line that shows the project from start to finish, demonstrating the open, elastic approach that is required. The focus is on the art of project management versus the more scientific and technical scheduling and planning. This approach creates several challenges we need to be aware of. It can be difficult to:

➤ Know how long to keep your options open

➤ Build options into the approach without undue cost and time

➤ Gather the right group of experts to discover, experiment, create, innovate, and:

  › Analyze the problem/opportunity

  › Conduct competitive, technical, and benchmark studies

  › Brainstorm to identify all possible solutions

  › Analyze the feasibility of each option

  › Design and test multiple solutions.

OPERATING ON THE EDGE OF CHAOS

Conventional business analysis practices that assume a stable and predictable environment encourage us to develop all the requirements up front, get them approved, and then fiercely control changes. As we have seen, conventional linear project cycles work well and should be used for predictable, repeatable projects; however, this approach has proven to be no match for chaotic 21st-century projects. Figure 3-6 compares the characteristics of projects on which conventional linear practices can be successfully used with the characteristics of projects that require a more adaptive model. A blend of the linear, adaptive, and eXtreme models is almost always the answer. The trick is to know when and how to apply which approach.

Conventional linear approaches work well for projects that...	Adaptive approaches work well for projects that...
Are structured, orderly, disciplined	Are spontaneous, disorganized
Rely heavily on plans	Evolve as more information is known
Are predictable, well defined, repeatable	Are surprising, ambiguous, unique, unstable, innovative, creative
Are built in an unwavering environment	Are built in a volatile and chaotic environment
Use proven technologies	Use unproven technologies
Have a realistic schedule	Have an aggressive schedule; there is an urgent need

FIGURE 3-6.   Conventional vs. Adaptive Approaches

What exactly does it mean to operate on the edge of chaos? Complex systems fluctuate between a static state of equilibrium and an adaptive state of chaos. If a system remains static, it will eventually result in paralysis and death. Whereas, if a complex system is in chaos, it is unable to function. So, here is the genius of complexity: it breeds and nourishes creativity, as complex systems adapt to changes in the environment for survival. Complexity scientists tell us that the most creative and productive state is at the *edge of chaos*. (Refer to Figure 3-7.)

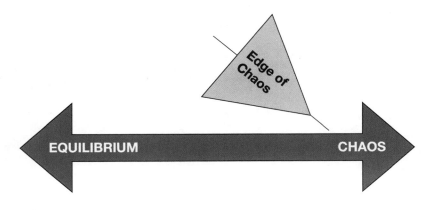

FIGURE 3-7.   The Edge of Chaos—The Most Creative State

Therefore, complex project teams must operate at the edge of chaos for a time in order to allow the creative process to flourish. The business analyst assigned to a complex project must use adaptive business analysis methods to foster an environment where creativity is possible. The next section explores the business analyst as creative leader of complex projects.

PUTTING IT ALL TOGETHER: WHAT DOES THIS MEAN TO THE BUSINESS ANALYST?

A business analyst who is an asset to highly complex projects is comfortable with lots of uncertainty and ambiguity in the early stages of a project. She leads and directs plenty of sessions of brainstorming, alternative analysis, experimentation, prototyping, out-of-the-box thinking, and trial and error, and encourages the team to keep options open until they have identified an innovative solution that will allow the organization to leap ahead of the competition.

What does this mean for the business analyst who has worked successfully on moderately complex projects but has the desire to become a critical strategic asset who works on highly complex endeavors? As you create your professional development plan, include education and experience in the following areas:

- ➤ Strategic planning, measurement scorecards, and portfolio management
- ➤ Business case development, return on project investment, and managing business benefits of project deliverables
- ➤ Creativity and innovation
- ➤ Complexity management

➤ Problem analysis, opportunity analysis, competitive analysis, and benchmark studies

➤ The industry within which your organization operates: best practices, key competitors, and trends, as well as your organization's strengths, weaknesses, opportunities, and threats.

NOTES

1. Martin Fowler, "The New Methodology," 2003. Online at http://www.martinfowler.com/articles/newMethodology.html (accessed July 2010).

2. Scott Ambler, "Agile Analysis," 2010. Online at http://www.agilemodeling.com/essays/agileAnalysis.htm (accessed July 2010).

3. Ibid.

4. Scott Ambler, "When Does(n't) Agile Modeling Make Sense?" 2010. Online at http://www.agilemodeling.com/essays/whenDoesAMWork.htm (accessed July 2010).

5. Ibid.

6. The Standish Group International, *CHAOS: A Recipe for Success* (West Yarmouth, MA: The Standish Group International, 1999): 12.

7. Ambler, "Agile Analysis."

8. Hal Mooz, Kevin Forsbert, and Howard Cotterman, *Communicating Project Management: The Integrated Vocabulary of Project Management and Systems Engineering* (Hoboken, NJ: John Wiley & Sons, Inc., 2003): 334.

9. Robert K. Wysocki, *Effective Project Management: Traditional, Adaptive, Extreme*, 4th ed. (Indianapolis: Wiley Publishing, Inc., 2007): 48.

10. Kathleen B. Hass, "An Eye for Value: What the Business Analyst Brings to the Agile Team," *Project Management World Today* (June 2007): 1–5.

11. Mike Cottmeyer, V. Lee Henson, and VersionOne, Inc., "The Agile Business Analyst," 2010. Online at http://www.versionone.com/pdf/Agile_Business_Analyst.pdf?mkt_tok=3RkMMJWWfF9wsRolv63JZKXonjHpfsXw6uUsW6%2Bg38431UFwdcjKPmjr1YEERMZ0dvycMRAVFZl5nRpdCPOcc45P9PA%3D (accessed July 2010).

12. D. Rind, "Complexity and Climate," *Science Magazine* 284, no. 5411 (April 2, 1999): 105–107.

13. Luay Alawneh, "A Unified Approach for Verification and Validation of Systems and Software Engineering Models," *Proceedings of the 13th Annual IEEE International Symposium and Workshop on Engineering of Computer-Based Systems* (2006): 409–418.

14. B. Michael Aucoin, *Right-Brain Project Management: A Complementary Approach* (Vienna, VA: Management Concepts, 2007): 132.

15. Doug DeCarlo, *eXtreme Project Management: Using Leadership, Principles, and Tools to Deliver Value in the Face of Volatility* (San Francisco: Jossey-Bass, 2004).

PART II

Unlocking the Secrets of Creative Leadership

In this part, we present the case for the growth and development of business analysts as creative leaders. Our goal is to arm business analysts with the principles, knowledge, practices, confidence, and courage they need to assume the roles of creative leader and innovation specialist in their organizations.

Although the belief that the business analyst is primarily responsible for writing and managing requirements remains prevalent, the numbers of business analysts serving as senior-level business/technology optimization and innovation consultants is growing rapidly. While business analysts acquire and sustain their requirements analysis knowledge and skills, organizations today need them to gain entry into the world of creative leadership as well.

➤ In Chapter 4, we examine how management differs from leadership and how creative leadership differs from conventional leadership in the world of business. In addition, we discuss how business analysts can begin to assume the mindset of creative leaders.

➤ In Chapter 5, we discuss the business analyst's role in leading innovation teams and building and sustaining creativity in team decision-making and problem-solving.

➤ In Chapter 6, we examine leadership strategies for fostering innovation and creativity when working with large, complex distributed teams.

➤ In Chapter 7, we examine the vast array of creativity-inducing techniques the business analyst can use to foster originality and inventiveness.

➤ In Chapter 8, we take the reader through the steps for planning and executing a requirements elicitation workshop, focusing heavily on ideas for requirements visualization techniques.

CHAPTER 4

Creative Leadership: What's All the Fuss About?

Leadership is a potent combination of strategy and character. But if you must be without one, be without strategy.

— GEN. H. NORMAN SCHWARZKOPF

Leadership is like genius; it is one of those concepts that is recognizable when you observe it in action, but is otherwise somewhat difficult to define. Books about leadership abound, each describing the concept in a different way. Leadership has been defined as:

➤ The art of persuading, influencing, or motivating other people to set aside their individual concerns and to pursue a common goal that is important for the welfare of the group

➤ The ability to elicit extraordinary performance from ordinary people

➤ The capacity to integrate the goals of the organization with the aspirations of its people through a shared vision and committed action.

While there are no gauges by which we can effectively measure the value of leadership, leadership is often the factor that makes one team more effective than another. Leaders are often held accountable for team successes and failures. When a team succeeds, we often remark about its leader's outstanding leadership abilities; when a team fails, the leader is likely to receive the blame.

Leadership is people-centered. And it is all about influence: it always involves actions by a leader (influencer) to affect (influence) the behavior of a follower or followers in a specific situation or activity. Three factors must be present for a person to act as a true leader:

➤ She must have certain inherited characteristics that impart the inclination to become a leader;

➤ She also must have learned knowledge and skills about becoming a leader; and

➤ The right situation must present itself.

We might not be able to do much to shape our inherent leadership disposition, but we certainly can create the appropriate learning opportunities and strive to influence our current situation and environment.

21ˢᵀ-CENTURY LEADERSHIP

In decades gone by, leadership in the business world was considered the province of just a few people who controlled the organization. By contrast, in today's demanding, challenging, and ever-changing business environment, organizations rely on a remarkable assortment of leaders that operate at varying levels of the enterprise. Twenty-first-century leadership looks very different from that of previous eras for several reasons: (1) the economic environment is more volatile and complex than ever before; (2) much of the work is accomplished in teams, so there is a stronger-than-ever need for more leadership at differing levels of the organization; and (3) lifelong learning is at the heart of professional success. The most valuable employees will no longer stay in narrow functional areas but will be likely to work broadly across the enterprise.

Teams that perform multiple activities on multiple projects are now more common than are multiple workers performing a single task. As we transition from the traditional stovepipe-shaped, function-centric structures to the team- and project-centric workplace, we are seeing the emergence of creative leadership at the nucleus of 21st-century business models. Because 21st-century projects are exceedingly complex, we cannot manage them with the traditional command and control leadership style.

21ST-CENTURY ORGANIZATIONAL CHANGE

Virtually all organizations of any size are investing in large-scale transformations of one kind or another. Contemporary changes add value to the organization through the development of breakthrough ideas, the optimization of business processes, and the use of information technology (IT) as a competitive advantage. These initiatives are often generated by mergers or acquisitions, new strategies, global competition, or the emergence of new technologies. Other programs are launched to implement new or reengineered business systems to drive waste out of business operations. Still others are spawned because of the need to innovate, adapt, or die.

Most of these changes are accompanied by pioneering product launches, organizational restructuring, new partnerships, cultural transformations, downsizing or right-sizing, and the development of value-added IT systems. Others involve implementing new lines of business and new ways of doing business (e.g., e-business). In addition to these business-driven changes, IT organizations are transforming themselves, striving to become more value-driven, service-oriented, and better aligned with the business—and to really contribute business benefits. In the 21st century, project teams no longer deal with IT projects in isolation but within the overarching process of business transformation and innovation. The reach of change affects all areas of the organization and beyond—to customers, suppliers, and business partners—making the complexity of projects unrelenting.

Rather than undertaking only a small number of projects, today's organizations are engaged in virtually hundreds of ongoing projects of varying sizes, durations, and levels of complexity. Since business strategy is largely achieved through projects, projects are essential to the growth and survival of organizations. They create value in the form of new products and services as a response to changes in the business environment, competition, and the marketplace.

To reap the rewards of significant, large-scale business transformation initiatives designed not only to keep organizations in the game but also to make them major players, organizations must be able to manage complex business transformation projects effectively. However, failed projects and projects with huge cost and schedule overruns have been commonplace in the past. According to leading research companies such as The Standish Group International, Inc., the Software Engineering Institute at Carnegie Mellon University, Gartner, Forrester Research, and Meta Group, vastly underperforming business transformation and IT projects have been the order of the day. The actual numbers are at best disappointing, at worst punishing and debilitating:

> ➤ The annual cost to the US economy is around $1.22 trillion per year. Sessions, Roger, the IT Complexity Crisis: Danger and opportunity (Houston Texas: ObjectWatch Inc. 2009); per year for failed and canceled projects.

➤ Twenty-five to 40 percent of all spending on projects is wasted as a result of rework.

➤ Fifty percent of new business solutions are rolled back out of production.

➤ Forty percent of problems are found by end users.

➤ Poorly defined applications have led to persistent miscommunication between business and IT, which is a major contributor to a 66 percent project failure rate for these applications and which costs U.S. businesses at least $30 billion every year.

➤ An estimated 60 to 80 percent of project failures can be attributed directly to poor requirements gathering, analysis, and management.

➤ A full two-thirds of all IT projects fail or run into trouble.

These dismal statistics and the increased importance of projects in executing business strategies have advanced the value and criticality of project leaders, including project managers, business analysts, technologists, and business visionaries. And make no mistake; project leadership is *very* different from project management, just as traditional management is very different from creative leadership.

MANAGEMENT VERSUS LEADERSHIP: WHO HAS THE POWER?

There are subtle differences between management and leadership and how they amass power and strength. The differences manifest themselves in how individuals motivate others. Managers have subordinates, while leaders have followers. Managers are often risk averse, whereas leaders are risk seekers.[1]

MANAGEMENT IS ABOUT OPERATING EFFECTIVELY

Management know-how involves establishing and executing a set of processes that keep complicated systems operating efficiently. Managers have authority by virtue of their title and position. Key facets of management involve strategic and business planning, budgeting, organizing, staffing, controlling, and problem-solving. Organizations tend to implement management processes to impose discipline and to control the looming chaos. At the same time, they have to avoid becoming so bureaucratic that they squash creativity and innovation. Some say management is just about keeping bureaucracies functioning.

LEADERSHIP IS ABOUT CHANGING EFFECTIVELY

Leadership is a different set of processes—those that create a new organization and change it when the business environment shifts. Leadership involves establishing direction and aligning, motivating, and inspiring people to produce change. The irony is that as new entrepreneurial organizations grow to a sustainable scale through creativity and innovation, managerial processes need to be put into place to cope with the growth and control the unruliness. As the organization succeeds and managerial processes are put in place, self-importance and arrogance surface, and a strong culture that is dead set against change emerges.[2]

By contrast, 21st-century *creative leadership* is all about welcoming and embracing change—in fact, creating *disruptive change*. The astute and influential business analyst is primed to play a strong role in resolving the inevitable tension and conflict between resistance to change and the need to innovate.

TO LEAD IS TO HAVE STRENGTH AND POWER

And then there is power. Power is something that is bestowed on an individual by someone else. It imparts the authority to get things done even when others resist, whereas leadership is about inspiring people to want to get the same things accomplished that you do and enabling them to do it. Val Williams, executive coach, tells us that:

> Power is often tied to position: being a CEO, a manager, partner, judge, parent, senator. If you have power, you can impact the lives of others. Strength is not dependent on any position: The concept of strength implies not what you can do to others; but what you can create from your own resources. Where power sometimes motivates people through fear, strength leads people through inspiration. Strength connotes charisma, attractiveness. People more naturally follow a strong person. They are motivated to act by something beyond that person's title.[3]

Strength is very much like leadership. People want to follow a strong person, one who is credible, attractive, results-oriented, fun to work with. Effective project leaders, including the business analyst, are effective through leadership and strength, not through power and authority.

THE GENIUS OF SHARED LEADERSHIP

Organizations use projects to add value to their products and services to better serve their clients and compete in the marketplace. To realize their goals, organizations tap into the talents and competencies of project leadership teams, consisting of the business analyst, the project manager, technologists, and business visionaries.

As discussed in Chapter 2, project-driven organizations develop a portfolio of valuable projects that collectively form the road map from strategy development to strategy execution. Executives spend a great deal of time identifying which projects might offer the greatest rewards with minimal risks. However, to make good project investment decisions, executives are discovering the need for real business analysis so that they have solid information backing their decisions.

DELIVERING VALUABLE CHANGE

The business analyst who is working at the strategy level provides processes, tools, and information to executives to help the organization develop a portfolio of valuable projects. The business analyst then transitions to focus on project execution to meet business needs and maximize the return on project investment.

It is not enough for executive teams to just select the right mix of projects to achieve their strategic imperatives. Executive teams must also establish the organizational capabilities to deliver. Specifically, they must ensure that project teams are capable of contributing to the organization's success. For optimal project execution, several elements are essential:

➤ Appropriate management support and decision-making at key control gates;

➤ Effective and targeted business analysis, information technology, process management, and project management processes, tools, and techniques;

➤ Technical infrastructure and software applications that are tightly aligned with the business; and

➤ High-performing teams.

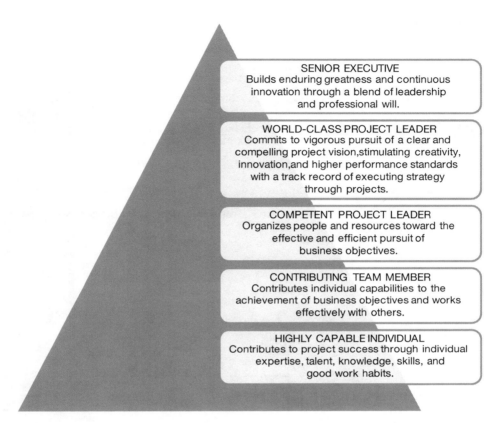

FIGURE 4-1. Business Analyst and Project Management Leadership Model

WORLD-CLASS PROJECT LEADERS

It is especially important for executives to groom exceptional project managers and business analysts so they can transition into effective leaders of complex innovation projects. Figure 4-1 depicts the transition from capable individual to world-class project leader and even to senior executive.

The performance of the business analyst is more critical than ever to keep project teams focused on the business benefits sought through project outcomes. With so much riding on successful projects, the business analyst is emerging to fill the gap in creativity, analysis of the business and the environment, and provision of information needed to execute strategy. At the same time, the project manager has risen to the role of strategic implementer, and cross-functional project teams have become management's strategic tool to convert strategy to achievement.

When project managers and business analysts form a strong partnership with business and technology teams, organizations will begin to reap the maximum value of both disciplines. As the business analysis and project management disciplines mature into strategic business practices, so must our project leaders evolve into strategic leaders of change.

THE 21ST-CENTURY PROJECT LEADER

As programs and projects are launched to realize critical strategic goals, leaders of strategic initiatives should be considered the executive officer team of a small enterprise. Just as a business leader must be multiskilled and strategically focused, a project leader must possess a broad range of knowledge

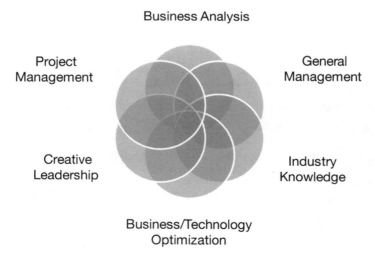

FIGURE 4-2. Project Leader Competency Groups

and experience, including competence in several distinct areas—general management, project management, business analysis, the application area (the domain), leadership, and business/technology optimization (see Figure 4-2).

THE CORE PROJECT LEADERSHIP TEAM

Clearly, a well-formed team of experts is better equipped to provide the requisite knowledge and skills than is a single individual. In the 21st century, small but mighty high-performing teams of experts are a vital strategic asset. It is now becoming obvious that successful projects are more the result of collaboration and leadership than management, command, and control.

Right now, the project team structure is transitioning from a traditional project management setup to one of team leadership. Consider the core project leadership team configuration represented in Figure 4-3. In this approach, the core team is small, multidisciplined, dedicated to the project

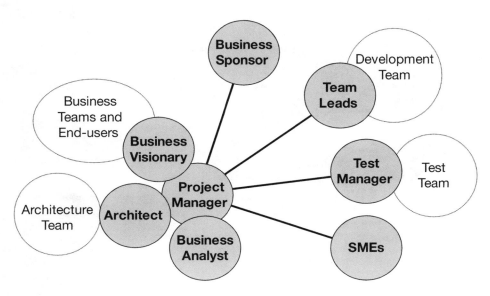

FIGURE 4-3. Core Project Team Configuration

full time, and collocated. The core team forms subteams and brings in subject matter experts when needed.

This core team shares the leadership of the project, each person taking the lead when his or her expertise is needed. Shared leadership does not mean there is no accountability. The project manager is still responsible for ensuring that the business solution is delivered on time, on budget, and with the full scope. The business analyst is responsible for ensuring that the project team fully understands the business need and the benefits expected from the new solution and for validating that the solution meets the requirements and will deliver the expected business value. The architect ensures that the solution is designed and developed according to specifications. And the business visionary continues to keep the team focused on the big picture, the strategic goal that will be advanced by the new solution; brings in the appropriate business experts when needed; and helps prepare the organization to operate in a new way once the business solution is deployed.

CAREER ADVICE
Shared Leadership

Projects today are too complex to succeed using conventional project management methods.

A Word to the Wise

Build strong relationships with project managers, business visionaries, influential technologists, and strong managers.

- Seek assignment on a critical project in need of strong leadership and a creative solution.
- Seek a mentor who has the power and influence you will need to become a creative facilitator of change.

SITUATIONAL PROJECT LEADERSHIP

In the past, project teams revolved around the project manager as their leader, but the very nature of project team leadership is changing. The team leadership style changes subtly based on the needs of the project. The project manager still leads the planning and budgeting activities. During requirements elicitation, the business analyst takes the lead, and the other core team members slide into more of a support role. As the project moves into solution design and development, the technical architect or developer often assumes the lead role. All core leadership team members support each other, and they get out of the way when their expertise is not the critical element needed. In Chapter 5, we will explore the role of the business analyst as creative team leader in more detail.

THE BUSINESS ANALYST AS PROJECT LEADER

The business analyst, serving as one of several project leaders, closes the gap in areas that have historically been woefully overlooked in business transformation and innovation projects. Some areas that are the purview of the business analyst and that require more diligence include:

➤ Integrating strategic planning with portfolio planning for information systems and technology efforts

➤ Defining business problems and identifying new business opportunities for achieving the strategic vision

➤ Understanding the business need and the effects of the proposed solution on all areas of business operations

➤ Maintaining a fierce focus on the value the project is expected to bring to the enterprise

➤ Using an integrated set of analysis and modeling techniques to make the as-is and to-be business visible for all to see, understand, and validate

➤ Translating the business objectives into business requirements using powerful modeling tools

➤ Validating that the new solution meets the business need

➤ Managing the benefits expected from the new solution.

Serving as a key project leader with a perpetual focus on adding value to the business, the business analyst becomes a powerful change agent.

THE BUSINESS ANALYST AS CHANGE AGENT

According to John P. Kotter, a professor at the Harvard Business School who is regarded as an authority on leadership and change, "The rate of change is not going to slow down anytime soon. If anything, competition in most industries will probably speed up even more in the next few decades."[4] Kotter predicts that as the rate of change increases, the willingness and ability of knowledge workers to acquire new knowledge and skills will become central to career success for individuals and to the economic success of organizations. Workers who are able to develop the capacity to handle a complex and changing business environment are vital to organizational survival. Along the way, these individuals grow to become unusually competent in advancing organizational transformation. They learn to be leaders.

As we have seen, the prevalence of large-scale organizational change has grown exponentially over the past two decades. Although some foresee (or perhaps wish) that the amount of change, in terms of reengineering, mergers and acquisitions, restructuring, downsizing, quality improvement efforts, and cultural transformation projects, will soon diminish, all indications are that change is here to stay. Powerful economic and social forces are at work to force innovation and change, including the rise of the Internet, global economic integration, maturation of markets in developed countries, emerging markets in developing countries, and the turbulent political landscape.

One of the critical roles of the business analyst (and the entire project leadership team) is to effect positive change—to become a creative leader who brings about innovation. Competitive pressures are forcing organizations to reassess their fundamental structures and operations. The amount of change today is formidable. Some react to this change with anger, confusion, and dismay, and it falls upon the project manager and business analyst to lead the transformations most organizations must undergo. In her role as change agent, effecting change through projects, the business analyst:

➤ Fosters the concept that projects are business problems, solved by teams of people using technology as a strategic tool

➤ Works as a strategic implementer of change, focusing on the business benefits expected from the project to achieve strategies

➤ Changes the way the business interacts with the technical team, often significantly increasing the amount of business resources/expertise dedicated to projects

➤ Encourages the technical team members to work collaboratively with the business representatives

➤ Builds high-performing teams that focus more on the business value of the project than on the "way cool" technology

➤ Prepares the organization to accept new business solutions and to operate them efficiently

➤ Measures the actual benefits new business solutions bring to the organization.

CHANGING THE WAY WE DO PROJECTS

An organization's culture is durable because it is "the way we do things around here." Changing the way it selects projects, develops and manages requirements, and manages projects, while focusing not only on business value but also on innovation, is often a significant shift for an organization. Even today, many organizational cultures still promote piling project requests, accompanied by sparse requirements, onto the IT and new-product development groups and then wondering why they cannot seem to deliver.

Conversely, mature organizations devote a significant amount of time and energy to conducting due diligence and encouraging experimentation and creativity before rushing to construction. These due diligence activities include enterprise analysis, competitive analysis, problem analysis, and creative solution alternative analysis, all performed before selecting and prioritizing projects. This new approach involves a significant cultural shift for most organizations—spending more time up front to make certain the solution is creative, innovative, and even disruptive.

IMPLEMENTING CULTURAL CHANGE

Rita Hadden, specialist in software best practices, process improvement, and corporate culture change, offers some insight into the enormity of the effort to truly change the way we do projects. To achieve culture change, Hadden suggests organizations must have a management plan to deal with the technical complexity of the change and a leadership plan to address the human aspects of the change. According to Hadden, successful culture change requires at a minimum the following elements:

➤ A compelling vision and call to action

➤ Credible knowledge and skills to guide the change

➤ A reward system aligned with the change

➤ Adequate resources to implement the change

➤ A detailed plan and schedule.

Hadden goes on to say that change agents need to understand the concerns and motivations of the people they hope to influence. They ought to clearly define the desired outcomes for the change and how to measure progress, assess the organization's readiness for change, and develop plans to minimize the barriers to success. The goal of the business analyst is to create a critical mass, a situation in which enough people in the organization integrate professional business analysis practices into their projects and maintain them as a standard. Therefore, to become leaders in their organizations, business analysts need to learn all about change management—becoming skilled change experts.[5]

THE BUSINESS ANALYST AS VISIONARY

A common vision is essential for an organization to bring about significant change. A clear vision helps to direct, align, and inspire people's actions. Without a clear vision, a lofty transformation plan can be reduced to a list of inconsequential projects that sap energy and drain valuable resources. Most importantly, a clear vision guides decision-making so that people do not arrive at every decision through unneeded debate and conflict. Yet we continue to underestimate the power of vision.

Whether she is implementing professional business analysis practices, a new innovative product, or a major new business solution, the business analyst needs to articulate a clear vision and then involve the stakeholders in the change initiative as early as possible. Executives and middle managers are essential allies in bringing about change of any magnitude. They all must deliver a consistent message about the need for the change. Select the most credible and influential members of your organization, seek their advice and counsel, and have them become the voice of change. The greater the number of influential managers, executives, and technical/business experts articulating the same vision, the better chance you have of being successful.

THE BUSINESS ANALYST AS CREDIBLE LEADER

When acting as a change agent, the business analyst needs to develop and sustain a high level of credibility. A credible leader is one that is trusted, one that is capable of being believed. Above all, a business analyst must strive to be a reliable source of information. Credibility is composed of both trustworthiness and expertise. In addition to these elements, colleagues often judge others' credibility on subjective factors, such as enthusiasm and even physical appearance, as well as the objective believability of the message. At the end of the day, professional presence, ethics, and integrity are the cornerstone of credibility.

Credible business professionals are sought out by all organizations. People want to be associated with them. They are thought of as being trustworthy, reliable, sincere—and creative. The business analyst can develop her credibility in bringing about organizational change by becoming proficient in these critical skills and competencies, all of which should be part of an organization's business analyst professional development program:

➤ Practicing business outcome thinking

➤ Conceptualizing and thinking creatively

➤ Demonstrating interpersonal skills

➤ Valuing ethics and integrity

➤ Using robust communication techniques to effectively keep all stakeholders informed

➤ Empowering team members and building high-performing teams

➤ Setting direction and providing vision

➤ Listening effectively and encouraging new ideas

➤ Seeking responsibility and accepting accountability

➤ Focusing and motivating a group to achieve what is important

➤ Capitalizing on and rewarding the contributions of various team members

➤ Managing complexity to reduce project risks and foster creativity

➤ Welcoming changes that promote the integrity of the solution or product.

CREATIVE LEADERSHIP

I must follow the people, am I not their leader?

—Benjamin Disraeli

CAREER ADVICE
Credible Leadership

Leaders rely on their credibility and ethics to succeed; never sacrifice your integrity.

A Word to the Wise

Create the most sophisticated professional development plan you have ever had. Include:

- Formal training and certifications
- Informal mentoring
- Experiences that stretch your capabilities
- Self study
- Reading, reading, reading.

Focus your plan on communications, creativity, innovation, facilitation, and team leadership.

Creativity has always been important in the world of business, but until now it hasn't been at the top of the management agenda. Perhaps this is because creativity was considered too vague, too hard to pin down. It is even more likely that creativity has not been the focus of management attention because concentrating on it produced a less immediate dividend than improving execution. Although there are similarities in the roles of manager, leader, and creative leader, there are subtle differences as well. Figure 4-4 shows the distinctions between these roles.

Objective	Manager	Leader	Creative Leader
Define what must be done	Planning and budgeting: • Short time frame • Detail oriented • Eliminate risk	Establishing direction: • Long time frame • Big picture • Calculated risk	Establishing breakthrough goals and objectives: • Envisioning the future mission and direction • Aligning with and forging new strategy
Create networks of people and relationships	Organizing and staffing: • Specialization • Getting the right people • Compliance	Aligning people: • Integration • Aligning the organization • Gaining commitment	Aligning teams and stakeholders to the future vision: • Innovation • Integration • Expectations • Political mastery • Gaining commitment
Ensure the job gets done	Controlling and problem-solving: • Containment • Control • Predictability • Outsourcing	Motivating and inspiring: • Empowerment • Expansion • Energizing	Building creative teams: • High performance • Trust development • Empowerment • Courageous disruption • Innovation

FIGURE 4-4. Comparison of Managers, Leaders, and Creative Leaders

SUSTAINING A CULTURE OF CREATIVITY

Because creativity is, in part, the ability to produce something novel, we have long acknowledged that creativity is essential to the entrepreneurship that starts new businesses. But what sustains the best companies as they try to achieve a global reach? We are now beginning to realize that in the 21st century, sustainability is about creativity, transformation, and innovation.

Although academia has focused on creativity for years (we have decades of research to draw on),[6] the shift to a more innovation-driven economy has been sudden, as evidenced by the fact that CEOs lament the absence of creative leaders. As competitive positioning turns into a contest of who can generate the best and greatest number of innovations, creativity scholars are being asked pointed questions about their research. What guidance is available for leaders in creativity-dependent businesses? How do we creatively manage the complexities of this new global environment? How do we find creative leaders, and how do we nurture and manage them? The conclusion of participants in the Harvard Business School colloquium "Creativity, Entrepreneurship, and Organizations of the Future" was that "one doesn't manage creativity; one manages *for creativity*."[7] Management's role is to get the creative people, position them at the right time and place, remove all barriers imposed upon them by the organization, and then *get out of their way*.

INNOVATING

Business analysts are now being challenged to rethink their approach—to not just record what the business is doing or wants to do, but to operate as a lightning rod to stimulate creativity and innovation. To do so, business analysts are also rethinking the role of the customers and users they facilitate, looking at them as creative resources that can contribute imagination and inventiveness, not just operational knowledge. The business analyst who works across and up and down the organization, getting the right people at the right time and in the right place, can fan the flames of creativity.

Good, sometimes great, ideas often come from operational levels of organizations when workers are given a large degree of autonomy. To stay competitive in the 21st century, CEOs are attempting to distribute creative responsibility up, down, and across the organization. Success is unsustainable if it depends too much on the ingenuity of a single person or a few people, as is too often seen in start-ups that flourish for a few years and then fall flat; they were not built to last, to continually innovate. Success is no longer about continuous improvement; it is about continuous innovation.

ENGAGING IN CONSTRUCTIVE DIALOGUE

Creative leaders have many distinguishing beliefs and observable behavioral characteristics. According to John McCann, educator, facilitator, and consultant, creative leaders:

➤ Believe in the capability of others, offer them challenging opportunities, and delegate responsibility to them

➤ Know that people feel a commitment to a decision if they believe they have participated in making it

➤ Understand that people strive to meet other people's expectations

➤ Value individuality

➤ Exemplify creativity in their own behavior and help build an environment that encourages and rewards creativity in others

➤ Are skillful in managing change

➤ Emphasize internal motivators over external motivators

➤ Encourage people to be self-directing.[8]

McCann believes that a skilled and credible facilitator can set the stage for groups to engage in productive dialogue that incorporates creativity, ambiguity, tension, and decisiveness. The business analyst is perfectly positioned to be that credible leader and facilitator, one who sets these conditions that lead to *creativity in motion*:

➤ Participants are willing to have their beliefs examined and reexamined.

➤ Participants look upon each other with respect and realize the benefits that come from open and candid discussion.[9]

FACILITATING CREATIVITY

As a creative leader, the business analyst combines open dialogue with expert facilitation as creativity-inducing tools for stimulating the sharing of unique ideas across the organization. Not only does the collective "IQ" of the groups the business analyst works with rise, so can the CQ, the *creativity quotient*. In fact, business analysts who encourage creativity and guide groups at all levels through the innovation process can increase an entire organization's CQ.

Business analysts would be prudent to take into account the views of John Kao, author of *Jamming: The Art and Discipline of Business Creativity*. According to Kao, drawing up a "Creativity Bill of Rights" can help team members feel as if they are truly responsible for their own decisions. The Creativity Bill of Rights proclaims the following:

➤ Everyone has the ability to be creative.

➤ All ideas deserve an impartial hearing.

➤ Similar to quality, creativity is part of every job description.

➤ Shutting down dialogue prematurely and excessive judgment are fundamental transgressions.

➤ Creativity is about finding balance between art and discipline.

➤ Creativity involves openness to an extensive variety of inputs.

➤ Experiments are always encouraged.

➤ Dignified failure is respectable, poor implementation or bad choices are not.

➤ Creativity involves mastery of change.

➤ Creativity involves a balance of intuition and facts.

➤ Creativity can and should be managed. The business analyst instinctively knows when to bring the dialogue to a close.

➤ Creative work is not an excuse for chaos, disarray, or sloppiness in execution.[10]

THINKING OUTSIDE THE BUILDING

The greatest future breakthroughs will come from leaders who encourage thinking outside a whole building full of boxes.

—Rosabeth Moss Kanter

What kinds of barriers should business analysts expect to encounter when they try to become the invaluable creative leaders organizations need today? The creative leader must learn to penetrate a formidable set of customs that exist in any organization. In a *Harvard Business Review* column, Rosabeth Kanter calls these organizational cultural barriers "inside the building thinking." These may pose the strongest obstruction to creativity and innovation.[11]

What does this mean for the business analyst in her role as facilitator, charged with helping groups engage in productive dialogue? Business analysts must be cognizant of the fact that their first inclination—and the first tendency of their stakeholders—will be to limit their options by focusing on similar companies doing comparable things. So it is up to the business analyst to be aware of and encourage the group to penetrate the inside-the-building boundaries.

To unleash creativity, business analysts must begin to challenge their stakeholders (users, customers, managers, project managers, developers, and executives) to use not only systems thinking, but also complexity thinking and out-of-the-building thinking—to look at the entire ecosystem that surrounds their organizations. It is only then that they can set the stage to bring about lasting innovation.

BECOMING A CREATIVE LEADER

Leadership is the capacity to mobilize people toward valued goals; that is, to produce sustainable change—sustainable because it's good for you and for the people who matter most to you.

—STEW FRIEDMAN

Stew Friedman, professor of management at the Wharton School, former head of Ford Motor's Leadership Development Center, and author of *Total Leadership: Be a Better Leader, Have a Richer Life*, posed this question to business leaders across the country: "What kind of leadership do we need now?" The most common response was *adaptive, flexible, and innovative*. Because of the current sense of turbulence in the business world and in our lives, the leadership attribute that comes to mind most often is a means for dealing with chaos, which Friedman calls *playful creativity*.[12]

Friedman believes that every person can have a capacity for leadership, regardless of organizational level or title. Friedman also teaches that leadership should not be confined to work but extended to one's personal life, community involvement, and family life.[13] So how do we become creative leaders? Friedman contends we need to actively work at it by experimenting with changing how things get done at work, as well as in other parts of our lives. He stresses that it is not the experiment that counts, but what we learn from it. Did we really create something new? What worked well, and what didn't?

Friedman believes that we must continually strive to overcome the three great inhibitors to creativity: fear of failure, guilt about appearing to be selfish, and ignorance of what's possible. If present and future leaders are not focusing on removing these barriers through experimenting, imagining, and continually trying new things, then they are "missing opportunities to strengthen their capacity to gain control in an increasingly uncertain world." Hence, Friedman asks: "So, what small wins are you pursuing these days? How will they improve your ability to be creative and to have greater capacity to adapt to the rapidly shifting realities of your life and work?"[14]

PUTTING IT ALL TOGETHER: WHAT DOES THIS MEAN TO THE BUSINESS ANALYST?

Creative leaders produce sustainable change. We have provided lots of food for thought as you strive to become a creative leader—and strive you must, because creative leadership is gravely needed for your organization to survive. Your power will come from your professional presence, your credibility and expertise, and your ability to get creative things done—to bring about *disruptive change*. As organizations mature in their use of business analysis, you may derive some of your power from positioning in the company, but without a doubt, it is through *creative leadership* that you will thrive.

CAREER ADVICE
Being Fun to Be With

Don't take yourself too seriously. People want to work with leaders who are credible and present themselves well, but they also want to have fun.

A Word to the Wise

Learn how to balance seriousness with *playful creativity*. Spend a lot of time planning your meetings, the techniques you will use, the outcomes you need. Then take a step back and make sure the experience will be fruitful, rewarding, and yes, fun for all participants.

NOTES

1. Val Williams, "Leadership: Strength vs. Power," (undated). Online at http://www.valwilliams .com/articles/Strength.html (accessed August 2010).
2. John P. Kotter, *Leading Change* (Boston: Harvard Business School Press, 1996): 27.
3. Williams.
4. Kotter, 161.
5. Rita Chao Hadden, *Leading Culture Change in Your Software Organization: Delivering Results Early* (Vienna, VA: Management Concepts, 2003): 133–226.
6. Po Bronson and Ashley Merryman, "The Creativity Crisis," *Newsweek* (July 19, 2010): 44–50.
7. Teresa M. Amabile and Mukti Khaire, "Creativity and the Role of the Leader," *Harvard Business Review* (October 2008). Online at http://hbr.org/2008/10/creativity-and-the-role-of-the-leader/ ar/1 (accessed July 2010).
8. John M. McCann, "Leadership as Creativity: Finding the Opportunity Hidden within Decision Making and Dialogue," *National Endowment for the Arts* (undated). Online at http://www.nea. gov/resources/Lessons/MCCANN2.HTML (accessed July 2010).
9. Ibid.
10. John Kao, *Jamming: The Art and Discipline of Business Creativity* (New York: HarperCollins, 1996): 75–93.
11. Rosabeth Moss Kanter, "Column: Think Outside the Building," *Harvard Business Review* (March 2010). Online at http://hbr.org/2010/03/column-think-outside-the-building/ar/1 (accessed August 2010).

12. Stew Friedman, "Become a More Creative Leader—Think Small," *Harvard Business Review* Blogs (June 15, 2009). Online at http://blogs.hbr.org/friedman/2009/06/become-a-more-creative-leader.html (accessed August 2010).

13. Marci Alboher, "Hot Ticket in B-School: Bringing Life Values to Corporate Ethics," *New York Times* (May 29, 2008). Online at http://www.nytimes.com/2008/05/29/business/smallbusiness/29shift.html?_r=1 (accessed August 2010).

14. Friedman.

CHAPTER 5

Fostering Team Creativity: The Business Analyst's Sweet Spot

As we look ahead into the next century, leaders will be those who empower others.

—Bill Gates

The need for effective team leadership in the business world can no longer be overlooked. Technology, techniques, and tools don't cause projects to fail. Projects fail because people fail to come together with a common vision, an understanding of complexity, and the right expertise. Team leadership is different from traditional management, and teams are different from operational work groups. Successfully leading a high-performing, creative team is not about command and control; it is more about collaboration, consensus, empowerment, confidence, and leadership.

EFFECTIVE TEAMS

If a business analyst is to step up to the task of becoming a credible project team leader, she must have an understanding of how teams work and the dynamics of team development. Team leaders cultivate specialized skills that are used to build and maintain high-performing teams and spur creativity and innovation. Traditional managers and technical leads cannot necessarily become effective team leaders without the appropriate mindset, training, and coaching.

As far back as 1995, Thomas Stewart, noted author and global management consultant, predicted that project management would be the profession of choice in the coming decade. As proof, he cited current trends that also spawned the need for the business analyst: trends toward global initiatives, virtual teams, mergers and acquisitions, downsizing and reengineering, and new types of alliances and partnerships—all of which have linked companies in new ways.[1]

The Project Management Institute has been warning us for years that cross-cultural training and awareness, interpersonal skills, and language facility will become conditions for professional success as a project manager. To manage 21st-century projects, these characteristics are not just nice to have. They are vital. Likewise, the ability to lead and inspire creative teams is recognized as the key to unlocking innovation in the new millennium.

> *A small group of thoughtful people could change the world.*
> *Indeed, it's the only thing that ever has.*
>
> —Margaret Mead

Teams are a critical asset used to improve performance in all kinds of organizations. Yet business leaders have consistently overlooked opportunities to exploit the potential of teams, confusing real teams with teamwork, team building, empowerment, or participative management.[2] We cannot meet 21st-century challenges—from business transformation to continuous innovation—without high-performing teams who are comfortable with turning uncertainty, complexity, and ambiguity into innovation.

THE POWER OF TEAMS

Examples of magnificent teams are all around us: emergency responders, symphony orchestras, and professional sports teams, to name just a few. When we see these teams in action, it feels like magic. These teams demonstrate their prowess, creativity, accomplishments, insights, and enthusiasm daily and are a persuasive testament to the power of teams. Yet the business project environment, especially the IT project environment, has been slow to make the most of the power of teams. It is imperative that business analysts who aspire to develop into creative leaders understand how to unleash this great power.

Business success stories based on the strategic use of teams for new product development are plentiful. For example, 3M relies on teams to develop its new products. These teams, led by product champions, are cross-functional, collaborative, autonomous, and self-organizing. The teams deal well with ambiguity, accept change, take initiative, and assume risks. The company has established a goal of generating half of each year's revenues from the previous five years' innovations and the other half from new products not yet invented. 3M's use of teams is critical to meeting that goal.[3]

Another success story is Toyota, despite the company's engineering problems that led to unprecedented recalls in 2009–2010. Toyota continues to boast the fastest product development times in the automotive industry, is a consistent leader in quality, has a large variety of products designed by a lean engineering staff, and has consistently grown its U.S. market share. Teams at Toyota are led by a chief engineer who is expected to understand the market and whose primary job is vehicle system design. The chief engineer is responsible for vehicle development, similar to the product champion at 3M.[4]

Economists have been warning us for years that success in a global marketplace is contingent upon our capability to produce products on a tight schedule to meet the growing demands of emerging markets. The same is true of projects to develop software products and solutions for business problems, improve business performance, and use IT as a competitive advantage. It's not enough to deliver projects on time and within budget, and scope; it is now necessary to deliver *value* to the organization faster, cheaper, and better.

For the business analyst who is struggling to understand how to build high-performing teams, a must-read is *The Wisdom of Teams* by Jon Katzenbach and Douglas Smith. The authors talked with hundreds of people on more than 50 different teams in 30 companies to discover what differentiates various levels of team performance, where and how teams work best, and how to enhance team effectiveness. Among their findings are elements of both common and uncommon sense:

➤ A commitment to performance goals and a common purpose is more important to team success than team building.

➤ Opportunities for teams exist in all parts of the organization.

➤ Formal hierarchy is actually good for teams and vice versa.

➤ Successful team leaders do not fit an ideal profile and are not necessarily the most senior people on the team.

➤ Real teams are the most common characteristic of successful change efforts at all levels.

➤ Top management teams are often difficult to sustain.

➤ Although companies are now using teams more often, team performance potential is largely unrecognized and underutilized.

➤ Managing the adjournment of teams can be just as important as managing their formation.

➤ Teams produce a unique blend of performance and personal learning results.

Wisdom lies in recognizing a team's unique potential to deliver creative results. Project leaders strive to understand the many benefits of teams and learn how to optimize team performance by developing individual members, fostering team cohesiveness, and rewarding team results. Katzenbach and Smith argue that teams are the primary building blocks of strong company performance.[5]

THE STAGES OF TEAM DEVELOPMENT

As a member of the project leadership team, the business analyst is partially responsible for building a high-performing team and fostering creativity and is fully responsible for building a high-performing requirements team and proposing innovative solutions. To successfully develop such a team, it is helpful to understand the key stages of team development. We use the classic team development model from Bruce Tuckman as a guide, since the Tuckman model has become an accepted standard for how teams develop.

THE TUCKMAN MODEL

The Tuckman model that outlines the five stages of team development—forming, storming, norming, performing, and adjourning—has become the gold standard for studying team dynamics.[6] As a team transitions from one stage to the next, the needs of the team and its individual members vary. A successful team leader knows which stage the team is in and skillfully manages transitions between the different stages. Figure 5-1 depicts the typical stages of team development.

In the ***forming*** stage, participants are introduced when the team is established and when new members join the team throughout the project. The goal of the project leadership team in this stage is to quickly transition the individuals from a *group* to a *team*. During the forming stage of team development, members are typically inclined to be a bit formal and reserved. They are beginning to assess their level of comfort as colleagues and teammates. There is likely to be some anxiety about the ability of the team to perform, and there might be hints about the beginnings of alliances between members.

During this stage, the project manager's job (with the support of the business analyst and other project leads) is to encourage people to not think of themselves as individuals but as team members by resolving issues about inclusion and trust. Team members may wonder why they were selected,

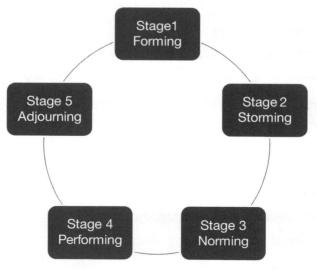

FIGURE 5-1. Stages of Team Development

what they have to offer, and how they will be accepted by colleagues new to them. Individuals have their own agendas at this stage because a team agenda does not yet exist. It is during this stage that the team leaders present, and give the team members the opportunity to refine, the team vision, mission, and measures of success. Allowing the team members time and opportunity to express their feelings and collaborate to build team plans will help members begin to make the transition from a group of individuals to an effective team. During this stage, team members form opinions about whom they can trust and how much or how little involvement they will commit to the project.

Storming is generally seen as the most difficult stage in team development. It is the time when the team members begin to realize that the task is different or more difficult than they had imagined. Individuals experience some discrepancy between their initial hopes for the project and the reality of the situation. A sense of annoyance or even panic can set in. There are fluctuations in attitude about the team, one's role on the team, and the team's chances for success.

The goal of the team leaders in this stage is to quickly determine a subset of leaders and followers and to clarify roles and responsibilities so that the team will begin to congeal. Individuals will exert their influence, choose to follow others, or decide not to participate actively on the team. For those who choose to participate actively and exert their influence, interpersonal conflict might arise. Conflicts also might result between the team leaders and team members, particularly if team members believe the leadership is threatening, vulnerable, or ineffective.

It is important to realize that conflict can lead to out-of-the-box or out-of-the-building thinking (described in Chapter 4), so the team leaders should encourage new ideas and viewpoints. For team leaders who do not like dealing with conflict, the storming stage is the most difficult period to navigate. Although the inevitable conflict is sometimes destructive if not managed well, it can be positive. Conflicting ideas, raised in an environment of trust and openness, lead to higher levels of creativity and innovation.

The job of team leaders is to build a positive working environment, collaboratively set and enforce team ground rules that lead to open communication, and gently steer the team through this stage. The common tendency is to rush through the storming stage as quickly as possible, often by pretending that a conflict does not exist, but it is important to manage conflicts so they are not destructive. It is also important, however, to allow some conflict because it is a necessary element of team maturation. If new ideas are not emerging, and if team members are not challenging each other's ideas, then creativity is not happening.

Norming is typically the stage in which work is being completed. The team members, individually and collectively, have come together and established a group identity that allows them to work effectively together. Roles and responsibilities are clear, project objectives are understood, and progress is being made. During this stage, communication channels are likely clear, and team members are adhering to agreed-upon rules of engagement during exchanges. Cooperation and collaboration replace the conflict and mistrust that characterized the previous stage.

As the project drags on, fatigue often sets in. Team leaders should look at both team composition and team processes to maintain continued motivation among members. Plan to deliver short-term successes to create enthusiasm and sustained momentum. Celebrate and reward success at key milestones rather than waiting until the end of a long project. Continually capture lessons learned about how well the team is working together and implement suggested improvements.

During the ***performing*** stage, team members tend to feel positive and excited about participating on the project. There is a sense of urgency and a sense of confidence about the team's results. Conflicts are resolved using accepted practices. The team knows what it wants to do and is reveling in a sense of accomplishment as progress is made. Relationships and expectations are well defined. There is genuine agreement among team members about their roles and responsibilities. Team members have discovered and accepted each other's strengths and weaknesses. Morale is at its peak during this stage, and the team has an opportunity to be highly creative.

The performing stage of team development is what every team strives to achieve. It is difficult, however, to sustain this high level of performance for a prolonged length of time, so capitalize on it while you can. The business analyst and project manager need to hone their team leadership skills to develop and sustain this most creative stage. The best course of action for the team leaders is to lightly facilitate the work: consult and coach when necessary, encourage creativity, reward performance and achievement of goals, and generally stay out of the way.

Adjourning can be thought of in the context of loss and closure. This stage of team development can be easily overlooked, as it occurs before and during a project or phase and for a short time after a project or phase is finished. During this stage of team development, the team conducts the tasks associated with disbanding the team and, to a certain extent, breaks the everyday rhythm of their contacts and transactions.

There is some discomfort associated with this stage. Surprisingly, even people whose teams have had performance issues can experience sadness or grief during this closing stage. The project leadership team should act quickly to recognize the accomplishments of individuals and the team as a whole and to help team members transition quickly to their next creative opportunity.

TRAVERSING THE TEAM DEVELOPMENT STAGES

The stages of team development are very much an iterative dynamic. Any change in the makeup of a team throws the team back to the very earliest stage of development, even if for a very short time. This is due to the natural evolution of teams, the addition of new members, removal of support, or changes in roles.

The balancing and leveling of power is another constant dynamic present in teams. The shifting of practical power among the core leadership team members might cause a team to revert back to the forming stage. Although this reversion might last only a short while, it is still significant; team members will have to accustom themselves to the new order. The time spent in any of the stages subsequent to the reentry into forming can vary, but make no mistake, the team will experience storming again before regaining a foothold in the norming or performing stage.

As a member of the project leadership team, you should acquaint yourself with the cycles of team development so that you can understand what the team is experiencing and manage any changes in the team's composition or dynamics. Figure 5-2 provides a quick reference on the characteristics of each team development stage.

Team Characteristics	Forming	Storming	Norming	Performing
Team Leader Style	Directing, presenting objectives, scope, and process to be followed	Supportive, active listening, managing conflict, driving consensus	Collaborative, shared leadership	Coaching, removing barriers, empowering, motivating, getting out of the way
Team Member Behaviors	Tentative, slow to participate	Vying for position, conflict	Trust and respect for team members, support for leaders	Positive, professional, creative, highly effective
Team Process	Driven by the team leader	Not working well due to conflict	Operating smoothly	Well-functioning and adapting as necessary
Trust	Low level	Alliances forming	Trusting relationships forming	High levels of trust, loyalty, respect
Decision-Making	Leaders make decisions	Difficulty making decisions, members unwilling to compromise	Consensus decision-making	Decisions made quickly by consensus, some decisions are delegated to subgroups or individuals

FIGURE 5-2. Characteristics of Team Development Stages

LEADERSHIP MODES THROUGH THE STAGES OF TEAM DEVELOPMENT

There are many team development models that one can use to guide team development at any given point in the project life cycle. David C. Kolb offers a five-stage team development model that suggests leadership strategies for each stage, from the team's initial formation through its actual performance.[7]

Each stage of Kolb's model suggests that the business analyst and project manager continually adjust their leadership styles to maximize team effectiveness and creativity. Kolb contends that a team leader subtly alters his or her style of team leadership depending on the group's composition and level of maturity. The seasoned business analyst moves seamlessly between these team leadership modes as he or she observes and diagnoses the team's performance.

The business analyst needs to strive to acquire the leadership prowess described by Kolb. In Figure 5-3, Kolb's stages are matched with essential leadership skills. It is particularly important for the business analyst to know when and how to assume a particular team leadership role as teams move in and out of development phases during the life of the project.

FACILITATOR

In the business analyst's function as a facilitator (the BA's sweet spot), the main goal is to provide a foundation for the team to make quality decisions. When the team first comes together, the business analyst uses expert facilitation skills to guide, direct, and develop the group. Skills required include understanding group dynamics, running effective meetings, facilitating dialogue, fostering creativity, and dealing with difficult behaviors. Expert facilitators possess these skills:

Kolb Team Development Stage	Team Leadership Mode
Building stage	Facilitator
Learning stage	Mediator
Trusting stage	Coach
Working stage	Consultant
Flowing stage	Collaborator

FIGURE 5-3. Kolb Team Development Model

➤ Understanding individual differences, work styles, and cultural nuances

➤ Leading discussions and driving the group to consensus

➤ Solving problems and clarifying ambiguities

➤ Building a sense of team

➤ Using and teaching collaborative skills

➤ Fostering experimentation, prototyping, emergence of many like and dissimilar ideas

➤ Managing meetings to drive to results

➤ Facilitating requirements workshops and focus groups.

To become more credible as a team leader, the business analyst ought to acquire professional facilitation credentials such as those offered by the International Association of Facilitators (IAF). IAF's work has identified the following six areas of core competency required for certification of facilitators. Each area is defined in more detail.

➤ Create Collaborative Client Relationships

➤ Plan Appropriate Group Processes

➤ Create and Sustain a Participatory Environment

➤ Guide Group to Appropriate and Useful Outcomes

➤ Build and Maintain Professional Knowledge

➤ Model Positive Professional Attitude.[8]

MEDIATOR

Transitioning from facilitator to mediator poses a challenge for new business analysts. It requires the business analyst to refrain from trying to control the team and lead the effort. The business analyst must be prepared to recognize when conflict is emerging (as it always does in teams) and be able to separate from it to mediate the situation. Although the mediator does not have to resolve the conflict, he or she must help the team members manage it. Meditation skills include:

➤ Conflict management and resolution

➤ Problem-solving and decision-making techniques

➤ Idea-generation techniques.

COACH

Coaching and mentoring take place at both the individual and team levels. Coaching is appropriate when trust has been established among the team members and communication is open and positive. The business analyst as coach uses experiences, perceptions, and intuition to help change team members' behaviors and thinking. Coaching tasks include:

➤ Setting goals

➤ Teaching others how to give and receive feedback

➤ Creating a team identity

➤ Developing team decision-making skills.

CONSULTANT

As the team begins to work well together, the business analyst transitions into the role of consultant, providing advice, tools, and interventions to help the team reach its potential. The business analyst then concentrates on nurturing the positive team environment, encouraging creativity and experimentation, removing barriers, and solving problems. Consulting tasks include:

➤ Assessing team opportunities

➤ Supporting and guiding the team to create a positive, effective team environment

➤ Aligning individual, team, and organizational values and strategic imperatives

➤ Fostering team spirit.

COLLABORATOR

Few teams achieve an optimized state and sustain it for long periods, because such a state is so intense. At this point, both the work and the leadership are shared equally among team members. The business analyst might hand off the lead role to team members when their expertise becomes a critical need during different project activities. Collaboration skills include:

➤ Leading softly

➤ Sharing the leadership role

➤ Assuming a peer relationship with team members.

Clearly, project team leaders need to understand the dynamics of team development and adjust their leadership styles accordingly. Once a high-performing team has emerged, it is often necessary for the team leader to simply step aside.

Figure 5-4 maps the variations in leadership modes to the two team development models we have presented.

Tuckman Team Development Model	Kolb Team Development Model	Team Leadership Mode
Forming stage	Building stage	Facilitator
Storming stage	Learning stage	Mediator
Norming stage	Trusting and working stages	Coach, consultant
Performing stage	Flowing stage	Collaborator

FIGURE 5-4. Mapping of the Team Development and Leadership Models

As you plan your professional development goals, it is wise for you to include training in facilitation, mediation, coaching and mentoring, consulting, and collaborating.

BEST TEAM LEADERSHIP PRACTICES FOR THE BUSINESS ANALYST

> *Coming together is a beginning. Keeping together is progress. Working together is success.*
>
> —HENRY FORD

The business analyst has dual team-leadership roles: (1) in general, he or she helps the other team leaders (the project manager, lead technologist, business visionary) build and sustain a high-performing project team; and (2) he or she is directly responsible for building a high-performing requirements ownership team—a team of business subject matter experts (SMEs) who take ownership of the business strategy to be advanced, the business need to be satisfied, and the business benefits to be realized by the solution. In addition, the business analyst instills in the requirements ownership team the understanding that it is their responsibility to spend enough time and energy to truly understand the business, to "think out of the building" by conducting research and analysis of the opportunity, and to collaboratively *create* to develop an innovative solution, as opposed to simply meeting requirements.

WHO SHOULD TAKE THE LEAD?

As a member of the project leadership team, the business analyst strives to help the team members determine who should take the lead depending on the expertise needed. For example, the project manager takes the lead during planning and statusing sessions. The business analyst leads during problem definition, opportunity analysis, solution and requirements trade-off analysis, requirements negotiation and conflict resolution, cost-benefit analysis, business requirements elicitation, solution requirements elicitation, and requirements analysis, review, and validation sessions. The project manager and business analyst may jointly lead discussions centered on issue resolution and risk analysis. The business representative should assume the lead when talking about the business vision, strategy, and benefits expected from the new solution. Then the business analyst again assumes the lead when the team is validating that the business benefits will actually be realized. Likewise, the lead architect or developer (or both) leads discussions on technology options and trade-offs. The challenge is for the core leadership team to seamlessly traverse through the leadership hand-offs so as not to interfere with the balance of the team.

THE REQUIREMENTS OWNERSHIP TEAM: A 21ST-CENTURY IMPERATIVE

The business analyst's leadership role undoubtedly involves forming, educating, developing, and maintaining a high-performing requirements team and keeping the team engaged throughout the project. The first task is determining the appropriate business and technical representatives needed to navigate through the requirements activities, then securing approval to involve them throughout the project. This is no small task, since business teams are accustomed to providing minimal amounts of information to project teams about the requirements (and these often are phrased in terms of the solution instead of the business need) and then sending the team off to do the real project work. The business analyst uses her influence, negotiating skills, and credibility to secure the participation of key business SMEs throughout the project. This involves building a strong relationship with the business owner, who is often the project sponsor, as well as other key business leaders who are influential in committing the essential SMEs.

As the requirements team comes together in workshops or other working sessions, they will inevitably pass through the same team development stages as the larger project team. The business analyst must navigate the team through the challenges of each stage of team development. The goal for the business analyst is to optimize the dynamics and expertise of the business SMEs to foster an innovative and creative atmosphere for determining the business opportunities and solutions. Remember: business analysts are not note takers—they are creative leaders.

What best practices should you as the business analyst employ as the requirements team leader?

➤ Meet face-to-face with business representatives, customers, and end users early and often.

➤ Devote time and energy to guide the requirements ownership team through the stages of team development, changing your leadership style as the team moves in and out of stages.

➤ When forming the requirements team, utilize the core team concept (small but mighty collocated teams that work collaboratively). Involve key technical SMEs (architect, lead developer, application portfolio manager) in the key working sessions of the requirements ownership team.

➤ Spend enough time training requirements team members on the requirements practices and tools the team will use so that they will be comfortable with the process before they jump in head first.

➤ Build a solid, trusting, collaborative relationship among the project team members and the requirements technical and business SMEs.

➤ Bring in additional SMEs and form subteams and committees when needed to augment the core requirements ownership team.

➤ Establish a requirements integration team to structure requirements into process groups and to manage interrelationships among requirement groups.

➤ Encourage frequent meetings among the core requirements and project team members to promote full disclosure and transparency as the inevitable trade-off decisions are made.

CAREER ADVICE
Requirements Ownership Team

Requirements alone are not complex. It is the interrelationships between and among requirements that bring about complexity. Form a requirements ownership team (also called a requirements integration team) to manage risks and complexities.

> **A WORD TO THE WISE**
>
> Limit or remove interrelationships between and among requirements whenever possible.
> - Assign a requirements owner for each category of requirements.
> - Bring all requirements owners together in a requirements integration team to manage interdependencies between and among requirements.

It is not enough for the business analyst to develop requirements engineering knowledge and skills. It is also important to understand—and use—the power of teams, which leads to much more creative solutions.

CREATIVITY: A RIGHT-BRAIN PURSUIT

A creative team that comes up with brilliant ideas is one of the most valuable resources any organization can have. If you want to give your creative team the best possible chance for success, give them clear ground rules and then let them run free.

—Bill Stainton

At this point, you might be questioning our assertion that business analysts should serve as creative leaders. You might be thinking that analysts are just that—analytical. Logical, methodical, questioning, reasoned, and rational. Isn't this left-brain stuff? In fact, the business analyst needs to learn how to optimize both sides of her brain. How is the business analyst to become a creativity catalyst? By using creativity-inducing tools and techniques that make use of structured, proven problem-solving and decision-making methods (left brain) and cleverly augmenting them with investigation, experimentation, and yes, experiencing a little bit of chaos along the way (right brain).

As business analysts rise to the top of their game, they will skillfully learn to balance both the left and right sides of the brains of their SMEs (see Figure 5-5) in addition to their own brains. They will inspire teams to invent, imagine, and experiment. But they also will have a keen understanding of the business opportunity, the customer desires, the market window, and the executive team's tolerance for ambiguity and research. The seasoned business analyst will instinctively know just the right moment to end experimentation and have the team put a stake in the ground. They will understand the concept of last responsible moment decision-making (i.e., do not shut down experimentation and lock into a design until it would be irresponsible to delay solution construction any longer; a delay would mean that the solution would be suboptimized and the opportunity lost.)

Left Brain	Right Brain
Verbal communication, uses words	Uses visual, spatial, tactile communication
Relies on logic	Processes emotions, offers intuition
Prefers to execute known rules	Seeks new associations, creative thought
Operates sequentially	Is comfortable with disconnected information
Prefers predictable behavior	Is comfortable with some ambiguity
Executes known patterns	Learns new unknown patterns
Prefers what is explicit, concrete	Prefers abstract concepts, metaphors
Operates with complete information	Operates with incomplete information
Unable to make decisions independently	Comfortable with critical decision-making

FIGURE 5-5. Right Brain vs. Left Brain Preferences

GETTING THERE: FROM AD HOC GROUP TO WORKING GROUP TO CREATIVE TEAM

According to Bill Stainton, whose presentations combine "business smarts with show biz sparks" (this is a great mental model for the creative business analyst leader), the only difference between creative and non-creative people is that creative people *believe* they are creative.[9] Stainton suggests that it is the job of the leader of a creative team to make its members believe that they too are creative. The leader of innovative teams does this by providing:

➤ *Direction.* Set down boundaries, rules, and clear targets for the team. Some believe rules and boundaries limit creativity. In fact, clear targets focus us on the task at hand and liberate us to be creative.

➤ *Freedom.* Do not tell your team *how* to achieve the targets. Creative people need the space to "play, explore, and discover."

➤ *Stimulation.* Creative people thrive in an inspirational environment, but their creativity dies in a sterile one.[10]

COMMONLY UNDERSTOOD BUT LITTLE-USED PRACTICES

The team leadership practices consultant Don Clark suggests are well known, but they are not implemented often enough. A great team leader is constantly assessing the extent to which his team possesses these critical elements:

➤ *Inspiration:* Continually reinforce the importance of the creative process to the organization as well as the value of the opportunity at hand.

➤ *Urgency:* Develop and maintain a sense of urgency; this keeps the creative juices flowing and time-boxes decision-making.

➤ *Empowerment:* Keep the team informed; challenge them with fresh facts and information. New knowledge just might redirect their effort or rekindle their creativity.

➤ *Togetherness:* Teams need formal and informal time together to build constructive relationships and trust each other. One team member remarked, "We did our most creative work on a sailboat." The team leader serves as the catalyst that brings the team together.

➤ *Recognition:* Recognize accomplishments and communicate enthusiastically about successes. Insist on working toward small wins to sustain motivation.

➤ *An overarching goal:* Although your team might have a number of goals, one of them must stand out as nonnegotiable.

➤ *Productive participation of all members:* If certain members of the team are not truly engaged, the team decisions will not benefit from their perspectives, and the team may miss out on creative ideas. Communication, trust, a sense of belonging, and valuing diversity of thought and approaches are all elements that encourage full team participation. Diversity is a vital ingredient that fosters team synergy. If team members are not all engaged in articulating new ideas and challenging each other, the team has not yet reached its most creative point.

➤ *Shared risk taking:* If no one individual fails (we all sink or swim together), then risk taking becomes a lot easier.

➤ *Change compatibility:* Being flexible and having the ability to self correct.[11]

COLLABORATION: THE GLUE THAT BINDS CREATIVE TEAMS

Perhaps the most essential element of great innovation teams is collaboration. Jim Tamm, a workplace expert specializing in building collaborative work environments and the co-author of *Radical Collaboration*, tells us that collaboration does not magically happen. He contends that collaboration is both a mindset and a skill set—both of which can be learned—that can make a big difference to a company's bottom line. After almost two decades of teaching collaborative skills in highly challenged and hierarchical organizations, Tamm discovered five essential skills for building successful collaborative environments:

➤ *Think win-win.* Foster a positive attitude among your team members; recruit and reward people who are fun to work with and aren't afraid of (and in fact, actually welcome) challenges and hard work.

➤ *Speak the truth.* Dishonesty is toxic in the workplace. Always be open and honest, and expect others to do the same.

➤ *Be accountable.* Take responsibility for your performance and interpersonal relationships. Focus on innovative solutions—the hallmark of successful teams.

➤ *Be self-aware—and aware of others.* Work hard to understand your own behaviors, and work just as hard to diagnose and optimize the behaviors of your team.

➤ *Learn from conflict.* Expect and capitalize on conflict—it happens whenever people come together. The secret to success is to use the conflict to learn and grow.[12]

THE INNOVATION IMPERATIVE

Every organization—not just business—needs one core competence: innovation.

—PETER DRUCKER

The United States has enjoyed a preeminent position in the world economy for decades, largely riding the wave of success brought about by the world's greatest innovators: Alexander Graham Bell, Henry Ford, George Eastman, Harvey Firestone, John D. Rockefeller, George Westinghouse, Andrew Carnegie, and of course, Thomas Edison. However, the 21st century brought with it immense global competitive pressure that is putting the U.S.'s economic domination at risk. Studies indicate that global innovation leadership is shifting away from the U.S., heading east to the emerging markets of China, India, and South Korea. Now is the time for us to revisit tried-and-true innovation skills and practices and once again seize competitive advantage. Business analysts are well positioned to play a vital role in this effort as they work with teams across the enterprise.

BUSINESS INNOVATION CHECKLIST

So how in the world does a business analyst develop the abilities needed to be an innovation leader? Innovation requires a systematic process. Edison taught us that innovation is much more than invention. An organization also needs to manufacture and market the new invention to convert a good idea into value for the consumer and revenue for the inventor.

A checklist is helpful for facilitators to begin the innovation decision-making process (see Figure 5-6). Business analysts can guide a team of experts to identify highly feasible innovative changes and then determine if the organization is ready to invest in far-reaching change. As innovators, we are keenly aware that breakthrough approaches are needed, but we are not always certain of the best course of action: when to change, what to change, if to change, or how to change.

A. Concept Selection

1. Strategy Assessment—Assess your organization's strategic plans, goals, and objectives. What are some unmet objectives/opportunities? Prioritize these according to level of innovation and the value of expected business benefits. Develop a corporate scorecard for the unmet objectives/opportunities.

2. Internal Current State Assessment—Assess your organization's internal environment (e.g., processes, organization, locations, data, applications, technology, project/program/portfolio management, business analysis). Are there unaddressed problems or opportunities? Are any of those unaddressed issues hindering strategic objectives? What are the barriers to your organization's success in those areas? How can you determine it's time to solve those particular problems? What solutions will have the greatest impact? Which solutions will help you gain a competitive advantage? Which offer the best business benefits? How will the organization monitor its progress toward these goals? Develop a corporate scorecard for the unmet objectives/opportunities.

3. External Current State Assessment—Assess your organization's external environment (e.g., well-known competitors, start-ups, recent failed products or service introductions, demand for your current product line, pent up or unspoken demand for innovative products/services). Do you have opportunities to create something new, innovate, and disrupt the current competitive positioning in your favor? By not pursuing opportunities, are you hindering strategic objectives? What has stopped you from pursuing the opportunities until now? When would be a good time to pursue the opportunity? Rank opportunities according to innovation, potential business value, and advancement of strategies. Are there significant differences? How will the organization monitor progress toward these opportunities? Develop a corporate scorecard for the most innovative and highest value opportunities.

4. **Select Concept for Further Review**—Select from among the opportunities identified during the assessments. Facilitate the group to reach agreement on a high-level plan to close the gaps between the current state and the future vision. Rank all opportunities documented in the corporate scorecard based on the expected level of innovation and business benefit. Conduct feasibility analysis for top-priority opportunities (e.g., economic feasibility, time-to-market feasibility, technological feasibility, market feasibility). Select the most feasible opportunity and prepare to build the business case.

B. Business Case Development (See Chapter 10)

C. Product Development (Chapter 9)

D. Commercial Launch

FIGURE 5-6. Business Innovation Checklist (Basic Outline)

Figure 5-6 provides the foundation for your facilitated innovation sessions. Enlist the participation of a small expert team. With the team's help, customize the checklist for your particular business and market and use it to start the innovation discussions. Do not feel as if you need to stick to the script precisely. If the session is lively and participants are identifying, challenging, building on, and experimenting with lots of creative ideas, let the session evolve itself. The checklist is intended to serve as a starting point for the discussion and as an inventory of items that teams may need to consider.

QUICK TEAM ASSESSMENT

Jim Clemmer writes, "Despite all the team talk of the last few years, few groups are real teams. Too often they're unfocused and uncoordinated in their efforts."[13] Clemmer developed the following set of questions based on his consulting and team development work. This team assessment and planning framework can be used to help newly formed teams come together and get productive quickly or to help existing teams refocus and renew themselves. Use this simple approach to assess team performance by having your team develop answers and action plans around each question. Perhaps add a question or two about creativity, innovation, and operating at the edge of chaos.

➤ Why do we exist (our purpose)?

➤ Where are we going (our vision)?

➤ How will we work together (our values)?

➤ Who do we serve (internal or external customers or partners)?

➤ What is expected of us?

➤ What are our performance gaps (difference between the expectations and our performance)?

➤ What are our goals and priorities?

➤ What's our improvement plan?

➤ What skills do we need to develop?

➤ What support is available?

➤ How will we track our performance?

➤ How/when will we review, assess, celebrate, and refocus?[14]

INNOVATION IS A TEAM SPORT

According to Jon R. Katzenbach, author of *Teams at the Top*, and Stacy Palestrant, a team is "a small group with complementary skills committed to a common purpose, performance goals, and working approach for which they hold themselves mutually accountable."[15] It may be easy to define what Katzenbach calls *real teams*, but they are very hard to build and even harder to keep going.

SUSTAINED INSPIRATION

Katzenbach and Palestrant write that teams can initially sustain their inspiration, motivation, and drive if they are presented with a compelling performance challenge. As BAs begin to work on mission-critical innovation projects, they are undoubtedly presented with a compelling performance challenge. At the outset, teams seem to ride on the wave of their instincts and desire to do good work. Real teams, however, succeed only if their leaders make sure the team members consistently apply what is referred to as *the essential discipline*. In a situation where performance challenges are changing rapidly, which is almost always the case in today's Internet-speed business cycles, it behooves team leaders to continually assess team health and instill team discipline.[16]

A TEAM CULTURE OF DISCIPLINE

As Jim Collins writes in *Good to Great*, it is important that organizations build a culture of discipline.[17] It is a commonly held misconception that the imposition of standards and discipline discourages creativity. A project team is like a start-up company. To truly innovate, the team needs to value creativity, imagination, and risk-taking. However, to maintain a sense of control over a large team, we often impose structure, insist on planning, and institutionalize coordination systems of meetings and reports.

THE ENTREPRENEURIAL DEATH SPIRAL

As we have discussed, the risk of requiring too much rigor is that the team becomes bureaucratic. Collins calls this the *entrepreneurial death spiral*. He contends that "bureaucracy is imposed to compensate for incompetence and lack of discipline—a problem that largely goes away if you have the right people in the first place." The goal is to learn how to use rigor and discipline to *enable* creativity. Great teams (think emergency responders and surgical teams) almost always have rigid standards; they practice the execution of those standards over and over again until they become second nature; and they work hard to examine each performance and improve the standards based upon experience. So, as Katzenbach tells us, "Team performance is characterized at least as much by discipline and hard work as it is by empowerment, togetherness, and positive group dynamics."[18]

PUTTING IT ALL TOGETHER: WHAT DOES THIS MEAN TO THE BUSINESS ANALYST?

The lesson for the business analyst is this: work hard with other project leaders to impose a culture of discipline in your project team. Build improvements into the team's interactions, imaginings, experimentations, problem-solving, and decision-making processes at every feedback point. Become an expert at developing and sustaining high-performing teams. To do this, you need to develop your unique leadership style, one that makes high performers want to be on your team.

To complete our discussion on leading creative teams, the next chapter looks at fostering creativity when leading complex, distributed, diverse teams. And Chapter 7 is chock full of creativity-inducing facilitation strategies, tools, and techniques to fill up your team-leading toolbox.

NOTES

1. Thomas A. Stewart, "The Corporate Jungle Spawns a New Species: The Project Manager," *Fortune* (July 1995): 179–80.
2. Jon R. Katzenbach and Douglas K. Smith, *The Wisdom of Teams: Creating the High-Performance Organization* (Boston: Harvard Business School Press, 1993): 20–21.
3. Mary Poppendieck, "Reflections on Development," December 18, 2001. Online at www.poppendieck.com/development1.htm (accessed May 2011).
4. Ibid.
5. Katzenbach and Smith, 24–26.
6. Bruce W. Tuckman, "Developmental Sequence in Small Groups," *Psychological Bulletin* 63, no. 6 (June 1965): 384–399.
7. David C. Kolb, *Team Leadership* (Durango, CO: Lore International Institute, 1999): 9–18.
8. International Association of Facilitators, "IAF Core Competencies for Certification," February 2003. Online at http://www.iaf-world.org/index/Certification/CompetenciesforCertification.aspx (accessed May 2011).
9. Bill Stainton, "How To Lead a Creative Team," January 5, 2010. Online at http://ovationconsulting.com/blog/how-to-lead-a-creative-team (accessed August 2010).
10. Ibid.
11. Don Clark, "Growing a Team," (undated). Online at http://www.nwlink.com/~donclark/leader/leadtem.html (accessed August 2010).
12. James W. Tamm, "The 'Red Zone' Organization," *Innovative Leader* 14, no. 5 (January–March 2006). Online at http://www.winstonbrill.com/bril001/html/article_index/articles.html (accessed August 2010).
13. Jim Clemmer, "Harnessing the Power of Teams," (undated). Online at http://ezinearticles.com/?Harnessing-the-Power-of-Teams&id=109593 (accessed August 2010).
14. Ibid.
15. Jon R. Katzenbach and Stacy Palestrant, "Team Leadership: Emerging Challenges," *Innovative Leader* 9, no. 8 (August 2000). Online at http://www.winstonbrill.com/bril001/html/article_index/articles/451-500/article482_body.html (accessed May 2010).
16. Ibid.
17. Jim Collins, *Good to Great* (New York: HarperCollins, 2001): 120–143.
18. Katzenbach and Palestrant.

CHAPTER 6

Igniting Creativity in Complex Distributed Teams

The boundaries of today's organizations are permeable. Organizations are fielding teams comprising elaborate networks of suppliers, contractors, migrant employees, customers, and even competitors. A number of drivers are pushing organizations to significantly change the way they do work. Global integration and the Internet have greatly expanded our ability to reach across the globe. New technologies, like cloud computing and social media, and the new technically savvy generation of workers are key drivers. Business analysts who combine their technical prowess with a broad, enterprise-wide business perspective have the opportunity to lead their organizations to use distributed teams as a competitive advantage.[1]

Business analysts are learning they must continually adapt their leadership style when working with large, geographically dispersed, diverse teams involving complex contractual agreements and using multiple methodologies. We use very large dispersed teams to expand our access to the talent we need. However, it is more important than ever to foster creativity and innovation to get the best possible return on project investments. We have learned from new product development efforts and research and development initiatives that innovation teams have unique complexities that require sophisticated team-leadership techniques. In this chapter, we recommend team-leadership practices that can help the complex project leadership team manage the complexities of distributed teams while establishing an environment of adaptability, innovation, and creativity.

WHAT MAKES LARGE, DISTRIBUTED TEAMS COMPLEX?

> *Fools ignore complexity. Pragmatists suffer it. Some can avoid it. Geniuses remove it.*
>
> —ALAN PERLIS, MATHEMATICIAN AND COMPUTER SCIENTIST

Complex projects almost always involve multiple layers and types of teams. We are currently seeing an explosion in the use of virtual workers; it is estimated that 70 percent of employees work in locations different from their supervisors. This exponential increase in itinerant workers around the globe has imposed immense complexity onto already stretched team leaders. While virtual work makes a wider pool of talent available to us, it also adds complexity to team interactions and leadership. Complicating factors include unpredictable interactions with team members, integration issues, and leadership and coordination challenges. Some of the other factors that work to increase uncertainty, ambiguity, and complexity in large distributed teams are shown in the right-hand column of Figure 6-1, which describes typical teams and performance factors for projects of different sizes.

On top of these factors, because we need to foster creativity and innovation to survive, leading these teams is more challenging than ever. How can we spark creativity in a team we can't see? Choosing the most appropriate practices, tools, and techniques when working with multiple contributors who are

	Independent Project	Moderately Complex Project	Highly Complex Project	Highly Complex Program or Megaproject
Size	3–4 team members	5–10 team members	> 10 team members	Multiple diverse teams
Time	< 3 months	3–6 months	6–12 months	Multiyear
Cost	< $250K	$250K–$1M	> $1M	Multiple millions
Team Composition and Past Performance	• PM: competent, experienced • Team: internal; worked together in past • Methodology: defined, proven	• PM: competent, inexperienced • Team: internal and external; worked together in past • Methodology: defined, unproven • Contracts: straightforward • Contractor past performance: good	• PM: competent; poor/no experience with complex projects • Team: internal and external; have not worked together in past • Methodology: somewhat defined, diverse • Contracts: complex • Contractor past performance: unknown	• PM: competent, poor/no experience with megaprojects • Team: complex structure of varying competencies and performance records (e.g., contractor, virtual, culturally diverse, outsourced teams) • Methodology: undefined • Diverse, highly complex contracts • Contractor past performance: poor

FIGURE 6-1. Project Complexity: Team and Performance Factors

scattered in different locations across the planet, at the right time, is in itself a complex endeavor. Successful teams are the result of many elements coming together, including team structure, composition, culture, location, collaboration, communication, coordination, and evolution—and most of all, team leadership.

It is the job of the business analyst to collaborate with the project manager and other key project leaders to establish the appropriate team-leadership approach. This involves developing a complex and rich assortment of relationships, integrating information in real time, and at the same time, bringing about innovation.

TEAMS ARE ALWAYS COMPLEX

All human groups and organizations are complex adaptive systems; teams are complex adaptive systems within a larger organization (which is also a complex adaptive system operating within the global economy). Leaders of a complex team cannot predict how their team members will react to each other, to the project requirements, to the call for creativity, and to their place within the team and the organization. Team members who have worked together in the past may bring biases or resentments toward one another. Team members who have not yet worked together are likely to reserve judgment and hold back interactions until they learn about each other. This concept, referred to as *interactional uncertainty*,[2] theorizes that if there is uncertainty in a relationship, the participants will tend to withhold information and calculate the effects of sharing information. The business analyst must guide the team members through the inevitable early stages of team growth discussed in Chapter 5 toward the certainty that leads to trust and transparency. Then, team members can focus their energies on positive interactions.

THE INEVITABLE INTEGRATION CHALLENGES

In addition to team dynamics, working with many disparate teams almost always leads to integration issues, which make it difficult to integrate interdependent solution components that have been designed and constructed by different teams. This issue is particularly common on innovation teams; different teams use dissimilar protocols, procedures, practices, and tools, which results in work products of varying quality and consistency.

LEADERSHIP AND COORDINATION CHALLENGES

In recent years, national responses to devastating natural disasters, including a large earthquake in Haiti and a massive oil spill and a ruinous hurricane in the Gulf of Mexico, have starkly illustrated the consequences of ineffective leadership and poor coordination of large, disparate teams. In the business world, deficiencies in team leadership can lead to rework to resolve integration issues.

FOSTERING CREATIVITY WHEN LEADING DISTRIBUTED TEAMS

To lead multilayered teams, project leaders must understand the potential power of teams, team leadership, and team collaboration, communication, and coordination.

CAPITALIZING ON TEAM POTENTIAL

> *Groups become great only when everyone in them, leaders and members alike, is free to do his or her absolute best ... The best thing a leader can do for a Great Group is to allow its members to discover their greatness.*
>
> —WARREN BENNIS AND PATRICIA WARD BIEDERMAN

As discussed in Chapter 5, the team is an essential configuration used to execute strategy, bring about innovation, and respond to crisis in all kinds of organizations. It is up the business analyst, in collaboration with the other team leaders, to exploit the potential of teams. We simply cannot meet the grand 21st-century innovation challenge without understanding and leveraging the creative muscle of teams.

HARNESSING THE WISDOM OF TEAMS

None of us is as smart as all of us.

— Japanese Proverb

LEADING COMPLEX TEAMS

In the 21st century, the ace in the hole for project success is high-performance teams.

A Word to the Wise

Learn everything you can about the power of teams. Leverage the talents of each and every member of your team. Learn to use virtual teams as a strategic advantage.

As we have argued, a team is much more effective than a single person when an organization is navigating complexity and striving for creativity. According to Warren Bennis, "One is too small a number to produce greatness." Bennis talks about teams as *great groups,* stating: "We must turn to Great Groups if we hope to begin to understand how that rarest of precious resources—genius—can be successfully combined with great effort to achieve results that enhance all our lives."[3] Along the way, members of these groups provide support and camaraderie for each other.

GREAT TEAMS: YOU'LL KNOW THEM
WHEN YOU SEE THEM

In *Organizing Genius: The Secrets of Creative Collaboration,* Bennis and coauthor Patricia Ward Biederman examine seven "Great Groups" systematically to reveal the secrets of their collaborative genius. These groups include the creative team at the Walt Disney animation studio; the groups at Xerox's Palo Alto Research Center and Apple that made computers suitable for home use; the 1992 Clinton campaign, which put the first Democrat in the White House in a decade; and the Manhattan Project, which brought us into the nuclear age.[4] What did these seven great groups have in common? They were "vibrant with energy and ideas, full of colorful, talented people playing for high stakes and often racing against a deadline . . . organizations fully engaged in the thrilling process of discovery." All great groups are engaged in creative problem solving.

A COMMON CAUSE

Bennis demonstrates that in a truly creative collaboration, "work is pleasure, and the only rules and procedures are those that advance the common cause."[5] Success is not about the heroics of the team leader, although all great groups have great leaders and often lose their way if they lose their leader. The leaders all seem to have an eye for talent, and the teams themselves seem to attract talent.

PASSION FIRST—GENIUS WILL FOLLOW

Jim Collins, author of *Good to Great,* suggests we look first for passion, and genius will follow. Recruiting the best talent is absolutely the first step in building a great team. Yes, the leader is essential, but greatness is really about the magic that happens within a group of talented individuals embarking on a critical problem that they are passionate about. An even better way to think of it, Bennis tells us, is that greatness is really a combination of great groups and great leaders. That is what we must learn to create in the business world: great groups and great leaders.

DECISION-MAKING ON DISTRIBUTED TEAMS

According to a host of studies, most successful 21st century companies have separate new-product teams for design, development, and manufacturing, with members in multiple locations and often in different countries and continents. The proliferation of distributed teams indicates that the barrier of distance has been removed, mostly due to the Internet and the abundance of effective communication and collaboration tools.

According to the research of Mario Bourgault, Jaoaud Daoudi, Nathalie Drouin, and Emilie Hamel, the accomplishments of distributed project teams are closely correlated to the level of autonomy a team is permitted.[6] However, since traditional models of corporate management are still prevalent and even dominant, it is the natural tendency of management to increase oversight as teams become more scattered. Since oversight reduces autonomy, it is likely to reduce creativity as well. Unfortunately, modern corporate management teams have not yet come to terms with the new management modes that are needed to build and sustain creative teams.

It should be noted, then, that the project manager and the business analyst are likely to disagree about how to manage geographically dispersed teams and how to make decisions within and across teams. The project manager is likely to want to impose a high degree of supervision and control, whereas the business analyst will argue for significant independence and self-sufficiency.

To determine the appropriate balance, the business analyst's negotiation and influence skills become critical for making a case for a management model that encourages a powerful creative climate.

WHEN TO MEET FACE-TO-FACE

Another consideration is when, if ever, distributed team members should meet face to face. People's preferences about collocation differ. Some studies indicate that distributed teams value face-to-face interaction during the early and final phases of a project, while other studies show that team members prefer not to meet until the project is well underway and roles are more clearly defined. We seem to think that for important decisions, collocation is the ideal. The study by Bourgault et al., however, reveals that "distributed teams are more likely to make good decisions than face-to-face teams because of better communications and better objectivity."[7] To make good decisions, the project manager and business analyst must discuss and come to an agreement on how the project team will be organized (distributed or centrally located), whether to make decisions in a centralized or decentralized manner, and the appropriate decision-making processes.[8]

SOLVING PROBLEMS AS A DISTRIBUTED TEAM

The Bourgault et al. study on decision-making within distributed teams revealed that an effective structured decision-making process becomes more important as teams become more spread out. Although the global scale of business, the constant instability and volatility of the marketplace, and the integration of business relationships has led to a rapid increase in distributed teams, the optimal management techniques to oversee these teams have not yet been determined. There does seem to be consensus, however, that structured problem solving and decision-making, coupled with formal communication strategies, are critical for distributed teams. It is imperative that the business analyst and the project manager experiment with different management approaches until the most effective strategies are discovered. Chapter 7 discusses structured problem-solving and decision-making approaches in greater detail.

STRATEGIES FOR DISTRIBUTED TEAM LEADERSHIP

Mario Bourgault and Nathalie Drouin authored a paper titled "How's Your Distributed Team Doing?" that is well worth downloading and reviewing with the project manager early in a project.[9] The paper proposes strategies to improve distributed team effectiveness. First and foremost, teams must communicate frequently, openly, and transparently. Because communication is widely viewed as the most important strategy for successful teams, whether they are distributed or collocated, the project manager and business analyst need to spend a great deal of time designing and executing the communication plan, taking into account the differing cultures and styles of the teams. Multiple rich communication channels are required; one size does not fit all.

The project manager and business analyst also must:

➤ Get the right communication and collaboration tools and make sure everyone knows how to use them effectively. When communicating virtually, it is more important than ever to make sure everyone is participating.

➤ Build trust and nurture it continually. It will likely take longer to build trusting relationship among members of dispersed teams.

➤ Ensure everyone agrees on the work rules, protocols, and practices.

➤ Spend time to build consensus on a common vision, and test and validate the vision often. Once the team is in full agreement, ensure that the management teams at each site are in agreement and will resoundingly communicate the vision to everyone within their organization.

➤ Recruit strong team leaders, but insist on shared leadership and real collaboration. Look for passion above all else, even before expertise. There are universal values that are found in almost all great team leaders. These include commitment to the team members as well as the project success; desire to serve the team; enthusiasm, expertise, and the ability to inspire the team to achieve more collectively than its members could alone; and acceptance of responsibility for successes as well as failures.[10]

➤ Collaboratively determine the decision-making process teams will use. It is important to establish the decision-making process early in the project and continually check to see if everyone thinks it is working and how it can be improved.

USING VIRTUAL TEAMS AS A STRATEGIC ADVANTAGE

Organizations that have adopted the virtual team model are experiencing increased innovation and competitiveness, which are vital benefits in today's marketplace. Virtual teams do not rely on traditional hierarchies and communication channels. Special business operations teams reach across geographical boundaries, organizational barriers, and cultural differences to assemble a team of experts like no other. According to a report from Cognizant Business Consulting, published in collaboration with *The Economist,* "Collaborative virtual teams, when used effectively, combine diverse skills to quickly carry out complex tasks and address novel market challenges. They also have the potential to foster more productive relationships with internal and external partners."[11]

These virtual teams, whose members are geographically dispersed, often multicultural, and cross-functional, yet who work on highly interdependent tasks, present unique leadership challenges. Leaders of all teams, whether dispersed or collocated, have responsibilities they must fulfill, including communicating the vision, establishing expectations and an achievable strategy to reach the vision, and creating a positive team environment. It can be difficult to carry out these responsibilities at a distance. Arvind Malhotra, Ann Majchrzak, and Benson Rosen conducted research and identified six practices of effective leaders of virtual teams:

➤ Establishing and maintaining trust through the use of communication technology

➤ Ensuring that distributed diversity is understood and appreciated

➤ Managing virtual work-life cycles (meetings)

➤ Monitoring team progress using technology

➤ Enhancing visibility of virtual members within the team and outside it, in the organization.

➤ Enabling individual members of the virtual team to benefit from the team.[12]

USE MULTIPLE COMMUNICATION TECHNIQUES

For complex projects involving team members from around the globe, communication and collaboration are the lifeblood of the team. The manner, methods, and frequency of communication are crucial factors in determining the success or failure of virtual teams, so it is essential to develop a communication strategy early in the project. The cofounder and CEO of an Internet start-up in Shanghai suggests, "First identify natural social interactions. Then develop techniques and choose technologies that seem instinctual and comfortable for users."[13] Don't make technology the defining feature of your virtual team management process; technology is simply part of your toolkit.

As the age-old adage suggests, a picture is worth a thousand words. When working virtually, depict your message visually whenever possible using rich modeling tools. Remember that there is no substitute for face-to-face sessions when the team is in the early formative stages or in crisis. Make the effort to travel to the virtual team location to collaborate and build strong relationships that can then be sustained virtually. If your sponsor indicates that travel is too expensive, explain that you can't afford *not* to establish a trusting relationship—and it can only be done in person.

USE EFFECTIVE COMMUNICATION TOOLS

In today's electronically borderless world, technology is an enabler for us to keep in close touch, manage interdependencies, and resolve issues. Audio conferencing, web meetings, testing, instant messaging, and email are the rule of the day for progress reporting and quick decision-making. Paper-based communication takes on enormous importance when virtual teams are involved since face-to-face communications is limited or nonexistent. Learn the art of keeping adequate documentation without overburdening the team. Formal procedures and processes for communications are necessary to set and maintain expectations.

FOCUS ON WORK CULTURE

According to Michelle LaBrosse, founder of Cheetah Learning, the challenge is not finding the right tools: "The biggest barriers are often around communications and work culture. Ground rules that focus on them can increase your team's productivity and let you reap the rewards of the virtual workforce." LaBrosse lists several best practices for working with virtual teams:

➤ *Build trust.* *Trust is the glue of the virtual workplace.* Trust is built when you bring your team together for training or team building and continues to grow when leaders set, and the team meets, clear expectations consistently.

➤ *Manage results, not activity.* In the virtual environment, when you can't see what people are doing, the key is to manage results. Set expectations and monitor results, not daily activities.

➤ *Schedule regular communication.* It is important to establish a regular time for reporting progress and managing issues.

➤ *Create communication that saves time, not that kills it.* With the empowerment created by email comes the weight of managing it. Clearly, email is a critical tool, but responding to hundreds of emails every day can become a barrier to effectiveness. The project leader's job is to ensure that the team's email communication is as efficient and productive as possible.

➤ *Create standards that build a culture of discipline.* On a virtual team, you need to focus on creating a sense of cohesion and pride in being part of the team and the larger enterprise. Make sure your teams know your quality standards and expectations to avoid rework, disappointments, and ultimately delays.

➤ *Define rules of responsiveness.* Whether your team is working remotely or is collocated, it is necessary to define rules of responsiveness. How quickly are people expected to return an email or a phone call? What is your protocol when people are out of the office or on vacation? If you're in a customer service environment, it's important to have clear expectations regarding how to respond to all customer inquiries.[14]

By implementing these commonsense practices, virtual teams can be more productive than traditional teams. Cultivate your virtual teams, and they will become a strategic advantage.

MANAGING DISTRIBUTED TEAMS WITH A LIGHT TOUCH

Business analysts and project managers need to develop new approaches to team leadership when using iterative and adaptive project management methodologies (detailed in Chapter 3). Sanjiv Augustine, a consultant, speaker, and trainer who helps companies implement agile management programs, offers several principles and practices for managing innovation project teams that are using iterative, incremental development and adaptable methods:

➤ Foster alignment and cooperation.

➤ Encourage emergence and self-organization.

➤ Institute learning and adaptation.[15]

Agile project management practices include:

➤ *Small teams.* Enable connections and adaptation through close relationships on small, flexible teams.

➤ *Vision.* Keep the team aligned and directed with a shared vision and clear targets.

➤ *Simple rules.* Establish a set of simple rules for the team to follow.

➤ *Transparency.* Provide full access to all information.

➤ *A light touch.* Apply light methods and tools to encourage standardization.

➤ *Situational leadership.* Steer the project by continuously learning, adapting, and adjusting your leadership style to meet the needs of the moment.

USE A STANDARD FORMAL METHODOLOGY

The Standish Group found that 46 percent of successful projects used a formal project management methodology.[16] For complex projects, using a standard methodology while encouraging each team to tailor it as needed, goes a long way toward eliminating undiscovered cross-team dependencies.

Do not overly burden the various teams with standards, but do insist on those that are needed to provide a realistic view of the overall project and to manage cross-team dependencies. Enforce the use of standard collaboration procedures, practices, and tools. Be firm about establishing decision check-points that involve all core project team members at critical junctures.

INSIST ON COLLABORATIVE PLANNING AND REQUIREMENTS DEVELOPMENT

Involve all core team members in the planning and requirements processes and seek feedback often to continually improve the performance of the team. Hold face-to-face working sessions during planning and requirements meetings, especially for scoping, scheduling, identifying risks and dependencies, and conducting critical control-gate reviews. Be sure to include adequate time and budget to bring core team members together for these critical sessions.

ACQUIRE STATE-OF-THE-ART COLLABORATION TOOLS

Secure and make easily available the best-in-class mobile tools (cell phones, mobile computing platforms, social media websites, web conferencing, wikis, group chats and chat logs, instant messaging, and other tools that have not yet been invented or are not yet widely available) to enable collaboration and document sharing. It is often best to keep it simple, going with tools everyone knows and uses on a daily basis, as opposed to more sophisticated hardware or software. Two general types of collaboration tools are available: professional service automation (PSA), which is designed to optimize service engagements; and enterprise project management (EPM) tool suites, which are used to manage multiple projects. In addition, provide your team members with personal communication and telecommunications tools so that they feel closely tied and connected. If these tools are an unconventional expense item for projects in your organizational culture, educate your project sponsor on the criticality of collaboration, stressing the need to manage the cross-project interdependencies that are known at the start of the project as well as those that will emerge along the way.

PUTTING IT ALL TOGETHER: WHAT DOES THIS MEAN TO THE BUSINESS ANALYST?

Great teams do not happen by accident; rather, they require hard work, planning, a sense of urgency, and disciplined effort to convert a group of people into a high-performing team. For complex innovation projects, the effort is magnified because multiple large, geographically dispersed, and culturally diverse teams are often involved. Leaders of complex projects cease to be business analysts and project managers and become leaders of teams.

What are the elements of superior team leadership? We have discovered that it takes an understanding of the complexities of large, diverse teams as well as a keen realization of the power, wisdom, and *potential* of teams. To be a great team leader, you must:

➤ Make sure you have the appropriate experience and are seasoned enough to be at the helm of a complex initiative.

➤ Insist that senior project leaders fill the other key project roles.

➤ Learn how to build a great team; devote a significant amount of your time to ensuring that your teams are healthy, well-structured, and consist of the right people.

➤ Nurture your teams, but also get out of the way and empower them to perform their magic.

➤ Pay special attention to contractor teams; lead them with the same degree of professionalism as your internal teams.

➤ Use virtual teams as a strategic advantage, but make sure you have adequate face time with them.

➤ Encourage experimentation, questioning, and innovation through edge-of-chaos leadership; the results will astound you.

➤ Lead the teams with a strong focus on collaboration, communications, and coordination.

➤ Learn the discipline and practices that lead to innovation, and model them with your teams.

NOTES

1. Cognizant, "Next-Generation CIOs: Change Agents for the Workplace," October 2010: 5. Online at http://www.cognizant.com/futureofwork/assets/whitepapers/Next-Gen-CIOs.pdf (accessed May 2011).

2. Christian Jensen, Staffan Johansson, and Mikael Lofstrom, "Project Relationships—A Model for Analyzing Interactional Uncertainty," *International Journal of Project Management* 24, no. 1 (2006): 4–12.

3. Ibid.

4. Bennis and Biederman, 3–4.

5. Bennis and Biederman, 8.

6. Mario Bourgault, Jaoaud Daoudi, Nathalie Drouin, and Emilie Hamel, *Understanding Decision Making within Distributed Teams* (Newtown Square, PA: Project Management Institute, 2009): 49.

7. Ibid.

8. Bourgault et al., 40.

9. Mario Bourgault and Nathalie Drouin, "How's Your Distributed Team Doing? Ten Suggestions From the Field," 2007. Online at http://students.depaul.edu/~skelly12/Distributed-Teams-Top-Ten.pdf (accessed August 2010).

10. The Teal Trust, "What makes a good team leader?" (undated). Online at http://www.teal.org.uk/et/page5.htm (accessed August 2010).

11. Cognizant, 3.

12. Arvind Malhotra, Ann Majchrzak, and Benson Rosen, "Leading Virtual Teams," *The Academy of Management Perspectives* 21, no. 1 (2007): 60–69.

13. Manuela S. Zoninsein, "Less Is More," *PMNetwork* 24, no. 10 (October 2010): 42–45.

14. Michelle LaBrosse, "Virtual Velocity: Effective Project Management Gives Virtual Teams the Edge," February 4, 2008. Online at http://www.projecttimes.com/project-teams/virtual-velocity-effective-project-management-gives-virtual-teams-the-edge.html (accessed April 2011).

15. Sanjiv Augustine, *Managing Agile Projects* (Upper Saddle River, NJ: Prentice Hall Professional Technical Reference, 2005): 25, 43–186.

16. James H. Johnson, "Micro Projects Cause Constant Change," *Extreme CHAOS* 2001 (West Yarmouth, MA: The Standish Group International, 2001): 134.

CHAPTER 7
Creativity-Inducing Facilitation

t is a tall order to ask 21ˢᵗ century business analysts to foster creativity throughout their organizations. Nonetheless, this goal is not as elusive as it seems. Business analysts' expertise in facilitation can foster constructive dialogue, and as we have learned in previous chapters, *dialogue cultivates creativity*. Creativity-provoking facilitation techniques are designed to discourage groups from to jumping immediately to the "right" answer, because there is really no right answer, only the most feasible and most valuable solution we have identified at the moment.

THE NUTS AND BOLTS OF CREATIVE FACILITATION

> *We cannot direct the winds, but we can set the sails to gather the wind that steer our course.*
>
> —Bertha Calloway

Without a doubt, creative teams have a keen appreciation for the fact that there is *no right answer*, only countless alternatives, some more viable than others. Skilled facilitators are highly responsive to participants' needs to drive to results, yet they defy these needs by challenging the participants to develop creative skills. It is in the "space between anxiety and boredom"[1] that creativity flourishes in middle-school-aged children—and the same can be said of adults. In the workplace, it is the job of the skilled facilitator to steer the group to find that *creative space*. Facilitators are taught to keep the conversation on track, tabling tangential conversations for later. However, the facilitator who fosters creativity strives to be tolerant of, and in fact encourages, unconventional answers, intermittent disruptions, and even diversions, never knowing where they might lead.

FACILITATION IS POWERFUL

To be a business analyst in the 21st century is an enviable position. Facilitating groups to solve problems and make decisions in an innovative way is the creative leader's most powerful role, and this endeavor is personified in the business analyst. It behooves the business analyst to become expert in facilitating groups to solve intractable problems and make ingenious decisions. Problem-solving and decision-making are closely linked, and each requires group members to use the creative process to identify and develop options.

FACILITATION TO FOSTER CREATIVITY IS EVEN MORE POWERFUL

So how do business analysts ensure they are fostering creativity and innovation in group sessions? First of all, we need to understand the subtle differences between creative thinking and critical thinking because we need to master both types of thinking to foster innovation.

➤ *Creative thinking* can be defined as making and communicating connections to brainstorm a variety of possibilities and new and unusual possibilities. It involves thinking and experiencing in various ways, taking different points of view, and guiding the generation and selection of alternatives.

➤ *Critical thinking* can be defined as analyzing and developing possibilities so that you can compare and contrast many ideas, improve and refine ideas, make effective decisions and judgments, and build a sound foundation for effective action.[2]

FACILITATED MEETINGS, WORKING SESSIONS, AND WORKSHOPS

For group problem-solving and decision-making, or when a consensus is required, facilitated sessions and formal workshops are the tools of choice. Innovative decision-making requires a mixture of skills: creative identification of remarkable ideas, clarity of conclusions and opinions, team resolve, and the ability to implement the best solution. In this chapter, we explore just a few tried-and-true techniques to foster creativity in decision-making. As you review these approaches, note that most of the problem-solving and decision-making processes discussed have accompanying activities designed to help the group identify as many alternative solutions as possible. These are the most creative part of the exercise, so do not cut them short.

CREATIVE AND CRITICAL THINKING

Expert facilitators know how to use both creative and critical thinking.

A Word to the Wise

Focus your professional development activities on learning to use both types of thinking to drive towards innovative results.

THE POWER OF THE AGENDA

The agenda is your friend! Do not hold a meeting without an agenda that includes, in addition to the agenda items, the expected outcome (a decision, information sharing, a context diagram, or the development of meeting ground rules), a list of the essential participants, and timing for each item. Successful meetings are the result of adequate planning and preparation. For all key meetings, the wise facilitator creates two agendas: (1) the typical meeting agenda (Figure 7-1), and (2) the facilitator agenda (Figure 7-2).

Meeting Logistics	
Team/Project Name:	
Purpose:	
Called By:	Scribe:
Date:	Time:
Place:	
Bridge # / Phone #:	
Pre-Meeting:	Please review all documents attached prior to the meeting. Documents attached for this meeting:

Distribution List				
Name	**Title/Role**	**Email**	**Telephone**	**Location**

Agenda Items					
	Topic	**Action/Expected Outcome**	**Supporting Documentation**	**Discussion Lead**	**Allotted Time**
1.	Opening	– Open meeting; review/approve agenda – Welcome guests – Approve minutes of last meeting			
2.	Agenda Item				
3.	Agenda Item				
4.	Agenda Item				
5.	Wrap-Up	– Date/time for next meeting – Agenda items – Meeting evaluation			

Action Items				
	Item Name	**Item Description**	**Status**	**Owner**	**Due Date**
1.					
2.					
3.					

FIGURE 7-1. Typical Meeting Agenda

Topic	Action	Supporting Documentation	Purpose/Output	Deliverable	Facilitation Technique
Opening	• Open meeting • Review/approve agenda • Welcome guests • Approve minutes of last meeting				
Agenda Item	Determine team ground rules	Business case	Decision; list of ground rules	Make a sample list of ground rules available.	Full group facilitation
Agenda Item	Define business objectives	Business case	Decision; list of objectives	Make a sample list of business objectives available.	• Three breakout groups • Report to plenary group • Full group reviews and refines
Agenda Item	Define requirements scope	Business case; project charter	Context scoping diagram	Make a sample context diagram available.	Full group facilitation
Agenda Item	Present overview of business analysis	Training slides	Group education; list of issues	Action items for follow-up	Presentation
Agenda Item	Present overview of requirements elicitation process	Training slides	Group education; list of issues	Action items for follow-up	Presentation
Wrap-Up	• Date/time for next meeting • Agenda items • Meeting evaluation				

FIGURE 7-2. Sample Facilitator Agenda

The business analyst uses the facilitator agenda to plan the meeting and design the facilitation approach and the output format for each significant agenda item. Only after the facilitator agenda is complete can the business analyst accurately predict timing for major agenda items and determine who needs to participate.

PROBLEM-SOLVING METHODS THAT FOSTER CREATIVITY

It is imprudent to attempt to solve problems without a tried and true problem-solving structure. The business analyst can choose from many problem-solving techniques. We provide a few here for consideration; this list is by no means exhaustive.

BEING CREATIVE

Chris Velden, author of the blog "Missing in Leadership," contends that being creative is sometimes out of our comfort zone.[3] Many of us have been socialized to be restrained, narrow, focused, hesitant, cautious, conservative, results oriented, and afraid to fail. Despite this tendency, certain techniques can elicit greater creativity, including a classic six-step problem-solving model depicted in Figure 7-3.

The steps include:

1. *Getting the right people*. Be sure you have invited the experts needed to truly analyze the problem area.

2. *Analyzing the problem*. All too often, groups devise brilliant solutions—for the wrong problem. Make sure the problem is well understood and documented.

3. *Researching and learning*. What has happened in the past to provide context and studying what other organizations do; brainstorming with others. Avoid in-the-building thinking here.

FIGURE 7-3. The Six-Step Problem-Solving Model

4. ***Searching for creative ideas***. This is the creative step, so encourage imagination, experimentation, combining known ideas to create new patterns. The breakthrough usually occurs when your group is in a relaxed, secure state.

5. ***Selecting using problem-solving techniques***. Choose one or more ideas to pilot and test. Examine the feasibility of each idea (economic feasibility, technical feasibility, cultural feasibility, time-to-market feasibility); select the most feasible idea to pilot and test first.

6. ***Experimenting and learning***. Experiment, build prototypes and mockup to incorporate learnings into the final solution.

THE CREATIVE PROBLEM-SOLVING MODEL

Another six-stage problem-solving process uses both creative and critical thinking and adapts well to a business environment (Figure 7-4).

1. *Identify the problem or opportunity*: What is the problem that needs fixing or the opportunity that needs to be explored? What is the situation that demands our attention? We have to identify and fully understand the problem first before we can proceed. (In Chapter 8, we suggest a number of techniques for analyzing the problem or opportunity to ensure we have a good understanding of the situation. These include root cause analysis, gap analysis, and SWOT analysis.)

2. *Find data*: This stage involves taking stock—unearthing and collecting information, knowledge, facts, feelings, opinions, and

FIGURE 7-4. The Creative Problem-Solving Model

thoughts to sort out and clarify the situation more specifically. What do we know about the situation, and what do we still need to find out?

3. ***Define the problem or opportunity***: Now that we have collected the data, we need to formulate a problem/opportunity statement that expresses the heart of the situation. We must try to put aside the common assumption that we already know what the problem is and try to state the problem in such a manner as to invite novel perspectives on it. (See Problem and Opportunity Analysis, Root Cause Analysis, Storyboard Analysis, and Gap Analysis in Chapter 8.)

4. ***Generate ideas***: This is the state in which we brainstorm as many ideas or alternatives as possible for dealing with the problem. Don't evaluate your ideas at this point; merely list them as an idea pool from which we will draw when putting together a variety of solutions to the problem. (We introduce lots of idea-generation techniques later in this chapter.)

5. ***Identify the solution***: Now that we have a number of ideas that can serve as possible solutions to our problem, we need to evaluate them systematically. To do this we have to generate a variety of criteria and select the most important for the problem. Is it cost? Innovation? Time to market? Simplicity? Expediency? In this way, we will be able to identify and evaluate the relative strengths and weaknesses of possible solutions. (See Feasibility Analysis later in this chapter.)

6. ***Implement the solution***: Having decided upon a solution, it's time to formulate a plan of action to implement it. Determine what kind of help we will need, what obstacles or difficulties might get in the way, and what specific short- and long-term steps we are going to take to solve the problem or capitalize on the opportunity. (Chapter 8 provides lots of techniques, including impact analysis and force field analysis, for analyzing the effects of the selected solution.)

THE FIVE-STEP PROBLEM-SOLVING MODEL

A very similar problem-solving approach that is based on research has proven useful when trying to make a difficult decision or solve an intractable problem (Figure 7-5).

FIGURE 7-5. The Five-Step Problem-Solving Model

This model involves a series of five steps:

1. ***Recognize the problem***. Recognize the problem exists and is worth solving. View the situation positively; treat it like an opportunity or challenge.

2. ***Define the problem***. Gather information about the problem; remember, many times we develop great solutions to the wrong problem. It is helpful to visualize what it will look like when the problem is solved and to develop success criteria.

3. ***Generate potential solutions***. This is the most creative part of the process. Think of as many options as you can; do not judge ideas; the goal is to generate as many alternatives as possible. Remember to engage in out-of-the-building thinking.

4. ***Make decisions***. Narrow down options by combining like ideas. Then use a prioritization approach to determine which ideas the group prefers. You can do this by taking an informal vote: ask each participant to mark the three ideas he considers best. Discard the ideas that did not receive any votes. Then analyze the feasibility of

each option in priority order (viability in terms of cost, time, complexity, probability of success, and level of change). Review the results as a group and determine the most viable option. List the options in order of feasibility.

5. ***Implement and verify solutions***. Pilot the solution on a small scale to validate assumptions and the feasibility assessment. During the pilot, continue to examine the chosen solution and the degree to which it is meeting success criteria. If the solution is not meeting expectations, revise it or try the next option.

THE STRUCTURED DECISION-MAKING MODEL (SDM)

The structured decision-making model is used in many industries. It consists of a set of six steps for problem analysis (Figure 7-6).

This approach to problem solving is rooted in decision theory and risk analysis. It is not a rigid approach to problem solving; rather, it is a straightforward set of steps. Decisions are made based on established objectives that take into account uncertainty, legal mandates, and community values, thus integrating science and policy. This problem-solving model is appropriate in the following scenarios:

➤ For decisions involving technical analysis with value-based discussions

➤ For facilitating multi-disciplinary technical planning and stakeholder involvement

➤ To inform difficult choices and to make them more transparent and efficient.

THE 11-STEP DECISION-MAKING MODEL

Creative problem solving is both an art and a science. It almost always involves the elements listed below, coupled with both creative and logical methods,

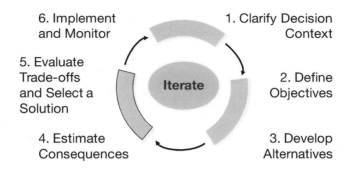

FIGURE 7-6. The Structured Problem-Solving Model

procedural principles and theories, and critical thinking skills. Decision Making.org offers a free worksheet to help users follow this 11-step process:

1. Analyze the environment to clarify the decision context.

2. Define the problem or opportunity in as much detail as possible.

3. Set goals and plans: what will success look like?

4. Search, explore, and gather evidence.

5. Generate as many ideas as possible: imagine, create, and originate.

6. Prioritize the ideas, and evaluate the high-priority ideas.

7. Make an educated guess (or hypothesis).

8. Challenge the hypothesis.

9. Reach a conclusion.

10. Keep your options open: experiment, prototype, and build mockups.

11. Take action.[4]

THE PLAN-DO-CHECK-ACT PROBLEM-SOLVING MODEL

Developed by W. Edwards Deming, the plan-do-check-act (PDCA) cycle is an iterative, easy, four-step problem-solving process typically used in quality control (Figure 7-7). It is also known as the Deming cycle, Shewhart cycle, and Deming Wheel. The PDCA cycle can be used in many situations:

➤ To manage a simple and well-understood problem-solving process

➤ As a routine management approach for an individual or team

➤ To manage a classic continuous-improvement project

➤ To guide the development of a relationship with a new partner or vendor

➤ To continually evaluate prototypes and solution components for a new product, process, or service development project.

The process goes like this:

1. *Plan*. Understand the problem; design or revise product, process, or service components to improve results:

   a. Clearly define the problem statement.

   b. Conduct root cause analysis to determine the actual source of the problem.

2. *Do*. Execute the plan:

   a. Pilot the changes and measure its performance.

   b. Implement corrective actions for all root causes of the problem.

3. *Check*. Monitor results:

   a. Evaluate the processes and results against objectives and specifications.

   b. Verify effectiveness of all corrective actions.

   c. Report the results to decisionmakers.

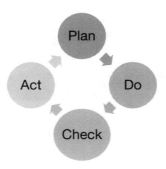

FIGURE 7-7. Plan-Do-Check-Act Problem-Solving Model

4. ***Act***. Determine the changes needed to correct the problem:

   a. Standardize the changes and apply actions to the outcome for necessary improvement.

   b. Apply corrections to standard processes, products, or services.

FIRST CREATE, THEN INNOVATE

As you can see, the business analyst can choose from a vast assortment of approaches to solve problems, make decisions, and foster creativity. Keep in mind that there are two basic required elements when using creative problem-solving and decision-making techniques (note their similarities to creative thinking and critical thinking, discussed earlier). The first is divergent thinking (to create), and the second is convergent thinking (to innovate):

1. ***Divergent Thinking: Generate Creative Ideas.*** When you are generating ideas, do not allow any judgment; the object is to identify as many options as possible. Encourage participants to think out of the box and even out of the building; accept all options and look for unusual possibilities and combinations. Combine like ideas; allow participants to build on others' ideas.

2. ***Convergent Thinking: Analyze, Refine, Prioritize, Decide— Innovate!*** When you shift to analyzing, refining, or choosing options, encourage a balanced approach. It helps to prioritize options

and eliminate the low-priority ones; conduct a feasibility analysis for each high-priority option. Consider affirmative as well as negative comments, and be purposeful and clear. Consider novel approaches, but also think about the appropriateness of each option. Keep the group focused until the appropriate course of action emerges.[5]

EXPERT FACILITATION

Expert facilitators create an environment where "real" dialogue takes place. Participants challenge each other respectfully, listen to each other, and build on each others' ideas.

A Word to the Wise

Focus your professional development activities on learning to use a multitude of facilitation techniques. Take facilitation classes. Become a certified professional facilitator. Join the International Association of Facilitators.

In the divergent approach, teams use creative idea-generating techniques to identify concepts and thoughts and then follow them wherever they lead. The process leads to one or more new ideas, and when the process takes hold, it leads to still more ideas. Convergent thinking is designed to solve a particular problem or help groups arrive at what is considered the most feasible option. Convergent thinking is creative thinking aimed at generating fresh new solutions.

Most methods designed to encourage creativity alternate divergent thinking with sessions of intense convergent thinking. The authors of *Creative Problem Solving: An Introduction* recommend this approach.[6] It is important to understand that both creative thinking and critical thinking are needed—they are not mutually exclusive. First, the business analyst should facilitate the group through divergent creative thinking, which involves "encountering gaps, paradoxes, opportunities, challenges, or concerns. Then search for meaningful connections by generating many varied possibilities, and unusual or original possibilities,and details to expand or enrich possibilities."[7] Then she should facilitate the group through convergent critical thinking, which involves "examining possibilities carefully, fairly, and constructively; then focusing your thoughts and actions by organization and analyzing possibilities, refining and developing promising possibilities; ranking or prioritizing options; and, choosing or deciding on certain options."[8]

DIVERGENT THINKING: GENERATE CREATIVE IDEAS

An extensive variety of creativity tools and techniques are at the business analyst's disposal. Use visualization techniques whenever possible, from stick figures to rich pictures, to ensure all team members are seeing the idea in the same way. Creativity is much more about technique and intelligence than it is about "creative talent." Business analysts should learn how to use a variety of creativity techniques to enhance their own capacity for creative thought and to develop innovation in their organizations.

BRAINSTORMING

Brainstorming is perhaps the most-used idea-generation tool in the business analyst's toolbox, so business analysts positively must become expert at facilitating brainstorming sessions. Brainstorming is a powerful method that is used to encourage a team to creatively and efficiently generate lots of ideas in a short period of time. It can be used for virtually any problem or issue that needs an innovative or creative solution. A word of caution: brainstorming sessions may actually shut down creativity if they are not conducted well. Brainstorming is a very fragile process. It is intended to be a free-flowing, nonjudgmental exchange and idea-list generator that sparks everyone's creative juices, but such an atmosphere can be very difficult to achieve.

MIND MAPPING

Mind mapping involves using diagrams to generate, structure, and classify ideas; visualize connections; study a problem; and organize information. Information is arranged around a central key word or idea. Use these maps during brainstorming or after brainstorming. Once the group has identified the most feasible option through a brainstorming session, mind mapping is a good way to ensure that the group has a deep understanding of the impacts and interdependencies of their proposed option. Mind maps support research, organization, problem-solving, decision-making, and writing. They inspire the visual thinking that leads to creativity.

CARDSTORMING

Cardstorming is another tool that can help you generate ideas. It is less interactive than brainstorming. This process calls for all participants to write their ideas on a card. The facilitator then collects the cards and guides the group in categorizing them. The group then uses prioritization techniques to limit the number of ideas for further consideration.

CONVERGENT THINKING: ANALYZE, REFINE, PRIORITIZE, DECIDE—INNOVATE!

Once you have successfully defined the problem and brainstormed to create a list of alternative solutions, your job is only half complete. Now decide which option to implement to bring about the innovation. To do so, prioritize and analyze the high-priority options.

THE NOMINAL GROUP TECHNIQUE

The nominal group technique is a method for condensing a list of brainstormed ideas and selecting the high-priority ideas the group would like to consider for further analysis.

1. ***Conduct a brainstorming session***. After the session, combine similar items.

2. ***Reduce the list***. Before condensing similar ideas, reduce the list to less than 50 ideas, if possible. You can do this by conducting one or two rounds of multi-voting (see below). You may also ask participants if they would like to withdraw any ideas, but no group member is allowed to remove an item that originated with another team member unless the originator agrees.

3. ***Distribute index cards***. Give each participant four to eight cards. The number of cards to be distributed depends on the number of ideas remaining on the list after step 2. (Distribute 4 cards for up to 20 ideas; 6 cards for 20–35 ideas; 8 cards for 35–50 ideas.)

4. ***Make selections***. Participants select ideas they like from the list and write down one per card.

5. ***Assign points***. Participants rank each idea based on their preferences. Each person assigns the highest point value to the item that will most positively impact him. Participants can award as many points to an idea as they have cards.

6. ***Tally votes***. The facilitator collects the cards and tallies the votes. The ideas that end up with the most points indicate the group's selections for feasibility analysis.

7. ***Discuss results***. Participants review the results and discuss their reactions. Some groups stop at this step if everyone agrees that the idea with the most votes is the most important. The group then performs a feasibility analysis and builds a business case for the selected idea. If the group does not agree on the clear superiority of the idea with the most votes, the group conducts a feasibility analysis (see below) of the top two to five ideas.

MULTI-VOTING

The multi-voting technique is another way to condense the list of brainstormed ideas and select the high-priority ideas the group would like to consider for further analysis.

1. ***Conduct a brainstorming session***. Conduct a classic brainstorming session, posting ideas on a whiteboard or chart and combining similar items.

2. ***Narrow the list***. Have participants select the most important ideas on the list. The number of ideas each person selects should be about one-third of the total number of items. (Example: If there are 15 items, each person should select 5.)

3. ***Tally the votes***. Using colored sticky dots or markers, participants mark their choices on the list.

4. ***Eliminate items with no or few votes***. As mentioned earlier, the objective is to choose no more than five to eight ideas. The rule of thumb is if it is a small group (5 or fewer members), cross off items with only one or two votes; if it is a medium group (6 to 15), eliminate anything with three or fewer votes; if it is large (more than 15), eliminate items with four votes or fewer.

FEASIBILITY ANALYSIS

After brainstorming and prioritizing, the business analyst guides the group in determining the most feasible solution. Make sure someone with requisite expertise in the problem area under consideration is in your group. Prepare a table similar to the one shown in Figure 7-8, listing the high-priority ideas down the first column and the feasibility criteria across the top row.

1. ***Analyze each option***. Facilitate the group through analysis of each option, capturing information about the economic, time-to-market, cultural, technical, success, and business process feasibility of each one, as well as the feasibility of achieving an innovative solution.

				<Problem, Opportunity, or Issue> <Expert Team Members Involved in Analysis>				
Option	Costs	Benefits	Innovation? (H, M, L)	Probability of Success	Process Complexity	Technical Complexity	Risks
1							
2							
3							
4							
5							

FIGURE 7-8. Feasibility Analysis Template

2. *Review results*. Step back and review the information. Ask the group if there is an obvious alternative that appears to be the most feasible. If not, ask if there are two most-feasible options.

3. *Analyze the most feasible option(s) in detail*. For the most feasible option(s), conduct more detailed analysis and capture the information in the matrix.

4. *Build the business case*. If significant investment is required to implement the top idea, prepare a business case to be used to propose the implementation of the solution.

5. *Present for approval*. Use the results of your feasibility analysis as decision-support information when presenting your recommended approach to decisionmakers. Include the names of those who participated in the analysis and all the options considered. You can present the results in a simple tabular template like the one you used to document the feasibility information.

TWENTY QUESTIONS

Twenty questions is a technique used to challenge assumptions and promote a thorough understanding of an idea or option. Once the group has chosen the most feasible alternative, this technique can help ensure the group fully understands the effects of the proposed option. The group should work together to answer the questions shown in Figure 7-9. Answering these questions quickly generates a lot of information about an idea.

The questions can be categorized as who, what, when, where, and how questions:

1. Who is participating?

2. What is happening? What has happened? What will happen?

	What?	**Where?**	**When?**	**Who?**	**How?**
Current State	What happens?	Where is the problem? Where is there confusion?	When does the problem occur?	Who does the work?	How are the activities sequenced and tasks performed?
Future State	What should the process look like?	Where will the process change?	When will it change?	Who will do the work?	How will the activities be performed, timed, and resourced?
Gap Indicators	What is different— what are the gap indicators?	Where in the process will the new solution make a difference?	When do the differences occur?	Who will identify the gaps?	How will the gaps be improved and managed?
Is There a Better Way?	What options are available?	Where in the process will the new solution make a difference?	When is the best window of opportunity?	Who makes the decision on the alternative solution?	How will the alternative solution be viewed by the organization?

FIGURE 7-9. Twenty Questions Grid

3. When is it going to happen? When did something happen?

4. Where is the action taking place?

5. How did something happen? What were the circumstances?

Finally, the group should discuss *why* these things happened.

LATERAL THINKING TECHNIQUE

Dr. Edward de Bono described a technique he called lateral thinking.[9] In his 1967 book on the subject, de Bono writes that normally, our thinking is pretty straightforward. But when a group engages in lateral thinking, it is not encouraged to find the "right" answer, or the most logical answer, but to come up with radical new approaches. The goal is to generate ridiculous or even provocative ideas—to truly think "out of the building." Lateral thinking is used to foster innovation, when it is important to explore multiple possibilities instead of a single approach.

THE SIX THINKING HATS TECHNIQUE

This technique, also attributed to Dr. Edward de Bono, uses colored hats as a metaphor for each area of focus, to encourage laser-like thinking when analyzing the impacts of a particular alternative (Figure 7-10).[10] The facilitator alerts the audience to a change in the focus of the discussion by putting on a different colored hat, literally or figuratively. This encourages the group to concentrate on a certain area of interest. To facilitate this technique:

➤ Use colored hats as a metaphor for each category.

➤ Identify the meaning of the colored hats.

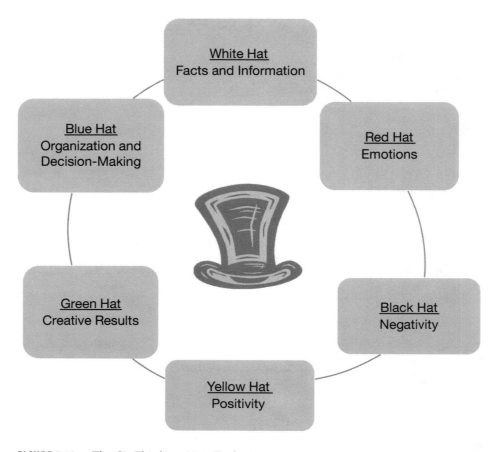

FIGURE 7-10. The Six Thinking Hats Technique

➤ Symbolize switching the discussion focus by putting on a different colored hat, literally or figuratively.

➤ Concentrate on different aspects of the option under consideration by changing the focus—or colored hat—periodically.

DECISION-MAKING—INNOVATING!

Notice that each problem-solving model involves a step to decide on the most feasible solution. Choosing a feasible solution converts the idea to value—true innovation. Selecting the appropriate decision-making approach will make the decision-making process more likely to succeed (Figure 7-11).

Consensus decision-making is the approach teams most frequently use when defining and agreeing on requirements. Clearly, in a business environment, where decisions should be made based on business value to the enterprise as a whole, the facilitator's job is to drive the group to consensus. There is a great deal of confusion about what defines consensus decision-making. A group reaches consensus when it debates, considers the interests of all participants, and makes a decision that *everyone is willing to support.*

Consensus does not mean that the decision is necessarily everyone's first choice. It does mean that everyone can live with it and commits to supporting it. If the decision did not come easily, the facilitator probes further by explaining that if anyone still has reservations about the decision, she has the responsibility to raise the issue to the group for further discussion before the final decision is made and the discussion is closed. In effect, everyone has

Method	When Is It Appropriate?
Total agreement	Full discussion is not required and everyone is united on the issue.
Assigned decision	One person will take full responsibility for the decision and is accountable for the results.
Voting	The stakeholders present options, and a division of the group as a result of the vote is acceptable.
Compromise	Opposite views prevent a decision, and a middle position incorporating ideas from both sides is developed.
Consensus	Buy-in of all affected stakeholders is essential.

FIGURE 7-11. Decision-Making Methods

veto power and should use it until she can truly support the decision in the future. Consensus means that all considerations have been discussed and resolved. For very important decisions, the facilitator polls the group one by one, posing the question, "Can you live with it, and will you support it?"

Consensus decision-making is difficult for newly formed teams, the members of which have not yet begun to trust one another. The skilled facilitator, however, uses the consensus-building process to unite the group, uncover various perspectives, and foster a collaborative approach to decisions to improve buy-in.

Once the decision is made, the facilitator moves quickly to action. Implementation strategies include:

➤ Assigning an owner or person responsible for acting on the decision

➤ Identifying activities and tasks that will support the decision and working with the project manager to identify resource requirements, timelines, and associated costs

➤ Determining whether there are any communication or training requirements during the implementation of the decision.

PUTTING IT ALL TOGETHER: WHAT DOES THIS MEAN TO THE BUSINESS ANALYST?

In addition to the creativity-inducing techniques described in this chapter, there are many others that the business analyst should explore. Many ideas are readily available on the Internet. It is important to change your facilitation style and techniques often to keep your meetings fresh, fun, and exciting.

NOTES

1. Po Bronson and Ashley Merryman, "The Creativity Crisis," *Newsweek* (July 19, 2010): 44–50. Online at http://www.newsweek.com/2010/07/10/the-creativity-crisis.html (accessed April 2011).

2. Mary Bellis, "Critical Thinking and Creative Thinking Skills," (undated). Online at http://inventors.about.com/library/lessons/bl_isaksen_treffinger.htm (accessed May 2011).

3. Chris Velden, "How to Be a Creative Leader," December 12, 2008. Online at http://ezinearticles.com/?How-to-Be-a-Creative-Leader&id=1765668 (accessed May 2011).

4. Norman W. Edmund, "Decision Making: The Best and Most Practical Guide Available," (undated). Online at http://decisionmaking.org (accessed May 27, 2011).

5. Donald J. Treffinger, Scott G. Isaksen, and K. Brian Dorval, *Creative Problem Solving: An Introduction*, 3rd ed. (Waco, TX: Prufrock Press, 2000): 3.

6. Ibid.

7. Ibid.

8. Ibid.

9. Edward De Bono, *New Think: The Use of Lateral Thinking in the Generation of New Ideas* (New York: Basic Books, 1967).

10. Edward De Bono, *Six Thinking Hats* (New York: Little, Brown and Company, 1985).

CHAPTER 8
Creatively Eliciting and Evolving Breakthrough Requirements

A requirements elicitation workshop is one of the most effective ways to gather information quickly and arrive at consensus on complicated requirements involving a large group of stakeholders. In this chapter, we discuss best practices for both formal and informal requirements elicitation working sessions.

RUNNING POWERFUL MEETINGS

We hear complaints about poorly run meetings all the time, perhaps because meeting management skills are often undervalued and underrated in the business environment, even though meetings consume so much valuable time and so many critical resources. Why is so little effort expended to make meetings more effective? Here are a few reasons to consider, although there are likely many more:

➤ Business leaders do not recognize the relationship between ineffective meetings and organizational productivity measures.

➤ Mid-level managers do not have the knowledge or the skills needed to plan, conduct, and facilitate an effective meeting and then follow up on decisions.

➤ Project managers and business analysts do not appreciate how important good meeting planning is for achieving better, more creative results.

➤ The organization does not acknowledge that ineffective meetings are a cost drain.

➤ Management does not hold functional managers, business analysts, project managers, or other people accountable for the effects of ineffective meetings.

PLANNING

A great deal of planning is necessary for a requirements elicitation workshop or other type of meeting to be effectively executed. For a significant event, enlist the help of a small planning team, consisting of a co-facilitator, a scribe/modeler, and the project manager, to prepare for the event. Prior to the event, it is important to:

➤ Review all project documentation that has been produced to date, including the business case, project charter and plans, business process documentation, and supporting application system documentation.

➤ Identify the scope of the requirements to be defined in the workshop, using a context diagram.

➤ Identify the participants needed, making sure that there will be a representative from all involved organizations and systems.

➤ Ensure needed resources are available and committed to conduct elicitation activities.

➤ Identify the goals of the workshop.

➤ Determine the project approach, i.e., whether it will be plan driven or change driven.

> A plan-driven approach to business analysis activities specifies all requirements up front.

> A change-driven approach to business analysis activities uses an iterative approach to requirements.

➤ Identify the artifacts to be produced during the workshop.

➤ Develop a participant agenda and a facilitator agenda.

➤ Determine the approach to be used at the workshop to resolve conflicting requirements with the end users and stakeholder participants.

➤ Determine the approach to be used to validate that the stated requirements resulting from the workshop meet business needs.

SCOPING

After all information relevant to the project has been reviewed, the planning team conducts a stakeholder analysis to determine the groups, organizations, and systems that are involved in or impacted by the project and should therefore be involved in the requirements elicitation workshop. Since the purpose of the workshop is to make key decisions about the business needs, it is important that the participants be empowered to make decisions for the organization they represent.

To identify all of the stakeholders, it is helpful to create a context diagram, which makes the scope of the requirements and players involved visible. The context diagram depicts the new or changed business system in

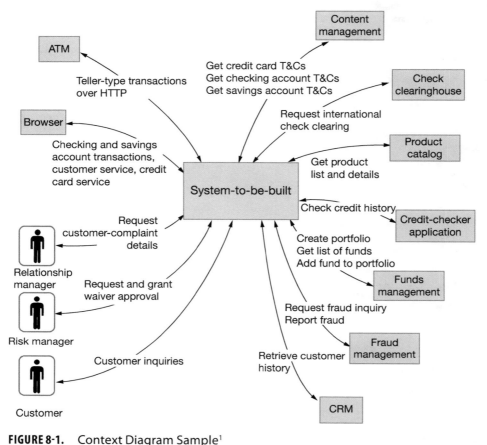

FIGURE 8-1. Context Diagram Sample[1]

Reprinted with permission from Tilak Mitra.

its environment, showing all external entities that interact with the system (including people, processes, and application systems). See Figure 8-1 for a sample context diagram and Chapter 11 for additional information on conducting a robust stakeholder analysis.

PREPARING FOR A MEETING

The business analyst facilitates multiple types of meetings. Following the same basic steps for each meeting helps it to be an effective and efficient use of participants' time and leads to a positive outcome for everyone.

ESTABLISH THE PURPOSE OF THE MEETING

Before you jump into planning a meeting, determine the objectives, purpose, and measures of success for the meeting by answering the following questions:

➤ Describe the purpose or goal of the meeting. Why have you decided to have a meeting?

➤ What are the objectives of the meeting?

➤ Describe the desired outcome of the meeting. What product or deliverable will be produced or decision made that constitutes meeting success?

➤ How will you measure the effectiveness or success of the meeting? Will the output contribute to innovation, wealth for the organization, value to the customer?

➤ Who needs the meeting deliverables? What exactly do they need? How will we involve them in the development and validation of the output?

➤ How will the meeting deliverables be used to add value to the project?

DESIGN THE MEETING TO MEET THE OBJECTIVES

Once the meeting's purpose, objectives, and outcomes are well understood, the business analyst selects the most appropriate meeting type from among the many alternatives. Do not hold a formal meeting with a large number of participants when a small, informal working session will accomplish the meeting objectives. Keep in mind the cost of large meetings, the difficulty in reaching consensus when the group is large, and the value of small-group interactions. Everyone invited to the meeting will expect and need ample time to air their viewpoints and participate fully in the discussion and the decisions. Sometimes it is helpful to first conduct a meeting with a small group of experts and then establish a review team to comment and provide feedback on the meeting results. So think before you hold a large meeting; carefully design the meeting on the basis of the objectives, purpose of the session, and number of participants who need to support the decisions that are made. Preparations for an informal working session are likely to be less rigorous than preparations for a formal requirements elicitation workshop. But no matter how small or informal the meeting, success is directly related to adequate meeting preparation.

LEVERAGE ORGANIZATIONAL MEETING CULTURE

The organization's meeting culture must also be considered when designing a meeting. The business analyst should take into account cultural considerations like those outlined below.

➤ *Meeting tolerance.* Don't expect participants to be taken away from their business unit for meetings too often, such as more than two or three days in a week.

➤ *Political agendas.* Conduct several meeting preparation interviews with key members of management and others who are influential within the organization to avoid political hazards. Political mistakes can be devastating to an effort to build a collaborative environment.

➤ *Meeting history.* There might be some unwritten rules about meetings. Again, conduct pre-meeting interviews to learn the meeting norms.

➤ *Team collaboration.* Take into account the amount of collaboration and team spirit that you have been able to engender to this point. Schedule less important meetings when the group is just coming together and critical meetings after you have had a chance to work with the group and gain its trust.

> ➤ **Management structure.** Be sure to respect the chain of command when considering the attendees. In addition, make sure you have management's approval to use their resources to capture, document, and validate requirements.

INVOLVE KEY PARTICIPANTS EARLY

To build a collaborative environment even before a meeting, enlist key participants to assist in developing the agenda, especially the project manager, technical lead, lead business representative, and key subject matter experts. Clearly state the overall outcome to be achieved at the end of the meeting and explain any preparations the participants are expected to make before the meeting. Consultant Carter McNamara offers these tips for designing effective agendas:

> ➤ Include something in the agenda for participants to do right away so they come on time and get involved early.

> ➤ Next to each major topic, note the type of action needed, the type of output expected (decision, vote, action assigned to someone), and time estimates for addressing each topic.

> ➤ Don't overdesign meetings; be willing to change the meeting agenda if members are making progress and are in the "creative zone."

> ➤ Think about how you label an event so people come in with the appropriate mindset. It might pay to have a short dialogue about the meeting with key stakeholders to develop a common mindset among attendees, particularly if they include representatives from various cultures.[2]

SCHEDULE THE MEETING

If the meeting requires broad participation, it is likely that it will have to be scheduled far in advance so that key attendees can block out the time on their calendars. Considerations include company, organization, and department calendars, as well as individual commitments and meeting room availability.

DETERMINE THE MEETING PARTICIPANTS

Identify the appropriate people to be invited to the meeting. Ensure that they have been authorized to dedicate time to your effort and that they are empowered not only to represent their organization but also to make decisions and commitments on behalf of it. When selecting meeting participants, consider the experience level, knowledge and skills, and availability of the people you need to accomplish the meeting objectives.

Ensure that all stakeholders who will be affected by the outcome of the meeting are represented, including members of management, business unit representatives, technical experts, and virtual team members. It is almost always necessary for the business analyst to include technical representatives and the project manager in requirements sessions in which key decisions are to be made. Technical experts develop prototypes and capture graphics in real time as decisions are made, and the project manager is needed to contribute to discussions about management expectations and constraints, both time and cost.

Collaborating with others when building the meeting attendee list is a good practice. As a courtesy, try to speak with participants before they receive your meeting invitation so that they will not be surprised. This small gesture goes a long way in building trust among the team members.

PREPARE THE MEETING AGENDA AND THE FACILITATOR AGENDA

When setting the meeting agenda, the business analyst strives to strike a balance between the meeting goals and outcomes needed, the meeting process or techniques to be used, and human behaviors, the dynamics of people working together. The agenda combines a structured set of activities designed to

➤ Establish an open and safe environment

➤ Transition the participants into a high-performing team

➤ Foster creative and critical thinking

➤ Produce work products that are innovative and will achieve the meeting objectives.

Knowing the purpose of the meeting is the first step in structuring the agenda. Having a firm idea of where you want to be by the end of the meeting suggests what must be covered during the meeting. The business analyst uses a very different set of agenda items to develop requirement functions or features than she uses to prioritize predefined requirements. Each step in reaching the desired meeting outcome is thought through carefully to determine the specific activity for that step, how it will be facilitated, and the amount of time it will take.

There are seven basic steps for developing a meeting agenda:

1. Establish how long the meeting is to last; shorter is better than longer.

2. List the agenda items that must be covered or process steps that need to occur.

3. Determine which facilitation technique to use for each agenda item. (See Chapter 7 for various facilitation models and techniques.)

4. Design the output format, which will be used as a template.

5. Build in time for key experts to be speak.

6. Estimate how long each agenda item will take, factoring in time for dialogue.

7. Leave a minimum of 15 minutes at the end for summary and agreement on what comes next.

If it is evident that more time will be needed to cover all of the agenda items than you have initially allotted, you might need to adjust the length of the meeting or cut back on what you expect to accomplish. Keep in mind that critical and creative thinking requires more time than what is typically allowed, especially if there is controversy. In addition, you need to allow more time if there is a large number of attendees so that everyone can participate. Opportunities to voice an opinion, ask questions, and explain reasons behind positions are critical to developing and achieving consensus. Taking shortcuts at this point could necessitate looping back or cause gridlock.

In the midst of making room reservations and sending out invitations, the business analyst also finalizes the facilitator agenda, which describes the tools, templates, visuals, supplies, and facilitation techniques he will use to facilitate each agenda item.

When finalizing the meeting and facilitator agendas, also consider these suggestions:

➤ Don't start with a clean piece of paper. If the outcome of the meeting is complex, the business analyst almost always works with small groups to create a draft version of the deliverables before the meeting and then facilitates the review and refinement of the deliverables during the meeting with the larger group.

➤ Confirm that the appropriate business and technical representatives will be available to attend the meeting and follow-up sessions. If not, the meeting should be rescheduled.

➤ For significant meetings, the business analyst invites the participants under the signature of the project or business sponsor. Attachments to the workshop invitation include a finalized agenda and summary-level project documents, which the participants should review before the meeting.

DEFINE OUTPUTS AND DELIVERABLES

Because the business analyst designs each meeting to produce an output or a deliverable, the stakes are high. Planning an effective requirements elicitation, analysis, specification, or validation meeting requires the business analyst to prepare extensively for each event. During these preparations, the business analyst should:

➤ Determine the appropriate requirements or other artifacts to be produced as a result of the meeting, including the method, tools, and templates that will be used. (An artifact is a requirement work product, such as a document, model, prototype, table, matrix, or diagram.)

➤ Establish an appropriate decision process, which attendees will use to arrive at consensus on the meeting results.

➤ Select appropriate facilitation activities and techniques. The business analyst will use these to guide the participants in creating and verifying results.

➤ Determine how to facilitate the interaction among meeting participants; for example, will the participants break out into small groups or work as a whole?

➤ Determine the appropriate visual media to facilitate understanding and consensus, such as flip charts, posters, sticky notes, cards on the wall, diagrams, and other visual aids. The more visuals used, the better.

➤ Ensure that the participants have prepared for the meeting. Preparations might include creating straw-man work products, which can be used as a starting point for creating deliverables.

SET UP THE ROOM TO FOSTER THE BEST POSSIBLE COLLABORATIVE DISCUSSIONS

The setup of the room is important to the success of a requirements elicitation session. Arrange the room for optimal efficiency and comfort during the session. For a requirements elicitation workshop, a U-shaped setup (see Figure 8-2) is the best possible arrangement to ensure effective communication and the participation of all workshop attendees. Also see Figure 8-3, Tips for Setting Up for a Formal Workshop.

STARTING THE MEETING

Set a positive tone for the workshop and establish a collaborative environment. Always start on time. Plan something notable at the start of the meeting as an incentive to showing up on time. As an incentive, serve refreshments prior to the meeting start; this encourages everyone to arrive on time.

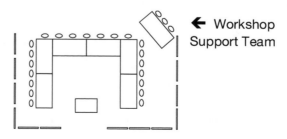

FIGURE 8-2. Room Setup

Setup Item	Description
Seating Arrangement	The participants should be seated around tables arranged in a U shape or in pods of teams.
Handouts	A packet of information, including requirements drafted to date and other key project information, should be placed at each participant's seat. In addition to the draft requirements, this packet may contain the agenda, the list of participants, a copy of the mission/business case, the project charter, the project management plan, the requirements management plan, the issues log, the risk log, the milestone schedule, and any other prepared information that is pertinent to the meeting.
Supplies	In addition to the project information, notepads, name tents, pens, ice water, and glasses should be readily available for each participant. The facilitators will need flip charts and paper, poster paper, sticky notes, markers, notepads, pens, an LCD/PC viewer/projector, and a printer. It's helpful to make a checklist of supplies and equipment ahead of time.
Workshop Support Team	A table should be set to the side or back of the room for the meeting facilitator/support team. They will need supplies such as laptop computers, a printer, and disks for capturing and printing all the information gathered during the workshop. The team will capture information in real time to present to the participants periodically for their review and refinement.

FIGURE 8-3. Tips for Setting Up for a Formal Workshop

SET THE STAGE

As participants arrive for the meeting, greet them by name and make introductions. Set a precedent to start the meetings on time, even if some participants have not arrived.

➤ Start by introducing yourself and describing your role as the business analyst and meeting facilitator. Also introduce other key members who helped prepare for the meeting, as well as those who will help conduct the meeting and capture the information.

➤ Review the agenda and discuss the goals of the meeting to get everyone prepared for the work ahead. Ask if the agenda as structured will meet everyone's needs. If not, ask if there are any recommended adjustments to the agenda. Be prepared to accommodate the recommendations if they help achieve the meeting objectives. This secures everyone's agreement to the agenda. You may even ask that everyone help manage the group's time by keeping to the agenda. Emphasize the need for creativity and innovation, and state that if the group is "in the zone," you will not interrupt or stop the meeting just to keep to the agenda.

➤ Review the project objectives in business terms, relate the meeting to the project objectives, and briefly discuss follow-on activities that are expected.

CONDUCT AN ICEBREAKER

If it is the first meeting of the group, plan a warm-up activity that helps the team members test their voices and get to know each other. Use an icebreaker to relax meeting participants, introduce them to each other, and energize the start of a meeting. Resist the temptation to use games as icebreakers. This may turn off some of your participants before you get a chance to engage them. Effective types of icebreakers include:

➤ Asking each participant to introduce themselves and provide answers to predefined questions

➤ Individual or group activities, such as determining a group name.

➤ Pairing the group and asking partners to exchange ideas on a relevant topic.

ESTABLISH GROUND RULES FOR THE MEETING

Ground rules are operating standards that determine how people conduct discussions and make decisions. At the beginning of the meeting, the business analyst should facilitate a discussion on ground rules, allowing the group to formulate its own operating standards. The facilitator might ask, "What team operating agreements should we adopt to make our work more efficient and of higher quality?" Or, simply, "What are some important guidelines we should all keep in mind as we work together in this and future meetings?" Use the multi-vote technique to gain approval of the rules if there are too many to deal with effectively. The group should review and revise the ground rules as needed.

Figure 8-4 presents typical ground rules.

CAPTURE AND SET EXPECTATIONS

The purpose of setting expectations is to uncover the participants' expectations and ensure they align with the objectives of the workshop. During this activity:

➤ Document expectations on a flip chart.

➤ Address expectations that are not aligned with the meeting purpose and objectives; perhaps write them on a flip chart for future actions.

➤ Reference the expectations throughout the meeting to validate meeting progress.

Setting expectations for the workshop is important for moving forward smoothly with the session. In the overview early in the meeting, the business analyst should state clearly what will be accomplished during the workshop and

Ground Rule Item	Suggested Description and Explanation
Meeting Management	• Team meeting attendance is mandatory. If a member misses a meeting, he or she must take the responsibility for finding out what decisions were made and either support them or raise any issues at the next meeting. • If a member must miss a meeting, are delegates allowed? • Team meetings will be conducted on a specific day and time to maintain consistency and facilitate full attendance. Team members are expected to arrive at the meeting on time. The facilitator will start and adjourn the meeting on time. • The facilitator will review the agenda at the start of each meeting and facilitate setting the agenda for the next meeting at the close. Meeting effectiveness will be evaluated at the end of each meeting.
Issue Management and Conflict Resolution	• If the team is unable to resolve an issue, the issue will be elevated to the next level of management. Prior to escalation, an analysis of the alternative resolutions will be conducted to formulate recommendations from the group.
Decision-Making	• Decisions will be made by consensus. Consensus means: "Although this solution might not be my first choice, I can live with the solution—and therefore I will support it. And if I can't live with it, it is my responsibility to the group to raise my concerns until they are satisfied." • Team decisions will be documented and archived.

FIGURE 8-4. Meeting Ground Rules

what will be left for other sessions. The business analyst also provides a brief overview of the requirements elicitation process to be used during the session.

➤ Briefly, and in general terms, review the requirements elicitation process that will be followed. Set clear expectations for the workshop deliverables and closeout activities that need to be completed after the workshop.

➤ Announce that the expectations that were captured at the beginning of the session will be reviewed at the end. If some have not been met, note an action item to make sure that these expectations are met at a later time. If it is obvious that some of the stated expectations cannot be covered in the session, discuss them very briefly, explain why they are out of scope for the session, and indicate how they will be addressed.

➤ You may need to conduct brief training sessions for activities that will be conducted that participants are not familiar with.

FACILITATING THE MEETING

Facilitators model and enable effective group interactions. They set the standards for group exchanges, listening carefully, directing and redirecting the discussion, and ensuring all participants are engaged and are contributing to the discussion. The best facilitators are relaxed, use humor to make others feel comfortable, and make sure group sessions are enjoyable.

One common pitfall is to plan too much for the time allowed. Following the facilitator agenda will go a long way in preventing this occurrence. Always remain flexible and plan for activities to take longer than you think they will. Constantly evaluate how the session is going, gauging energy levels and watching group behaviors and body language.

To lead your participants into the "creative zone," encourage both critical and creative thinking. Each requires a different mindset and leads to different outcomes. According to *Teacher Tap,* a free professional development resource:

➤ *Critical thinking* involves logical thinking and reasoning, including techniques such as comparison, classification, sequencing, cause/effect, patterning, webbing, analogies, deductive and inductive reasoning, forecasting, planning, hypothesizing, and critiquing.

➤ *Creative thinking* involves creating something new or original. It involves the flexibility, originality, fluency, elaboration, brainstorming, modification, imagery, associative thinking, attribute listing, metaphorical thinking, and forced relationships. The aim of creative thinking is to stimulate curiosity and promote divergence.[3]

Always maintain control of your meetings. If you invite a member of senior management to kick off a meeting, he may "get on a roll" and take much more time than allotted. You may avoid this by preparing your guest for the situation: list the key points you would like him to cover and tell him how much time you have allotted for his brief remarks and a few questions that will likely follow.

When you open any meeting or presentation to group participation, there is a risk of losing control. If you think a question or comment is not relevant, say so, but try hard to be patient with those who take the discussion off track. You might say, "Actually, that comment isn't within the scope of our discussion today."

To help the team stick to the agenda, consider the following time-management techniques:

➤ *Parking lot.* Use a flipchart labeled "Parking Lot" to list ideas that come up during discussion but are outside the scope of the meeting. Ask the individual who brought up the item for permission to "park" the item until the end of the session. At the end of the session, disposition the items by scheduling another meeting with the appropriate participants, putting the "parked" items on a list of action items or issue log, and assigning ownership and a due date to each item. Ask those whose ideas have been "parked" if they are satisfied with the follow-up plan.

➤ *Refocusing questions.* If the discussion begins to digress, take a moment to reword and refocus the question that is under consideration. This can often put the group back on track.

➤ *Timekeeping.* Use the power of the agenda to keep the meeting on track. If an item is going over the allotted time but very valuable discussions are taking place, do not stop the meeting. At a breaking point, note that the time has been exceeded, and arrive at a consensus on how to use the remaining time and reschedule items that have not been covered.

➤ *Placement.* Place high-priority topics that require rigorous discussion and interaction at the very beginning of the agenda to ensure they get the time and attention they need, and allow flexibility in the agenda if more time is needed.

FACILITATING VIRTUAL MEETINGS

In this borderless world, there is no getting around it: business analysts will be called upon to facilitate multisite teams. Special facilitation approaches are needed when facilitating teleconference, video-teleconference, and web meetings. All meetings require supporting materials, such as the agenda and other documentation relevant to agenda items. Many virtual teams rely heavily on paper-based communication to ensure that everyone is fully informed and working from the same information. The materials should be as visual as possible so that everyone sees the same picture and is talking about the same concept.

For important training, elicitation, or validation sessions, a very effective approach is to have a lead facilitator and an onsite facilitator at each location, all directing the discussions at their respective venue. The facilitators collaborate beforehand to establish detailed plans and to design the event. They test for meeting effectiveness by polling participants during and at the end of the meeting and incorporate the suggestions into future sessions.

TOOLS FOR PROCESS IMPROVEMENT SESSIONS

When determining requirements for a business process improvement project, process improvement tools create a common vision for improving business results. While facilitating process improvement sessions, consider using a process map, flow chart, or process chart. To focus everyone on the scope of the process under review, offer an early draft of the process map, flow chart, or process chart before the meeting. Throughout the requirements-gathering sessions, challenge the group to innovate by asking questions like, Are we making breakthrough changes that will result in increased value to our customers and/or our organization? Or is this pretty much business as usual?

PROCESS MAP

A process map shows how specific work gets done in an organization. It is also referred to as a swim lane diagram (Figure 8-5). Each box in the diagram represents a step in the process, and a textual definition for each box or step is usually included along with the diagram.

FLOW CHART

A flow chart is a graphic representation of the sequence of steps to be followed to execute a process.

Requirements Definition

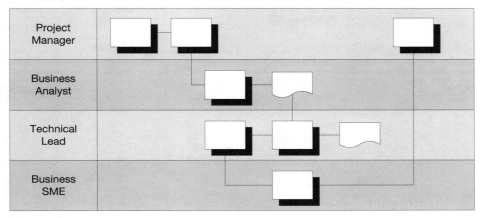

FIGURE 8-5. Process Map

PROCESS CHART

A process chart is a tool to help teams manage, improve, and control processes.

TOOLS FOR ANALYSIS SESSIONS

Analysis facilitation tools are used to identify and study factors when improving and making organizational changes. Again, the facilitator should be sure to encourage creative and critical thinking, as opposed to business as usual.

PROBLEM AND OPPORTUNITY ANALYSIS

In our rush to results, sometimes groups come up with great solutions for the wrong problem. Prior to problem solving, be certain you truly understand the problem by following these steps:

1. Document the problem in detail.

2. Determine the adverse effects the problem is causing.

3. Determine how soon the problem must be solved and the cost of doing nothing.

4. Conduct root cause analysis to determine the underlying source of the issues.

5. Determine the kinds of analysis required to address the issues.

6. Draft a requirements statement describing the business need for a solution.

ROOT CAUSE ANALYSIS

A root cause diagram (also called a cause-and-effect or fishbone diagram) is used to identify and organize the actual causes of a problem. It is like a map that depicts possible cause-and-effect relationships. It helps groups organize ideas for further analysis.

There are six steps to developing a root cause diagram:

1. Write the issue or problem under discussion in a box at the top of the diagram.

2. Draw a line from the box across the paper or white board (this forms the spine of the fishbone).

3. Draw diagonal lines from the spine to represent categories of potential causes of the problem. Categories may include people, processes, tools, and policies. Don't label the lines yet.

4. Draw smaller lines extending from the diagonal lines to represent specific causes in each category; again, don't label these lines yet.

5. Brainstorm relevant categories and potential causes of the problem, label each diagonal line with a category, and note the specific causes under the appropriate category.

6. Analyze the results. Remember, the group has only identified potential causes of the problem. Further analysis, ideally with data, is needed to validate the actual cause or causes.

Once the actual cause or causes have been identified, the group brainstorms potential solutions, either in the same or a follow-on session.

STORYBOARD ANALYSIS

A storyboard is a visualization tool that graphically organizes process steps in sequence (see Figure 8-6). A storyboard can be used:

➤ As an accompaniment to a project proposal, to show how a project to develop a new business solution will look

➤ To depict how a business process will function

➤ To describe the steps in a process, using one box for each major activity.

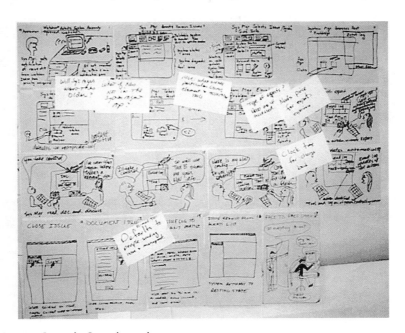

FIGURE 8-6. Sample Storyboard

Requirement	Met	Not Met	Action
Requirement #1			
Requirement #2			
Requirement #3			

FIGURE 8-7. Gap Analysis Template

GAP ANALYSIS

A gap analysis is a tool used to compare actual performance with desired performance. It answers two questions: "Where are we?" and "Where do we want to be?" Figure 8-7 is a simple template for a gap analysis. Gap analysis can be used to:

➤ Benchmark or otherwise assess general expectations of performance in industry, compared with current organizational capabilities.

➤ Determine, document, and evaluate the variance or distance between a current and desired future business process.

➤ Determine, document, and approve the variance between business requirements and system capabilities in terms of COTS (commercial off-the-shelf) packaged application features (this is also referred to as a deficiency assessment).

➤ Discover discrepancies between two or more sets of diagrams.

➤ Analyze the gap between requirements that are met and not met (this also can be called a deficiency assessment).

➤ Compare actual performance against potential performance and then determine the areas in which improvement must be achieved.

Strengths	Weaknesses
Opportunities	Threats

FIGURE 8-8. SWOT Analysis Template

SWOT ANALYSIS

A SWOT—strengths, weaknesses, opportunities, and threats—analysis is used to capture aspects of the current state of the business as a whole, or a specific line of business or business process that is undergoing change (see Figure 8-8). Be sure to focus the discussion on creative opportunities and ways to leverage strengths.

IMPACT ANALYSIS

An impact analysis is a process to determine the costs and benefits, or other competing demands, of a proposed alternative (see Figure 8-9). Each letter represents one of the options under consideration.

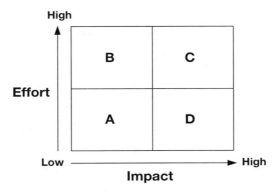

FIGURE 8-9. Impact Analysis Template

<Idea/Concept>	
Driving Forces	**Restraining Forces**
• Xxx • Xxx • Xxx	• Xxx • Xxx • Xxx
Actions to Leverage Driving Forces	**Actions to Manage Restraining Forces**
• Xxx • Xxx • Xxx	• Xxx • Xxx • Xxx

FIGURE 8-10. Force Field Analysis Template

FORCE FIELD ANALYSIS

A force field analysis is a problem-solving technique used to identify and address driving and restraining factors when making an organizational change (see Figure 8-10). Driving forces help the option succeed, while restraining forces pose barriers to the success of the option.

QUESTION AND ANSWER SESSIONS

Question and answer (Q&A) sessions are used to assess understanding and validate consensus. There are two types of questions: closed and open. A closed question is usually used to check participants' comprehension. It requires a factual answer and allows little opportunity for dissent. The answer will be either correct or incorrect. An open, or higher-order, question offers participants much more opportunity to speculate, draw inferences, extrapolate from data, or contribute their own opinions. Open questions are frequently used as springboards for lively discussion, so learn to use open questions liberally. It is a good idea to think of some possible answers to an open question before you ask it to ensure you are eliciting the correct thought process.[4]

ASKING QUESTIONS

➤ Be sure to ask only one question at a time.

➤ Give the group time for deliberation. Wait 10–15 seconds for a response.

➤ If there is no answer, rephrase the question and ask it again. Jumping to a different topic may cause confusion.

➤ If there is still no answer, you have just discovered that no one in the room has the requisite expertise to provide the background and information needed to move on. You may need to adjourn the meeting and reconvene after conducting research or when experts are available to join the discussion.

ANSWERING QUESTIONS

In his article, "Question and Answer Session after the Presentation," Dr. Stephen D. Boyd, a professor of speech communication, offers the following guidelines:

➤ Answering participants' questions can be unnerving at first. If you do not know the answer, say so and put it in the "parking lot" so you will remember to find the answer later. It is better to be honest than to give an inaccurate answer that will have to be retracted later. Tell the participants you will answer the question by the next meeting; better still, invite the questioner to find the answer and report it at the next meeting.

➤ Listen to questions carefully. Some questions may indicate that a participant is having difficulty with the concepts being discussed. You may wish to answer with another question until you discover where the questioner's misunderstanding begins.

➤ If a question requires a very lengthy response or indicates that the questioner has missed some meetings, you may wish to ask the participant to stay behind after the meeting or come see you at another time to get the answer.

➤ Invite questions by saying, "Who has the first question?" Look expectant after you ask the question. If no one asks a question, engage the group and encourage discussion by saying something like, "A question I'm often asked is…." You may answer the question you posed or see if anyone would like to attempt a response. If there are still no questions, you can finish with "Are there any other questions?"

➤ Always repeat the question before you begin to respond to ensure you understand the intent. This is essential if there is a large audience; it also helps if you need a moment to think. Look at the entire audience when responding, and then look at the questioner as you complete your response to see if it was adequate.

➤ Stand in a place where you are equally distant from all members of your audience.

➤ Be concise; don't let your response turn into a presentation.

➤ Don't answer a loaded question designed to throw you off guard. Before answering, say something like, "I sense your frustration with . . . and I think you are asking. . . ." Then answer that question. If the questioner is not satisfied, invite her to meet with you after the session.

➤ Manage comments that are not questions. Do not allow anyone to hijack the Q&A session. When the speaker pauses to take a breath or regroup, thank him for his comment and move to a questioner on the other side of the room.

➤ Don't say, "That was a great question." You can't say it for every question, and others will think their question was not so good. You could say, "Thanks for asking that question."[5]

EVALUATING THE MEETING

It is important to evaluate a meeting early and often. Get participant feedback during the meeting when you can improve the meeting in process immediately. (Evaluating a meeting only at the end will usually only help future meetings.) At key points during the meeting, informally ask what is working well and what can be improved in the conduct of the meeting. Be prepared to incorporate improvements immediately.

At the end of the meeting, allow five to ten minutes to evaluate the session. This evaluation should focus on how the group did as a whole working together, not on your performance as the facilitator. Go around the room and ask each participant to rate the meeting from 1–7, with a rating of 1 meaning that the participant thought it was a waste of time, and a rating of 7 meaning that the meeting far exceeded the participant's expectations. (Use the same scale each time so that you can determine if participants' satisfaction is increasing as the group gels.) Next, ask each participant what he or she liked most about the group's work, and what opportunities he or she sees to improve either team interactions or the quality of the output in future meetings (participants can pass if they do not have a comment). Always have the senior person in the room evaluate the meeting last. Be sure to incorporate suggestions into future events. In that way you are continually improving the ability of the group to work together toward common goals.

CLOSING THE MEETING

Always end meetings on time. It is also important to end a meeting on a positive note. Typical meeting wrap-up steps include:

➤ *Issues and action items.* Review action items, issues, and unmet expectations. Assign an owner and due date for each action item and issue. Explain that the owner of each issue is charged with enlisting the help of a small team of experts to discuss the issue, identify alternatives for resolution of the issue, conduct a feasibility analysis of each alternative, and propose the most feasible (and most innovative) resolution to the group at the next meeting.

➤ *Next meeting.* Set the date, time, and main agenda items for the next meeting.

➤ *Next steps.* Ask that the meeting outputs, including all requirements artifacts, minutes, and the issue/action logs, be reported back to participants within one week; this is important to keep the momentum.

➤ *Meeting evaluation.* Evaluate the success of the event, meaning how well the group worked together and the quality of the outputs, as described earlier.

PUTTING IT ALL TOGETHER: WHAT DOES THIS MEAN TO THE BUSINESS ANALYST?

Regardless of the meeting facilitation approach you use, following these guidelines will go a long way toward improving your facilitation skills:

➤ Use humor, stories, and examples that directly relate to the work of the group.

➤ Evaluate how the session is going after each major agenda item and at the end of the day; incorporate feedback into the next part of the session and future events.

➤ Use lots of visual tools to keep everyone engaged and on the same page.

And avoid these common pitfalls:

➤ Pushing toward a preconceived "right" answer; there is no right answer.

➤ Appearing to be dominating; ignoring a participant's suggestion.

➤ Reading from a document or delivering a lengthy presentation.

➤ Favoring one group's perspective.

As you plan and conduct your workshops and working sessions, always remember that requirements elicitation is an iterative process. Although it is imperative to capture, continually refine, and validate requirements using visualization techniques whenever possible, textual descriptions are also needed for clarity and to precisely describe technical requirements. Visual graphs and diagrams are necessary to depict sequences and dependencies.

Remember, requirements alone are not complex; it is the interrelationships and interdependencies among requirements that impose complexities that are difficult to understand, and the impacts of which are difficult to predict.

NOTES

1. Tilak Mitra, "Figure 1: System context diagram," May 13, 2008. Online at http://www.ibm .com/developerworks/library/ar-archdoc2/index.html?S_TACT=105AGX20&S_CMP=EDU (accessed April 2011).
2. Carter McNamara, "Basic Guide to Conducting Effective Meetings," *Free Management Library* (undated). Online at http://www.managementhelp.org/misc/mtgmgmnt.htm (accessed February 2011).

3. Larry Johnson and Annette Lamb, "Critical and Creative Thinking—Bloom's Taxonomy," *Teacher Tap* (2011). Online at http://eduscapes.com/tap/topic69.htm (accessed February 2011).

4. Dalhousie University Center for Learning and Teaching, "Question and Answer Techniques," (undated). Online at http://learningandteaching.dal.ca/taguide/QandATechniques.htm (accessed February 2011).

5. Stephen D. Boyd, "Question and Answer Session after the Presentation," *Ron Kurtus' School for Champions* (2011). Online at http://www.school-for-champions.com/speaking/boyd_q_a_after_pres.htm (accessed February 2011). Copyright © 2011 by Ron Kurtus and School for Champions LLC.

PART III
Strategies to Foster Innovation

n this part, we explore the world of smart products and learn about complexity management strategies we can use when leading innovation teams.

- ➤ In Chapter 9, we explore the nature of innovative products, specifically their increasing reliance on software as the discriminator. We discuss best practices for innovative product development, and we explore the nature of the complexity of IT product development and propose both technical and managerial strategies to manage and capitalize on this complexity.

- ➤ In Chapter 10, we present a case for the business analyst's becoming a major player in helping companies transition to innovation-driven organizations.

- ➤ In Chapter 11, we propose strategic communication techniques to drive innovative decisions.

CHAPTER 9
Developing Products for Competitive Advantage

What are smart products? Well, we are already familiar with smartphones, so we know that smart products can do things for us that we don't even know we want to do yet. Smart products are intelligent, interconnected, and instrumented business solutions and products. They include communications networks, enterprise resource planning applications, online navigation systems, traffic and fleet logistics management systems, point-of-sale retail systems, and health care information management systems.

Here is how IBM explains the philosophy behind and general functions of smart products:

> On a smarter planet, intelligence is infused into the products, systems and processes that comprise the modern world. These include the delivery of services; the development, manufacturing, buying and selling of physical goods; and the way people actually work and live. Nowhere may this transformation be more evident than in the creation of smarter products. Smarter products are the building blocks for a smarter planet. Embedded with increasingly sophisticated software and instrumentation, they can connect and communicate with other devices and respond intelligently to user needs.[1]

It is clear that smart products rely heavily on software to operate "smartly"; hardware is no longer the discriminator.

We might wonder how technology vendors continue to deploy innovative software products year after year. The intense competitive pressures in the marketplace demand that all industries innovate. Regardless of the industry you are in, it is almost certain that information technology and software development have become critically important for your organization to create innovative business processes, products, and services.

SYSTEMS THINKING

According to IBM, a holistic approach to product and IT system development is needed to be able to react to, and hopefully preempt, the market changes that have led to delivering value through smarter products. Keep in mind that it is no longer enough to incrementally add value to existing products to maintain a competitive edge in the marketplace. In this environment, we must look across the enterprise and outside the enterprise, across companies and business ecosystems, as we develop the creative solutions we need for survival. Your challenge as the business analyst is to refine process-, product-, and service-development efforts to deliver the smarter solutions that employees and customers demand—before your competitors do it.[2]

Since smart products often combine a physical product with additional services, they are a kind of product service system, which is a set of products and services capable of jointly fulfilling a customer's needs.[3] Realizing that profit can be made by bundling products with valuable services, companies reacting to the changes in market conditions have begun to augment their product suite with services.[4]

BEST PRACTICES FOR INNOVATIVE PRODUCT DEVELOPMENT

IBM proposes several practices that businesses can employ to build smarter products and drive innovative technologies:

➤ Employ a holistic design process that includes requirements management and traceability through all engineering disciplines.

➤ Become value driven and continually assess how to optimize your products, services, and projects.

➤ Understand your product in the context of a system.

➤ Provide all business disciplines across your enterprise with a single, shared view of all product requirements.

➤ Perform extensive modelling early in the development process and use it to evaluate the impact of changes across the entire system.[5]

PRODUCT COMPLEXITY

Remember, complexity breeds creativity. And software projects are always complex!

A Word to the Wise

Truly innovative new products and services will rely on software to make them "smart." Pay special attention to the recommendations in this chapter to not only manage the complexity inherent in developing such products but to capitalize on it.

Standout companies not only manage and capitalize on complexity, but they *hide* the complexity of their products and services from their employees and customers.

These sound very much like business analysis best practices! We can see, then, how important it is for business analysts to master the disciplines needed to successfully deliver innovative solutions on highly complex IT projects. So let's examine the nature of complex IT and software development projects.

WHAT MAKES INNOVATION PROJECTS COMPLEX?

For every complex problem there is a simple solution. And it is wrong.

—H. L. MENCKEN

Virtually all projects that involve significant new IT products and services are highly complex. There are many technical and managerial factors behind this complexity. IT organizations are structured so that hardware and the software components are provided by different technical teams, which can lead to bandwidth, performance, and compatibility issues. These teams are often unable to manage the dependencies and integration risks, resulting in (1) schedule and cost overruns to fix the issues; (2) defects, discovered by the customer in the field; and (3) erosion of the business benefits expected from the new solution.

In addition to these common problems, there is a great deal of pressure to build agility and ease of change into the next generation of IT systems. With complexity accelerating, far-reaching new managerial techniques, partnerships, and technologies are needed if our economic competitiveness is not to be compromised.

TECHNICAL COMPLEXITIES

There are several sources of technical complexity in IT product development.

➤ A solution is considered technically complex if it involves a broad collection of systems functioning together to achieve a common mission, which creates complex system integration issues.

➤ Innovative IT solutions often require unproven technology.

➤ Significant integration issues also affect solutions that involve multiple products from diverse vendors, as these often do not follow the same protocol.

MANAGERIAL COMPLEXITIES

Projects to design and build complex IT solutions are usually affected by several complexity dimensions related to management, including:

➤ Multiple contractors providing solution components that must be integrated

➤ A large and diverse complex project team, with a program office to coordinate subprojects and a large collection of subject matter experts (e.g., technical, administrative, finance, and legal)

➤ A central master plan with separate plans for subprojects

➤ Formal bureaucracy that is highly visible and sensitive to political, environmental, and social issues.[6]

> *Most business applications are too inflexible to keep pace with the businesses they support.*
>
> —JOHN RYMER AND CONNIE MOORE

To remain competitive, organizations need flexible, adaptable business solutions that rely on embedded IT systems. There is a sweeping realization in the business world that our inflexible business processes and IT business applications form barriers to business agility at every turn.

Successful 21ˢᵗ century businesses need to streamline their processes and applications, making them more nimble, adaptable, and agile to keep pace with the changes in the competitive landscape and in customer preferences.

HARNESSING IT COMPLEXITY FOR COMPETITIVE ADVANTAGE

For the past twenty years, *CIO Magazine* has recognized the "CIO 100," a list of chief information officers who run standout companies across multiple industries. In 2007, the winners were dubbed "The Transformers" for their contributions to their companies in terms of innovation and increased business value. According to the article on the winners, companies that strive to harness technology for competitive advantage need:

> *IT departments that understand what makes their companies tick and IT leaders who know how to translate visions into actions.... This year's CIO 100 Awards honorees understand. They've embraced IT innovation as a tool for transformation, their winning projects motivated by critical business needs and the conviction, backed by solid analysis, that technology-enabled change can create new value. The CIOs at these companies define themselves not as technology suppliers but as facilitators of corporate growth.*[7]

Organizations innovate in many different ways, ranging from product innovation to process innovation to customer-experience innovation. To design, build, and maintain innovative, adaptive products and business solutions that are dependent on highly complex IT applications, you must understand and account for the strategies of your business as they evolve, your customer inclinations as they transform, and the competitive environment as it changes. You also must be able to build and support nested systems within systems, complex business rules, and the intricate feedback loops that are characteristic of software-rich systems.

ADAPTIVE MANAGEMENT APPROACHES

Thought leaders in the IT industry suggest that radical new approaches are required to build complex adaptive products and business solutions. While building software-intensive systems is an engineering specialty all its own, we offer some up-and-coming management approaches to foster innovation and customer empowerment.

Jim Highsmith, a guru in the agile project management arena, tells us that today's development teams must strive to adopt the objectives of reliable innovation:

➤ *Continuous innovation:* delivering on current customer requirements

➤ *Product adaptability:* delivering on future customer requirements

➤ *Reduced delivery schedules:* meeting market windows and improving return on investment

➤ *People and process adaptability:* responding rapidly to product and business change

➤ *Reliable results:* supporting business growth and profitability.[8]

BUILD SOLUTIONS THAT EMPOWER THE CUSTOMER

To design and build complex adaptive products and business systems that are responsive to changes in customer desires and the global marketplace, IT leaders are focusing their teams on new success criteria: innovation, adaptability, customer empowerment, and benefit generation. IT business solutions are seldom about cost savings anymore (we have done most of those projects already); they are about revenue generation and empowering customers to drive the system so that they get what they want, when and how they want it. Forward-thinking CIOs say that there are three important steps to building solutions that empower the customer:

1. Find out everything you can about the customer.

2. Build a system that anticipates his every wish.

3. Step back, get your own business processes out of the way, and let him do his thing.[9]

To find out everything you can about your customers, conduct extensive research to gather information on their preferences, likes, and dislikes. It takes a creative team to then anticipate what customers' desires will be in the future. Since it is virtually impossible to predict the future precisely, lots of experimentation and prototyping will be needed to bring into focus a solution that will be adaptable as customers' desires change.

EXPLOIT THE ADVANTAGES OF EDGE-OF-CHAOS MANAGEMENT

Profound new solutions can emerge from instability and even from near chaos.

—Hugh Crail

When facilitating groups, the business analyst must encourage his or her team to operate on the edge of chaos by brainstorming, creating, studying, examining ideas, experimenting, prototyping, and evaluating the flexibility, adaptability, and interdependencies of solution options to select the most innovative, revenue-generating, customer-empowering solution. In some cases, expert designers will begin to design and develop more than one solution to determine which one is truly the most elegant and adaptable. Spending adequate time in this creative zone can lead to outcomes that are more innovative and creative then ever imagined.

INTRODUCE A LAST RESPONSIBLE MOMENT DECISION-MAKING PROCESS

So how do you know when to wind down experimentation and get down to building something? In *Lean Software Development: An Agile Toolkit,* Mary Poppendieck and Tom Poppendieck describe a technique for making better decisions.[10] They advocate that teams dealing with ambiguity and constant change start development when only partial requirements are known, develop partial solutions in small components iteratively, and schedule feedback and learnings after each iteration so that the solution *emerges*. This approach obviously allows for solution design decisions to be made iteratively as more is learned, and it encourages the development team to delay commitment to a design concept until the last responsible moment. Design decisions are deferred until all viable options are explored as fully as possible. The goal is to increase solution adaptability and customer value.

This approach prevents teams from making decisions too early, when not much is known and more risk is involved. However, be mindful that if decisions are delayed beyond this point, they are likely to be made by default, which is highly undesirable. It is up to the complex project team, architects, and the business analyst to intuitively guide the timing of team decisions.

STRUCTURE THE EFFORT INTO MICROPROJECTS

The Standish Group predicts that microprojects will dominate the IT landscape in the 21st century. Microprojects are the ultimate in minimization; they last no more than four months, involve no more than four people, and cost around $100K. The Standish Group's CHAOS research indicates that microprojects are more successful than are customary large-scale

IT projects.[11] The web has made it easier to standardize the technical development infrastructure, thus making microprojects plausible.

There are many positive aspects of microprojects: valuable solution components are delivered early and often, learnings occur with each deployment, benefits can be realized immediately, and problems are identified and fixed quickly. However, there are downsides, too: it takes considerable effort to manage resources across many small projects, configuration management may be made more difficult, and dependencies between projects are difficult to manage.

CREATE COMMUNITIES OF PRACTICE AND FOSTER DIVERSITY OF THOUGHT

To leverage the diverse expertise needed to build complex adaptive products and business systems, project leaders often establish an integrated solution design team comprising empowered experts who have clear roles, responsibilities, and authority, as well as a common understanding of the project vision. Diversity of core solution design team members is critical if a team is to come up with the best solution, one that can react to changes in the environment. These teams typically include a project manager, a business analyst, an IT technologist, and a business visionary and process expert.

On complex projects, communication is of utmost importance. Within any expert group, members hold a significant amount of unspoken knowledge in their heads. This sometimes vital information may be intuitive, experiential, and judgmental, and it is often context sensitive. In addition, it may be difficult to articulate and is almost never recorded. Establishing formal communities of practice to share this knowledge facilitates the emergence of collaborative solutions that are much more innovative than ones designed by a single architect.[12]

ENSURE YOUR IT ARCHITECT IS SEASONED

The vital role of the IT architect has been woefully underutilized in the IT world. As a result, there is a shortage of individuals who are skilled and seasoned IT architects—an expertise that is essential when building complex IT systems. But IT architects are becoming pivotal to complex IT projects because there are so many technology options (hardware, software, and communications) to choose from.

The job of the architect is not just about IT; it is about achieving the needed business benefits. The architect creates a vision of how the new solution will look when it is all put together—when business processes, policies, manual procedures, training, desktop tools, and personnel are in place to optimally use the new technology.

Strive to recruit a certified IT architect experienced in specifying, designing, implementing, testing, releasing, and driving maintenance of either semi-custom or custom software. Embed the solution architect in the project team from the very beginning, when the team is defining the solution concept and lots of experimentation is expected.

FORGE NEW PARTNERSHIPS

On every project, we're working with suppliers and other manufacturers, and IT is there to help us collaborate with third parties.

—Chris Coupland

When multiple development teams, consisting of both internal and external members dispersed geographically, are involved in a project, the teams must put an end to viewing themselves as individual entities and commit to establishing strong partnerships. Their focus should be on understanding what is needed (instead of on negotiating the best contract), clearly defining roles and responsibilities, and intensely collaborating every step of the way.

A stunning example of 21st century partnerships is the outsourcing agreement between BAE Systems, the combination of British Aerospace (BAE) and Marconi Electronic Systems (MES), and Computer Sciences Corporation (CSC), one of the longest-running alliances of its kind. According to CSC, "The two companies have successfully grappled with the biggest challenges in any outsourcing agreement: building mutual trust over the long haul and creating an effective deal management structure. And they have kept a focus on the business even while doing some highly complex IT implementations." The collaboration allowed the companies to cut IT costs by 30 percent in the first 18 months.[13]

Building a trusting relationship comes from working closely together, slowly earning each other's trust and confidence. CSC asserts that "establishing shared expectations and a requirements management process involving all stakeholders will break the cycle of misunderstanding and unfulfilled expectations."[14]

SET UP SYSTEM INTEGRATION TEAMS

System integration is all about managing dependencies. Dependencies and interrelationships bring about complexity. When there are multiple development teams, integration is *the* major complexity. Integration involves combining system entities, proving the system works as specified, and confirming that the right system has been built and that the customers or users are satisfied.[15] Because software development is riddled with complexity, establish joint integration, verification, and validation (IV&V)

teams to bring together the software and hardware components, subsystems, elements, and segments to "build up" the integrated IT system.

Techniques for the integration team to consider that are intended to limit integration complexities include planning the integration of various workflows as an "upstream" activity, planning interfaces early to anticipate integration obstacles, reusing modules whenever possible, and using simulation and layer-based testing to establish a strong platform concept that limits dependencies.[16]

STRIKE THE RIGHT BALANCE BETWEEN DISCIPLINE AND AGILITY

In most discussions about what project cycle to use, we tend to weigh agile versus plan-based approaches as if they are mutually exclusive. The best approach to managing a project is to use a blend of adaptive project management approaches and conventional plan-based disciplines. The trick is for the complex project team to determine when each approach is appropriate.

According to two experts, Barry Boehm of the University of Southern California and Richard Turner of George Washington University:

> *Agile development methodologies promise higher customer satisfaction, lower defect rates, faster development times, and a solution to rapidly changing requirements. Plan-driven approaches promise predictability, stability, and high assurance. However, both approaches have shortcomings that, if left unaddressed, can lead to project failure. The challenge is to balance the two approaches to take advantage of their strengths and compensate for their weaknesses. We believe this can be accomplished using a risk-based approach for structuring projects to incorporate both agile and disciplined approaches in proportion to a project's needs.[17]*

So how do Boehm and Turner suggest determining the right balance between agility and discipline? They propose conducting a risk-based analysis of your project using a simple framework based on five key project dimensions affecting method selection:

➤ Size (number of personnel)

➤ Criticality (value of loss due to defects)

➤ Personnel (skilled vs. novice)

➤ Dynamism (percent of requirements that change per month)

➤ Culture (percent of team members thriving on chaos vs. order).[18]

Once the analysis is complete, it may be apparent that either the agile approach or the disciplined method is needed. More likely, a mixture of the two will strike the right balance, and the team will have to adjust its methods to address identified risks in each project dimension.

COMPLEXITY MANAGEMENT DESIGN TECHNIQUES

Because the business analyst works with the design team to identify the most feasible solution, it is imperative that she be familiar with complexity-reducing design techniques. Indeed, the requirements should be structured to mirror the overall solution design. Innovative design approaches for systems that are driven by the customer and adapt to environmental changes are emerging; we discuss some of these next.

LIMIT DEPENDENCIES BETWEEN SOLUTION COMPONENTS

When a technical solution is complex, it is prudent to divide the development into a core system (the operative part of the system), and special components (elements that are separate from the core and add functionality. This approach is often referred to as a *wheel and spoke design*. Further divide the core system into extension levels, building the foundation platform first and then extending system capabilities incrementally. While the core system is developed and implemented, different technical teams work on specialized functional components.

The secret to the success of this design approach is to build the specialized components with only a one-way dependency with the core system; therefore, specialized components are independent of each other and can be created in any order or even in parallel. This approach also limits the cost of changes, since components can easily be changed without impacting other specialized functional components of the system.[19]

MAKE USE OF CONTEMPORARY SOLUTION DESIGN TOOLS

When there is a high degree of uncertainty (e.g., requirements, technology, or even the business model are rapidly changing) and a need for interoperability across a complex network of suppliers and customers, the use of architecture tools is virtually essential.

Architecture tools capture, organize, and link complex information about the organization and the supporting technology; they help guide decision-making and monitor design decision implementation and success. In addition, architecture tools institutionalize standards that facilitate communication, a common language, common references, and common work products and data. When designing complex systems, a number of architectural views may be created to capture information about the operations, the business systems, and the supporting hardware and software technologies. The tool documents interrelationships between the views. This allows for a keener understanding of the dependencies within the solution that must be identified, made visible, understood, and managed.

DESIGN FOR PEOPLE, BUILD FOR CHANGE

John Rymer and Connie Moore of Forrester Research, Inc., an independent technology and market research company, present the case that our current IT systems are sadly inadequate when it comes to keeping up with the pace of change: "Most business applications are too inflexible to keep pace with the businesses they support. Today's applications force people to figure out how to map isolated pools of information and functions to their tasks and processes, and they force IT pros to spend too much budget to keep up with evolving markets, policies, regulations, and business models."[20] Their proposed solution is quite futuristic: IT innovators should make it their "primary goal" to invent the next generation of "enterprise software that adapts to the business and its work and evolves with it." Rymer and Moore call such software *Dynamic Business Applications*.

Adaptable software can be said to be designed for people and built for change. Designing for people is all about customer empowerment, collaboration, and easy access to information. Building for change is concerned with making organizations and their business solutions flexible, agile, and adaptive. These tools will undoubtedly change people's jobs, how we build and change business processes, and how we design and build software-rich products and business solutions.[21]

Peter Sterpe, a senior analyst at Forrester, surmises that the changes in how people work together will be formidable, and his predictions sound much like agile and extreme project methods:

Some people's jobs will have to change. To conceive and build applications that are context-aware and process-aware, IT will need resources that are also context-aware and process-aware. Likely changes include:

➤ Business analysts will finally come into their own, bridging the divide between the business and technical communities.

➤ Developers will become experts in how their business works, and they'll start to work more closely with their business analysts and architecture experts. For developers, this also means the likely end of the waterfall model as the project cycle of choice.

➤ Business customers will have to get more intimate with both end users and the development team; in many ways, they'll start to resemble product managers.[22]

COMPLEXITY MANAGEMENT TECHNOLOGIES

Advanced solution design and development technologies are rapidly emerging in the IT world. These do not use the traditional feature-based approach to building 21st century solutions. Business analysts need to become intimately familiar with these technologies and adapt their requirements approach to the new principles.

SERVICE-ORIENTED ARCHITECTURE

One development method that is designed to reduce system dependencies and interrelationships is service-oriented architecture (SOA). SOA is a breakthrough software design technique that calls for the development of smaller services, or groups of software components that perform business processes. The services are then hooked together with other services to perform larger tasks. The services are loosely coupled, have an independent interface to the core system, and are reusable. An SOA project is a type of microproject.

Web services, one of the important strategies for increasing business while reducing transaction costs, are an example of SOA. This development approach represents a transformation in how businesses and IT collaboratively develop business solutions. It is an effort to drive down to total cost of ownership of IT systems, thus freeing scarce resources to develop even more innovative IT applications and infrastructures.[23]

Using SOA and microprojects forever changes the business analyst's work. At the tactical project level, the business analyst builds requirements as services. (Keep in mind that once the development team is "on a roll," there is a risk that it will continue its work long after the basic business need is met. At the more strategic enterprise level, the business analyst's job is to continually perform enterprise analysis, managing the business case so that the development team stops building services when the ROI and business objectives have been met, or redirecting the development team if the business need has changed.

BUSINESS PROCESS MANAGEMENT

Business process management (BPM) is a vital business analysis specialization. The practice is supported by vendor tool suites that are designed to standardize methods that align organizational processes with the needs of the customers. BPM strives to promote business effectiveness by optimizing business processes while focusing on flexibility and innovation—just the ingredients we need when building complex innovative products, services, and business solutions.

A difficult decision needs to be made about ownership of cross-functional business processes: someone in the organization needs to be responsible for enterprise business processes, those that cross functional boundaries. Many argue that the effort must be driven from the top, by a senior officer of the company. Often, the CIO is the most appropriate person to get the effort going. Forrester suggests organizations form teams, aligned with each line of business and channel, that are responsible for governing processes. These governance teams comprise representatives from all areas that support customers (e.g., marketing, sales, servicing, cross-selling, and retention). The goal is to build customer-centric processes and technology.[24]

WEB 2.0 DEVELOPMENT

There is no single definition that is widely accepted for the term *Web 2.0*; however, we can describe it a set of design patterns and business models that have come into widespread use in the 21st century, using the web as a platform.

Web 2.0 is more about customer participation than about simply publishing information. The emergence of Web 2.0 (no one person actually designed the web as we know it today) is a spectacular example of a complex adaptive system. Dynamic websites replaced static web pages a decade ago; today, it is the links in current web applications that increases the adaptive nature of the web. Blogging, which drives new value chains, is an example of a Web 2.0 technology. The power of the web in its current form is that it harnesses collective intelligence and houses it on relatively small sites.

SOCIAL NETWORKING

Social networking is an phenomenon that has effectively taken over the web, enabling connectivity and interaction between people all over the world.

Networking sites like Facebook and MySpace are "virtual communities" that provide valuable consumer data to those interested in reaching groups of people with certain interests. The potential of social networking "teams" to bring about innovation for businesses is largely untapped and unknown, but businesses in industries as diverse as insurance, financial services, and electronics are exploring the potential.

UNIFIED COMMUNICATIONS

Unified communications (UC) is a software platform that brings multiple communications technologies together into a single solution. Elizabeth Herrell of Forrester Research writes:

> *UC generates interest as a potentially important business tool to improve existing business processes and reduce costly business delays for time-sensitive situations. An intelligent software platform, it connects people to people and to applications directly and easily. UC also connects desktop collaboration technologies, such as presence, email, instant messaging, and web conferencing with communication applications (e.g., telephony, audio conferencing, voice messaging, and video). Its intuitive user interface promotes adoption and usage of UC across the enterprise. To justify UC investments, organizations should evaluate UC's business benefits and IT improvements, and explain its full value—for example, how it enables faster response to critical situations, allows employees to collaborate more easily, and reduces overhead such as travel and conferencing expenses.*[25]

UC is an emerging technology designed to improve collaboration, speed up decision-making, reduce customer response time, and increase enterprise agility—all of which are elements of managing complexity in the 21st century.

PUTTING IT ALL TOGETHER: WHAT DOES THIS MEAN TO THE BUSINESS ANALYST?

A system-thinking, much more business- and customer-focused approach to product and IT system development is needed if companies are to be able to react to, and hopefully preempt, the market changes that have led to delivering value through smarter products. We must look across the enterprise and outside the enterprise, across companies and business eco-systems, as we determine and develop the creative solutions our businesses need for economic survival. The business analyst's challenge: to become a key player in your organization's efforts to transform process, product, and service development practices for delivering the smarter solutions that your employees and customer demand—before your competitors do it first.

The road ahead is daunting. The task at hand is complex. That is why we presented for your consideration several relatively forward-looking managerial, design, and development techniques to build innovative business solutions, products, and services. Many of these technologies are rather immature right now, but they are emerging in the IT industry in response to our need for radical new methods and tools that meet the challenges we are facing. A summary of these suggestions:

> ➤ *Expert unconventional management approaches:* maintaining a fierce customer focus, fostering edge-of-chaos management, adopting a last responsible moment decision-making process, structuring the work into microprojects, establishing communities of practice and encouraging diversity of thought, recruiting and developing professional IT systems architects, striking new vendor and contractor partnerships, and forming integration teams.

➤ *Innovative design approaches:* limiting solution-component dependencies, using solution design tools, and adopting a practice of designing for people but building for change.

➤ *New design and development technologies:* using the service-oriented architecture approach, adopting business process management principles and tool suites, pursuing Web 2.0 development practices, and using unified communication software.

NOTES

1. IBM Corporation, "Four Key Strategies for Enabling Innovation in the Age of Smart," 2010: 2.
2. IBM Corporation, "Turning Product Development into Competitive Advantage," 2009: 16.
3. Cees Van Halen, Carlo Vezzoli, and Robert Wimmer, *Methodology for Product Service System Innovation* (Assen, NL: Uitgeverij Van Gorcum, 2005): 21.
4. Ken Bates, Hilary Bates, and Robert Johnston, "Linking Service to Profit: The Business Case for Service Excellence," *International Journal of Service Industry Management* 14, no. 2 (2003): 173–183. Rogelio Oliva and Robert Kallenberg, "Managing the Transition from Products to Services," *International Journal of Service Industry Management* 14, no. 2 (2003): 160–72.
5. IBM Corporation (2009), 2.
6. The Royal Academy of Engineering, "The Challenges of Complex IT Projects," April 2004: 8. Online at http://www.raeng.org.uk/news/publications/list/reports/Complex_IT_Projects.pdf (accessed January 2011).
7. Elana Varon, "2007 CIO 100 Winners: How IT Can Harness the Power of Innovation," *CIO* (August 6, 2007). Online at http://www.cio.com/article/127400 (accessed June 2011).
8. Jim Highsmith, *Agile Project Management: Creating Innovative Products* (Boston: Addison-Wesley, 2004): 6.
9. Katherine Walsh, "IT Innovations That Generate Revenue and Get You More Customers," *CIO* (August 6, 2007). Online at http://www.cio.com/article/print/127651 (accessed January 2011).
10. Mary Poppendieck and Tom Poppendieck, *Lean Software Development: An Agile Toolkit* (Boston: Addison-Wesley, 2003): 2–42.
11. James H. Johnson, "Micro Projects Cause Constant Change," *Extreme CHAOS 2001* (West Yarmouth, MA: The Standish Group International, 2001): 132–135.
12. Linda J. Vandergriff, "Complex Venture Acquisition," 2006: 9–14. Online at http://cs.calstatela.edu/wiki/images/1/1e/Vandergriff.pdf (accessed May 2011).
13. Louise Baverstock, "An Enduring Partnership," *CSC World* (July–September 2006): 6–9. Online at http://assets1.csc.com/cscworld/downloads/cscworld_july_sep_2006.pdf (accessed May 2011).
14. Computer Sciences Corporation, "Managing a Transatlantic Relationship: Chris Coupland: Director, IT and e-Business, BAE Systems," *CSC World* (July–September 2006): 10–13. Online at http://assets1.csc.com/cscworld/downloads/cscworld_july_sep_2006.pdf (accessed April 2011).

15. Hal Mooz, Kevin Forsberg, and Howard Cotterman, *Communicating Project Management: The Integrated Vocabulary of Project Management and Systems Engineering* (Hoboken, NJ: John Wiley & Sons, 2003): 202.

16. Birgit Seeger, "Tackling Complexities of In-car Embedded Systems," *The PA Consulting Group's Viewpoint on Complexity* (2005). Online at http://www.paconsulting.com/insights/managing_complex_projects (accessed February 2008).

17. Barry Boehm and Richard Turner, "Observations on Balancing Discipline and Agility," Agile Development Conference (2003): 1–8. Online at http://agile2003.agilealliance.org/files/P4Paper.pdf (accessed April 2011).

18. Ibid.

19. Martin Lippert, Stefan Roock, Robert Tunkel, and Henning Wolf, "XP in Complex Project Settings: Some Extensions," *Schweizerischer Verband der Informatikorganisationen*, no. 2 (April 2002): 33–37.

20. John Rymer, Connie Moore, and Forrester Research, Inc., "The Dynamic Business Applications Imperative," September 24, 2007. Online at http://www.forrester.com/Research/Document/Excerpt/0,7211,41397,00.html (accessed May 2011).

21. Ibid.

22. Peter Sterpe and Forrester Research, Inc., "Application Development and Program Management First Look," November 15, 2007. Online at http://www.forrester.com/FirstLook/Print/Vertical/Issue/0,,940,00.html (accessed January 2011).

23. Mark Frederick Davis, "SOA: Providing Flexibility for the Health and Life Sciences Industry," July 2006: 2–5. Online at http://h20247.www2.hp.com/publicsector/downloads/Technology_Davis_VB.pdf (accessed April 2011).

24. Mary Pilecki and Forrester Research, Inc., "Organizational Silos: Can't Live With Them and Can't Live Without Them," October 2, 2007. Online at http://www.forrester.com/rb/Research/organizational_silos_cant_live_with_them,_cant/q/id/43457/t/2 (accessed Mary 2011).

25. Elizabeth Herrell and Forrester Research, Inc., "How To Evaluate Business Value For Unified Communications," December 27, 2007. Online at http://www.forrester.com/Research/Document/Excerpt/0,7211,42895,00.html (accessed May 2011).

CHAPTER 10

Strategies to Foster Innovation

We cannot manage and capitalize on complexity if we cannot close the wide and costly gaps in our business practices. A very important—and, too often, missing—component of the business environment is the ability of executives to select, prioritize, and provide oversight to a valuable portfolio of projects. Although many leadership teams are attempting to do just that, enterprise analysis, facilitated by the business analyst and culminating in the business case, is often shortchanged or totally missing. As a result, decisionmakers do not have the information they need to make informed decisions.

But organizations must not shy away from the challenge of determining the most effective structures, processes, and practices for executing complex projects just because they don't have a total solution right away. Senior managers, project managers, and business analysts all possess the power and influence to make the needed changes, and only they can build and nourish the empowering organizational culture and flexible infrastructure needed to deploy complex, creative, innovative solutions.

STANDOUT COMPANIES HAVE PAVED THE WAY

Standout companies, those businesses that have flourished in spite of the financial crisis of late, have learned to capitalize on complexity to drive innovation. The first thing they did was to admit that:

➤ Projects execute strategy by implementing the changes needed to respond to the relentlessly changing dynamics of the marketplace.

➤ Successful projects are critical to organizations' economic survival.

➤ Strategy execution is the job of everyone involved in projects, especially the leadership team of a complex project: the project manager, business analyst, solution architect/lead technologist, and business visionary.

➤ Projects are investments and part of a portfolio that has an investment strategy. The portfolio needs attention, support, and expertise.

➤ Complexity is here to stay and is only going to get worse, and we must learn to not just manage complexity, but also capitalize on it to remain competitive.

➤ It is through creativity and innovation that we will enable our company to capitalize on complexity.

So how do we establish an organizational infrastructure to accommodate the challenges we face and to effectively support complex projects? Implementing the business practices needed to support complex projects is a learning process that demands an understanding of complexity, a focus on creativity, and business practices that are adaptive and flexible. For senior management teams, the objective is clear: risk reduction and increased return on project investments (ROI). For complex project, program, and portfolio management teams, the objective is no different.

Four professional disciplines must converge to bring success on complex projects: project management, business analysis, business process management, and information technology (see the core project leadership team presented in Chapter 6).[1] Through a real collaborative effort relying on the synergies of these four professional groups, whose members have different expertise and different perspectives, the complex project team will have the technical skill and leadership prowess to bring about innovation.

A new definition of a requirement relates it to something that generates business benefits, either in the form of value to the customer or wealth to the organization. Once we understand that business benefits are the only real measure of project success, we can more easily establish critical business requirements early in the project—requirements that the Standish Group refers to as "firm basic requirements" that are not expected to change.[2] Approaching business requirements in terms of their business value makes it appreciably easier to make important decisions about a project's scope.

The complex project team, and particularly the business analyst, is uniquely positioned to transform the way we do projects. In this chapter we will explore the BA role on three levels:

THE NEED FOR CHANGE

Transforming your organization into one that focuses on innovation can require significant changes.

A Word to the Wise

As you hone your ability to influence others, work with BAs and PMs to foster innovation at three levels:

- Project
- Portfolio
- Project support offices and centers of excellence.

➤ Projects—the hotbed of creativity

➤ Portfolios—the strategy-execution framework needed to achieve innovation

➤ Project support offices and centers of excellence—the hub for mature practices that foster creativity.

TRANSFORMING PROJECTS INTO HOTBEDS OF CREATIVITY

As the core complex-project leadership team comes together, the first order of business is to diagnose the complexity of the assignment, whether it is a project, program, or portfolio.[3] The business analyst or the project manager typically facilitates the complexity analysis. The same small expert team, the core complex-project leadership team, also must participate. You may want to augment the group with other SMEs to ensure that the team understands the business area undergoing change and the technology that enables the business to operate.

Before diagnosing the level of complexity, the expert team should take these steps, which are essentially a review of the analysis of the enterprise, so the members can fully understand the task at hand.

1. Review the business case for the initiative. If it is deficient or out of date, update the business case. Be sure the business need, problem, or opportunity is clearly defined.

2. Revisit the solution approach outlined in the business case. Guide the team in identifying all possible options to meet the business need. Conduct a feasibility analysis for all options. This is where the business analyst can foster creativity. She must facilitate a "creativity zone," an atmosphere that helps the team engage in real dialogue.

The business analyst should encourage all ideas, challenge and build on them, and even experiment with, model, and prototype ideas. (For more on creativity-inducing skills the business analyst needs, see Chapters 5 and 7.)

3. Review the current-state business and technical architecture for the area of the business to be changed to gain an understanding of its complexity and scope.

4. Develop a high-level work breakdown structure and product breakdown structure to understand the scope of the project.

5. Develop a context diagram to help the team visualize the scope of the project.

6. Develop firm basic requirements in terms of business value. These should be the critical business requirements that are not expected to change. Approaching business requirements in terms of business value helps to minimize the scope, keeping it to only what is sufficient to meet the real business need.

7. Develop quantifiable business measures of success, in terms of adding value for customers and wealth to the organization.

At this point, your expert team is ready to diagnose project complexity and determine which management strategies to use to capitalize on complexity and foster innovation (see Figure 10-1).

APPLYING COMPLEXITY THINKING TO MANAGE PROJECTS

Applying complexity thinking to projects involves selecting methods and techniques and assigning project leadership to suit the project's profile

PROJECT COMPLEXITY MODEL 2.0

Complexity Dimensions	Project Profile			
	Independent Project Low Complexity	Moderately Complex Project	Highly Complex Project	Highly Complex Program "Megaproject"
Size/Time/Cost	**Size:** 3–4 team members **Time:** < 3 months **Cost:** < $250K	**Size:** 5–10 team members **Time:** 3–6 months **Cost:** $250–$1M	**Size:** > 10 team members **Time:** 6 – 12 months **Cost:** > $1M	**Size:** multiple diverse teams **Time:** multi-year **Cost:** multiple millions
Team Composition and Past Performance	**PM:** competent, experienced **Team:** internal; worked together in past **Methodology:** defined, proven	**PM:** competent, inexperienced **Team:** internal and external, worked together in past **Methodology:** defined, unproven **Contracts:** straightforward **Contractor Past Performance:** good	**PM:** competent; poor/no experience with complex projects **Team:** internal and external, have not worked together in past **Methodology:** somewhat defined, diverse **Contracts:** complex **Contractor Past Performance:** unknown	**PM:** competent, poor/no experience with megaprojects **Team:** complex structure of varying competencies and performance records (e.g., contractor, virtual, culturally diverse, outsourced teams) **Methodology:** undefined, diverse **Contracts:** highly complex **Contractor Past Performance:** poor

Complexity Dimensions	Project Profile			
	Independent Project Low Complexity	**Moderately Complex Project**	**Highly Complex Project**	**Highly Complex Program "Megaproject"**
Urgency and Flexibility of Cost, Time, and Scope	**Scope:** minimized **Milestones:** small **Schedule/Budget:** flexible	**Scope:** achievable **Milestones:** achievable **Schedule/Budget:** minor variations	**Scope:** over-ambitious **Milestones:** over-ambitious, firm **Schedule/Budget:** inflexible	**Scope:** aggressive **Milestones:** aggressive, urgent **Schedule/Budget:** aggressive
Clarity of Problem, Opportunity, Solution	**Objectives:** defined and clear **Opportunity/Solution:** easily understood	**Objectives:** defined, unclear **Opportunity/ Solution:** partially understood	**Objectives:** defined, ambiguous **Opportunity/ Solution:** ambiguous	**Objectives:** undefined, uncertain **Opportunity/ Solution:** undefined, groundbreaking, unprecedented
Requirements Volatility and Risk	**Customer Support:** strong **Requirements:** understood, straightforward, stable **Functionality:** straightforward	**Customer Support:** adequate **Requirements:** understood, unstable **Functionality:** moderately complex	**Customer Support:** unknown **Requirements:** poorly understood, volatile **Functionality:** highly complex	**Customer Support:** inadequate **Requirements:** uncertain, evolving **Functionality:** many complex "functions of functions"

Continued on next page

Complexity Dimensions	Project Profile			
	Independent Project Low Complexity	Moderately Complex Project	Highly Complex Project	Highly Complex Program "Megaproject"
Strategic Importance, Political Implications, Stakeholders	**Executive Support:** strong **Political Implications:** none **Communications:** straightforward **Stakeholder Management:** straightforward	**Executive Support:** adequate **Political Implications:** minor **Communications:** challenging **Stakeholder Management:** 2–3 stakeholder groups	**Executive Support:** inadequate **Political Implications:** major, impacts core mission **Communications:** complex **Stakeholder Management:** multiple stakeholder groups with conflicting expectations; visible at high levels of the organization	**Executive Support:** unknown **Political Implications:** impacts core mission of multiple programs, organizations, states, countries; success critical for competitive or physical survival **Communications:** arduous **Stakeholder Management:** multiple organizations, states, countries, regulatory groups; visible at high internal and external levels

Complexity Dimensions	Project Profile				
	Independent Project Low Complexity	**Moderately Complex Project**	**Highly Complex Project**	**Highly Complex Program "Megaproject"**	
Level of Change	**Organizational Change:** impacts a single business unit, one familiar business process, and one IT system **Commercial Change:** no changes to existing commercial practices	**Organizational Change:** impacts 2–3 familiar business units, processes, and IT systems **Commercial Change:** enhancements to existing commercial practices	**Organizational Change:** impacts the enterprise, spans functional groups or agencies; shifts or transforms many business processes and IT systems **Commercial Change:** new commercial and cultural practices	**Organizational Change:** impacts multiple organizations, states, countries; transformative new venture **Commercial Change:** ground-breaking commercial and cultural practices	
Risks, Dependencies, and External Constraints	**Risk Level:** low **External Constraints:** no external influences **Integration:** no integration issues **Potential Damages:** no punitive exposure	**Risk Level:** moderate **External Constraints:** some external factors **Integration:** challenging integration effort **Potential Damages:** acceptable exposure	**Risk Level:** high **External Constraints:** key objectives depend on external factors **Integration:** significant integration required **Potential Damages:** significant exposure	**Risk Level:** very high **External Constraints:** project success depends largely on multiple external organizations, states, countries, regulators **Integration:** unprecedented integration effort **Potential Damages:** unacceptable exposure	

Continued on next page

Complexity Dimensions	Project Profile			
	Independent Project Low Complexity	**Moderately Complex Project**	**Highly Complex Project**	**Highly Complex Program "Megaproject"**
Level of IT Complexity	**Technology:** technology is proven and well-understood **IT Complexity:** application development and legacy integration easily understood	**Technology:** technology is proven but new to the organization **IT Complexity:** application development and legacy integration largely understood	**Technology:** technology is likely to be immature, unproven, complex, and provided by outside vendors **IT Complexity:** application development and legacy integration poorly understood	**Technology:** technology requires groundbreaking innovation and unprecedented engineering accomplishments **IT Complexity:** multiple "systems of systems" to be developed and integrated

PROJECT COMPLEXITY FORMULA

Highly Complex Program "Megaproject"	Highly Complex Project	Moderately Complex	Independent
Size: Multiple diverse teams, **Time:** Multi-year, **Cost:** Multiple Millions *Or* 2 or more in the **Highly Complex Program/Megaproject** column	**Organizational Change:** impacts the enterprise, spans functional groups or agencies, shifts or transforms many business processes and IT systems *Or* 3 or more categories in the **Highly Complex Project** column *And* No more than 1 category in the **Highly Complex Program/ Megaproject** column	3 or more categories in the **Moderately Complex Project** column *Or* No more than 2 categories in the **Highly Complex Project** column and	No more than 2 categories in the **Moderately Complex Project** column *And* No categories in the **Highly Complex Project** or the **Highly Complex Program/Megaproject** column

FIGURE 10-1. Project Complexity Model 2.0

and complexity dimensions. Here I suggest a three-step process, which is also described in detail in *Managing Complex Projects: A New Model.*[4]

1. ***Select the project cycle to suit the project profile.*** Based on the project profile, the project team first determines the appropriate project cycle to use. All projects pass through a cycle or sequence of stages. Typical cycles have a series of periods and phases, each with a defined output that guides discovery, requirements, design, construction, and/or acquisition of goods and services. As projects have become more complex, project cycles have evolved to address the various levels of complexity.

2. ***Select appropriate management techniques to suit the project's complexity dimensions.*** Projects sometimes fail because of a misapplication of good methods and techniques. Applying complexity thinking to determine which techniques to use is the key to success when managing complex projects. Successful managers use situational project management by adapting their leadership style and project management, systems engineering, and business analysis techniques to manage the project's unique complexity dimensions.

3. ***Assign project managers and business analysts to suit the project's profile.*** A project can fail if its leadership doesn't adequately suit the characteristics of the project. The project's manager and business analyst have critical project leadership positions. Once an organization chooses a project cycle and identifies project complexity dimensions, it should also apply complexity thinking to project leadership assignments.

FOSTERING A CREATIVE PROJECT TEAM ENVIRONMENT

Once the complexity of a project is well understood, there are a number of specific activities that the complex project team in general, and the business analyst in particular, can engage in, including matching project staff to the complexity profile; securing the physical space that is needed for the team to collaborate and interact; minimizing the key team leaders' distractions and other assignments; and understanding, accepting, and informing management and business partners that the team will adapt its approach as more is learned.

For more on fostering creativity and building a high-performing innovation team, revisit Chapter 4, on creative leadership; Chapter 5, on fostering team creativity; and Chapter 6, on igniting creativity in complex distributed teams.

EXECUTING STRATEGIES THROUGH VALUABLE PORTFOLIOS

Organizations often have to undergo significant changes to improve the way they select projects, develop creative requirements, and manage projects while focusing not only on business value, but also on innovation. Even today, many organizations still pile project requests onto IT and new-product development groups with only sparse requirements and then wonder why those groups cannot deliver.

Conversely, mature organizations devote a significant amount of time and energy to conducting enterprise analysis and encouraging experimentation and creativity before rushing to construction. This means selecting and prioritizing projects only after performing rigorous competitive analysis, problem analysis, and creative-solution-alternative analysis. This also means spending more time up front to make certain that the solution is creative, innovative, valuable, and even disruptive.

As a key leader of a project or program, the business analyst should periodically (usually on a quarterly basis) conduct rigorous analysis of the enterprise, including the current state of the project or program and the current state of the business. She should review the value expected from the project or program and the other benefits forecasted in the business case. The business analyst is responsible for continually validating the business case throughout a project. If the assumptions and forecasted benefits are no longer valid, the business analyst needs to alert the project leadership team and facilitate working sessions to determine the most appropriate course of action through analysis of alternative options. These discussions result in a recommendation for a course correction to the portfolio manager and often to the senior decision-making team.

Portfolio oversight is the "sweet spot" of the senior management team. It is how they capitalize on complexity to achieve innovation. It is through complex project portfolios that strategy is executed, innovation is achieved, value is added for the customer, wealth is earned for the organization, and competitiveness is maintained or advanced. However, the senior team cannot do its job without good, solid information, which the complex project team leadership presents after robust enterprise analysis facilitated by the business analyst. We can see, then, that the business analyst is critical to effective portfolio management.

ESTABLISHING PROJECT SUPPORT OFFICES AND CENTERS OF EXCELLENCE

Most standout organizations maintain and support some kind of office or center that provides a collection of services to the enterprise and to complex project, program, and portfolio teams. The goal is for the senior team to tolerate and encourage different project-support models, depending on the complexity of the team structure, the number of different business lines, and the impact to key business applications. For the senior team to tolerate and encourage different models, it again needs project leaders to provide information that is based on structured analysis, which is most often facilitated by the business analyst.

Over the last two decades, we have made progress in improving project performance, which is mostly due to improved project management and to reducing the size of projects (smaller projects are much more likely to succeed). But as we've learned from the Standish Group's CHAOS research, even with these improvements, nearly two-thirds of IT projects continue to fail (nothing of value is delivered) or are challenged (they run over time and cost and likely do not deliver the full scope of functionality).

These problems are significantly affecting our ability to compete in the marketplace. We know that failed and challenged projects often have significant negative effects on companies' finances. A study by TechRepublic, Inc., and its parent Gartner Group, Inc., revealed only *32 percent* of IT projects are successful, which is extremely costly. The annual cost to the U.S. economy is around $1.22 trillion per year. Worldwide, we are losing over $500 billion per month on IT failure and the problem is getting worse.[5] Clearly, we must do better.

So what is the root cause of our continued inability to flawlessly deliver new business solutions that hit the mark and add significant business benefit? Many experts have made the case that our *gap in business analysis and complex project management capabilities and competencies* is at the heart of the problem (Figure 10-2).

The challenge to close the gap in BA capabilities and competencies is formidable, and at the same time, we need to build complex project management

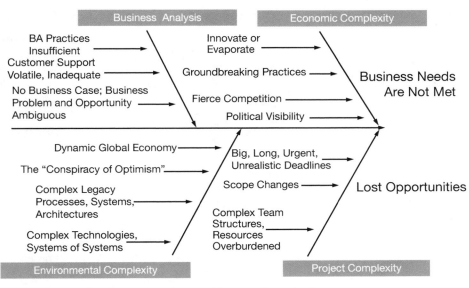

FIGURE 10-2. Why Businesses Cannot Manage Complexity

capabilities. To make the systemic improvements that are needed, an entity needs to be responsible and accountable for advancing BA and CPM practices. It is through this entity, often called a project support office or center of excellence, that the needed improvements can be made.

WHERE IS THE BA PROFESSION HEADING?

Clearly, BAs who are focusing on multiple roles and tasks involving diverse disciplines cannot devote the time and attention needed to build a mature BA practice and a world-class BA workforce. The current hybrid role is tactically focused, deep into project tasks. How can the BA transition from a tactical player into a more strategic asset (see Figure 10-3)?

According to a 2008 study conducted by Forrester, the BA will retain the current tactical roles that are both IT and business oriented.[6] IT-oriented business analysts mostly improve operations through changes to technology.

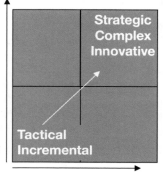

IT Improvements
Improve operations through changes to technology.

Business Improvements
Improve operations through changes to policy and process.

Business Architects
Make the enterprise visible.

Enterprise Analysts
Convert business opportunities into innovative business solutions.

Translate strategy into breakthrough process and technological change.

FIGURE 10-3. The BA's Transition from Tactical to Strategic Asset

These are mostly generalists, but some specialize as data analysts, process analysts, or rules analysts. Business-focused analysts are usually functionally focused and mostly improve operations through changes to policy and process; they specialize in business process management, business rules management, or Six Sigma.

At the same time, the industry is expected to begin grooming and fielding more strategic BA roles, driving BA practice maturity to meet our organizations' needs for innovation. These roles include the business architect and the enterprise analyst. The business architect makes the enterprise visible through diagrams, models, and rich pictures. As the current-state architecture comes into view and the future-state architecture takes shape, the gaps in capabilities to meet business strategies become clear. The enterprise analyst then conducts rigorous enterprise and competitive analysis, works to convert business opportunities into innovative business solutions, and translates strategy into breakthrough process and technology change.

Experienced and influential business analysts should champion the transition from a tactical to a strategic focus for their business analysis practice. Developing compelling business cases that are stated in very simple business terms, identifying the outcome to be achieved, and linking the outcome to implementation strategies can help them make this transition.

As businesses acknowledge the value of business analysis, they must ask themselves four questions:

➤ What are the characteristics of our current BA workforce?

➤ What kind of BA workforce do we need?

➤ How can we build a mature BA practice?

➤ How long will it take to get there?

As you can see in Figure 10-4, many elements need to be in place to implement a mature BA practice. This comprehensive maturity framework

FIGURE 10-4. BA Practice Maturity Framework

describes the elements of a mature business analysis practice. The journey begins by acknowledging that business analysis is a critical business management practice in the 21st century. It will take an investment of resources, a structured approach, and expert change management skills. The framework involves a three-pronged approach to build a mature BA practice, develop a competent BA workforce, and establish a BA center of excellence to plant the seeds and steer the course.

THE LIVING BUSINESS CASE: A VEHICLE FOR INNOVATION AND STRATEGY EXECUTION

In most organizations, the business case is treated as an annoyance, not as a critical component of strategy execution. It is typically created as quickly as possible (if it is created at all), not as a product of serious enterprise analysis, and is simply used to secure resources and funding. Once funding for a project is secured, it is often discarded, never to be looked at again, so only enough effort, expertise, and analysis to get the funding are expended.

It is the responsibility of the business analyst to conduct rigorous enterprise analysis, which then culminates in the development of a sound business case. According to the *BABOK® Guide*, the BA drives creation of the business case, through leadership, coordination, and facilitation of these steps:

1. Defining the business need

2. Assessing capability gaps

3. Determining the solution approach

4. Defining the solution scope

5. Defining the business case

6. Assessing the proposed solution

7. Validating the solution

8. Evaluating the performance of the solution.

USING THE BUSINESS CASE TO ESTABLISH
A STRATEGY-EXECUTION FRAMEWORK

> *Controlling costs is still a major business pressure. But cost cutting alone doesn't foster growth, energize employees, or attract new customers. Investments do—if they're well-conceived, solid, and deliver results. Brilliant business cases can facilitate that.*
>
> —GARTNER GROUP, INC.

How well do organizations actually execute strategy by making investments that are well-conceived, solid, and deliver results? Research shows that less than 10 percent of well-formed strategies are effectively executed. Why would this be so?

➤ 85 percent of executives spend less than one hour per month on strategy.

➤ 95 percent of the workforce doesn't understand the strategy.

➤ 60 percent of organizations do not link strategies to budgets.

➤ 70 percent of organizations do not link strategies to incentives.[7]

The root cause behind these statistics is this: executives do not have a framework for strategy execution. An effective framework for strategy execution would look something like this four-step portfolio management process:

1. ***The executive team receives critical information in the business case,*** which is based on strategy and goal decomposition, enterprise analysis, research, competitive analysis, benchmark studies, analysis of business problems and opportunities, and the generation of moral ideas to faster innovation.

2. *The business case serves as a new-project proposal* during strategy, project selection, and prioritization sessions, when project investment decisions are made. Investment decisions are only as good as the business case.

3. *The strategy-focused program and project teams execute against goals, objectives, and business benefits described in the business case.* Therefore, the business case needs to be high caliber to serve as a solid guide for the subsequent work.

4. *Project, program, and portfolio managers continually validate information updated in the business case* to ensure that the investment is still warranted, desired innovation will be achieved, and the business benefits will be realized.

The business case is, of course, the common element in these steps. It is the foundation for a strategy-execution framework. Only after the business analyst facilitates the development of a solid business case can the portfolio management team prioritize projects based on innovation, value to the customer, and wealth to the organization.

OVERCOMING BARRIERS TO INNOVATION AND STRATEGY EXECUTION

Figure 10-5 lists some of the barriers to strategy execution and symptoms of a defective strategy, as well as what the BA can do to eliminate them.

BRINGING THE BUSINESS CASE TO LIFE

Without a living business case, several unintended consequences can affect the project's chance of success:

➤ Project creep sets in.

Barriers to Strategy Execution	Symptoms of a Defective Strategy[8]	BA Actions to Enable Strategy Execution
Strategy is not actionable.	Strategy is not executed. The strategic plan is not a living, breathing document.	The BA fields a small expert team and facilitates them to analyze and decompose strategy into actionable, measurable goals and objectives; identify gaps in capabilities needed to achieve the goals; determine the most feasible solution; and build the business case.
Strategy not linked to resource allocation process.	PMs fight over resources. Projects are launched regardless of the availability of resources.	The BA requests the business case to the sponsor to propose the new project or program, describing resource needs and the resource acquisition process.
Strategy is not linked to departmental, team, and individual goals.	Project priorities frequently change. Managers have authority to unilaterally approve and fund pet projects.	The BA links goals and objectives to program and project teams' objectives in the business case. Using the information in the business case, a senior team prioritizes projects based on predetermined criteria linked to strategic goals and innovation targets.
Feedback measures are tactical, bottom-up, not strategic, heavily weighted toward short-term financials.	Even when a project is completed "successfully," the expected improvement is not achieved.	The BA and expert team create a balanced scorecard from the actionable goals and objectives, including business benefit metrics: • Program and project managers report on progress against strategic measures, including time to market, cost to develop the new solution, and scope/quality of the solution. • BA keeps the business case alive: updates the business case at key points in the project, reports on the probability of achieving business benefit forecasts during the project, decides whether a course correction is needed to achieve business objectives, and finally, reports the actual benefits achieved after the solution is delivered.
Projects are not viewed as an executive tool for strategy execution.	No linkage between projects and strategy.	Through a living business case, the BA continually communicates that the project is a strategy execution vehicle.

FIGURE 10-5. Barriers to Strategy Execution

➤ Project leaders are appointed by accident.

➤ Training is seen as a cure-all.

➤ Conflicts develop between project teams.

➤ Few projects are completed in a timely manner.

➤ Project investments continue even when the return on investment becomes marginal.

➤ Business benefits are not realized.

It is evident that a living business case is vital to project success and strategic direction. We suggest nothing short of a full-court press to elevate the importance and use of the business case. It is the business case that provides direction for project teams, drives all decisions, improves inter-project cooperation, and drives focus on innovation and strategy execution. A living business case has three distinct phases or "lives":

1. Life before project funding

2. Life during solution development

3. Life after solution delivery.

Life before Project Funding: Charting the Course

As discussed, the business analyst leads the enterprise analysis activities. With an expert team of SMEs, including an experienced project manager, a business visionary, an architect and/or lead developer, and a financial analyst, the business analysts facilitates:

➤ Competitive and benchmark studies

➤ Current- and future-state business architecture and gap analysis

➤ Business problem and opportunity analysis

➤ Solution feasibility analysis

➤ Cost/benefit analysis and business case development

➤ Review/approval by executive sponsor; the sponsor uses the business case to propose investment in a new project.

Life during Solution Development: Managing Changes

The second phase (after approval) focuses on maintaining momentum, keeping the project positioned in a proactive and positive light, and conditioning stakeholders to accept the changes the project's implementation will deliver. It is during this "life" that requirements are managed to minimize the scope of the solution, while still innovating, which will allow the business to reap benefits as quickly as possible. The business analyst continually validates assumptions and forecasts in the business case during:

➤ *Requirements definition,* when the BA and the requirements team elicit, analyze, and specify business requirements

➤ *Solution validation,* to ensure the solution continues to meet business needs and is truly innovative

➤ *Requirements communication,* to constantly relate requirements to strategy and value

➤ *Change management,* to welcome changes that add value and to determine the cost versus benefit of change requests

➤ *Business case validation,* in which the expert team reviews changes to the business case and determines any needed course corrections to recommend to the sponsor.

Life after Solution Delivery: Measuring Benefits

During solution deployment, the business analyst focuses on the organization's readiness to accept the new business solution and do its work in a new way. The BA documents any needed organizational changes as change management requirements. In addition, the business analyst develops any required business artifacts, including procedures, processes, skill requirements, position descriptions, and an optimal organization structure.

After the solution is operational, the business analyst captures actual business benefits as compared to those forecasted in the business case. If actual business benefits fall short of expectations, the BA conducts root cause analysis to determine why the benefits were not achieved and to identify corrective actions and process improvements to ensure benefit realization on future projects.

DELIVERING THE BUSINESS CASE TO ALL STAKEHOLDERS

There is value in a living business case for virtually all stakeholders, including business analysts, project managers, business units, and the executive team. A living business case benefits the business analyst in several ways:

➤ The BA is elevated to a strategic role.

➤ The BA becomes a key player in strategy execution.

➤ The BA is able to focus the team on business priorities.

➤ The BA clearly documents the business-value basis of her decisions.

A living business case also benefits the project manager in various ways:

➤ It gives the PM clear business-benefit information on which she can base decisions.

➤ The PM transitions from a tactical solution developer to a strategic implementer of change.

➤ The PM can rely on the BA as a strong advocate for the business, and each party understands what she is accountable for:

> ❯ PM: to deliver the solution on time, on budget, with the full scope of features and functions
>
> ❯ BA: to meet business needs.

A living business case benefits executives, too. It:

➤ Gives them confidence that they are investing in the most valuable projects

➤ Helps them make decisions about projects based on business value throughout the project life cycle, allowing them to "protect their investment"

➤ Shows them the expected value of the portfolio of projects, as well as the actual value of the benefits that were realized through newly deployed solutions.

Finally, a living business case benefits the business itself by:

➤ Showing the ROI for the project

➤ Helping the organization meet business objectives and achieve business strategy

➤ Helping the organization salvage, maintain, or greatly improve its competitive position.

BEST PRACTICES FOR BUSINESS CASES

We present three best practices for building "brilliant business cases" suggested by Gartner Group, Inc., the research and advisory firm.[9]

1. ***Develop business cases collaboratively.*** Use a business-driven inclusive process that:

   › Involves all stakeholders to ensure approval and ongoing support

   › Focuses on how the business will achieve innovation related to both processes and people

   › Identifies all potential benefits and who will achieve them.

2. ***Fully document business cases.*** Clearly present the information decisionmakers need.

   › Link the business case to business plans.

   › Describe the major risks and how they will be mitigated.

   › Package the business case well, boosting its credibility.

3. ***Leverage business cases after approval.*** Use the business case throughout the project to:

   › Guide and assess project execution

   › Track how well process and people changes are being institutionalized, as well as the realization of benefits.

PUTTING IT ALL TOGETHER: WHAT DOES THIS MEAN TO THE BUSINESS ANALYST?

The challenge for you as a business analyst is to become a key player in your organization's efforts to implement a center of excellence or project support office, an entity that will be responsible and accountable for transforming process, product, and service-development practices to deliver the smarter solutions that your employees and customer demand—before your competitors do it.

In addition to fostering creativity throughout the organization and honing your leadership, relationship-building, and influence skills, we recommend that business analysts focus on working with a support office or center of excellence to institutionalize the following practices.

RIGOROUS ENTERPRISE ANALYSIS PRACTICES

Enterprise analysis comprises the critical practices that the business analyst performs to ensure that a project is innovative and will deliver real business value. In too many organizations, these activities are not considered part of the business analyst's scope of work, but when they are performed before project approval, after project funding, or throughout the project, enterprise analysis is the very heart and soul of business analysis.

Once again we prevent enterprise analysis activities.

➤ Building the current- and future-state business architecture

➤ Conducting rigorous opportunity analysis and problem analysis with a small expert team to ensure an understanding of the business need

➤ Conducting feasibility analysis with a small expert influential team to identify the most valuable, feasible, and innovative solution to propose

➤ Developing a business case with a small expert team to propose a new project to build the solution

➤ Continually validating the assumptions and forecasts made in the business case throughout the project; recommending course corrections when the ROI elements of the business case have changed

➤ Conducting solution assessment and validation throughout the project

➤ Measuring the business benefits of the deployed solution as compared to the forecasts made in the business case; business benefits can include increased value to the customer and/or increased wealth for the organization.

Experienced business analysts should champion the transition from a tactical to a strategic focus for their business analysis practice. This requires a compelling business case for a mature BA practice, stated in very simple business terms that identifies the outcome to be achieved through business analysis practices, linked to strategies, along with the associated investment.

As we've seen, a living business case serves as a tool for the business analyst to drive the project team from a tactical focus to a focus on innovation and strategy execution. What should you do if you don't have a business case? Facilitate an expert team (probably your core project leadership team) to help you develop one. If your current project does not have an executive sponsor, recruit one and ask him to review and approve the business case. If your business case is no longer valid, facilitate a team of experts to update it.

INNOVATIVE REQUIREMENTS MANAGEMENT PRACTICES

Requirements definition and management comprise the traditional activities thought to compose business analysis. The business analyst and the rest of the complex project management leadership team must focus exclusively on value, creativity, innovation, and competitive positioning when performing these activities, which include:

➤ Planning the requirements approach and activities

➤ Eliciting requirements using multiple elicitation techniques that encourage creativity and innovation and validating the requirements

➤ Defining and specifying requirements, using multiple techniques to make the requirements visible (e.g., text, models, tables, matrices)

➤ Analyzing requirements to ensure they are creative, leading-edge, innovative, accurate, complete, and testable

➤ Validating that the emerging solution meets the business need and that it will add value for the customer and wealth to the organization throughout the project

➤ Managing changes to requirements; welcoming changes that add business value; reducing the cost of change through iterative development

➤ Communicating requirements to stakeholders, customizing the message as needed.

THOROUGH CHANGE MANAGEMENT PRACTICES

Change management is a critical practice that is too often inadequately understood and poorly implemented. The business analyst is the ideal person to work with all key stakeholders, including suppliers, employees, external partners, and end customers, to ensure the new solution will meet their needs, be deployed effectively, and return value to the customer and wealth to the organization. Specifically, the business analyst should:

➤ Ensure the organization is ready to operate the new business solution efficiently and effectively

➤ Manage the organizational changes required to ensure the new business solution is implemented efficiently and effectively

➤ Develop the necessary business artifacts: business policies, procedures, rules, training, retooling, restructuring

➤ Implement an effective benefits measurement and management program.

NOTES

1. Bob Wysocki, *The Executive Guide to Project Management* (Hoboken, NJ: John Wiley & Sons, Inc., 2011): 91–101.

2. James H. Johnson, "Micro Projects Cause Constant Change," *Extreme CHAOS 2001* (West Yarmouth, MA: The Standish Group International, 2001): 5.

3. Kathleen B. Hass, *Managing Complex Projects: A New Model* (Vienna, VA: Management Concepts, 2009).

4. Ibid.

5. Roger Sessions, *The IT Complexity Crisis: Danger and Opportunity* (Houston, TX: Object Watch, Inc., 2009): 2.

6. Carey Schwaber, Rob Karel, and Forrester Research, Inc., "The New Business Analyst," April 8, 2008. Online at http://www.forrester.com/rb/Research/new_business_analyst/q/id/43178/t/2 (accessed April 2011).

7. David Norton, "Project Balanced Scorecards—A Tool for Alignment, Teamwork, and Results," a presentation given at *ProjectWorld & The World Congress for Business Analysts Conference Proceedings* (November 2005).

8. Gerald I. Kendall and Steven C. Rollins, *Advanced Project Portfolio Management and the PMO: Multiplying ROI at Warp Speed* (Boca Raton, FL: J. Ross Publishing, 2003): 73.

9. Gartner, Inc., "Building Brilliant Business Cases," *EXP Premier Report* (January 2004).

CHAPTER 11

Communication and Political Management Strategies to Enable Innovation

What is strategic communication, and why does the business analyst need to use it? For business analysts to communicate effectively with all key stakeholders, they need to be both credible and influential. They need to respect the valuable time of stakeholders, think holistically, strive for innovation, continually focus on business benefits, and make themselves not only heard, but also memorable (see Figure 11-1).

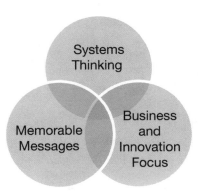

FIGURE 11-1. Elements of Strategic Communication

Before building a communication plan, the wise business analyst works with other project team leaders to assess the political landscape, including the organization's culture, decision models, and the project stakeholders and customers.

ASSESSING THE POLITICAL LANDSCAPE

Make no mistake, organizational politics will impact your effectiveness. *Politics* is defined as dealings related to power and influence within an organization. Politics is neither good nor bad; it just is. Things happen when politics works. Decisions are made, projects move forward, goals are met, and innovation is achieved. How can that be bad? Positive politics is about getting positive results for the team, for the organization, and ultimately for you. The positive politician uses influence rather than authority or manipulation to achieve tasks or goals. She starts from a solid basis from which to influence: status, trust, integrity, consistency, and knowledge.

To effectively negotiate your organization's politics, seek out opportunities to help your project team and the business manage organizational politics. First, gather information about your organization, specifically:

➤ Your customers and stakeholders

➤ The political environment

➤ Your personal political capabilities and those of your team members

➤ The landmines and risks.

Work closely with the project manager and other core project leaders to identify customers and stakeholders who provide budget, oversight, requirements, and input to your project and who receive output, depend on your deliverables, and benefit or suffer from your project's success. For each, key customer/stakeholder, capture pertinent information, including:

➤ Role

➤ Awareness

➤ Opinion

➤ Importance

➤ Current level of support

➤ Level of support needed.

Document the information in a simple tabular template (see Figure 11-2). This and the other templates presented in the section can be customized to meet the unique needs of your project.

Stakeholder or Customer	Role in Project	Awareness	Opinion	Importance	Support Needed	Existing Support
Stakeholder #1						
Stakeholder #2						
Stakeholder #3						
Legend						
Awareness	1 = Unaware		2 = Basic understanding		3 = Informed	
Opinion	1 = Opposed		2 = Disinterested		3 = Champion	
Importance	1 = Unimportant		2 = Pertinent		3 = Critical	
Support Needed	1 = Not needed		2 = Helpful		3 = Critical	
Existing Support	+ = Active		0 = Neutral		– = Opposes	

FIGURE 11-2. Stakeholder and Customer Intelligence

Then, as a project leadership team, identify the issues and concerns about the project that are important to each stakeholder. Ask, What's in it for stakeholder #1? What does stakeholder #1 need to view the project positively and actively support it? What innovation does stakeholder #1 need to succeed? Develop an influence strategy for each key stakeholder (see Figure 11-3).

THE POLITICAL ENVIRONMENT

Work with your project leadership team to determine the answers to these questions:

➤ Is the business case solid? Is there a need for innovation to meet the business objectives?

➤ Will the proposed solution bring about innovation?

➤ Is the project politically sensitive? If so, what are the major political implications?

➤ Will the project affect the core mission?

➤ Do you have a strong executive sponsor?

➤ What are the unspoken expectations for the project?

➤ What is the organization's decision-making process? Is it effective?

➤ What are the cultural norms?

➤ What are the challenges to communication and stakeholder management?

Capture the information in a simple tabular template (see Figure 11-4).

Stakeholder	Role in Project	Awareness	Opinion	Importance	Support Needed	Existing Support	Influence Strategies	Innovation Concerns
Stakeholder #1								
Stakeholder #2								
Stakeholder #3								

FIGURE 11-3. Stakeholder and Customer Influence Strategies

Political Environment	Business Case Cost vs. Benefit	Political Implications	Mission Impacts	Executive Sponsors	Expectations	Decisionmakers	Preferred Mode of Communication	Need for Innovation
Enterprise								
Business Unit #1								
Business Unit #2								

FIGURE 11-4. Organizational Political Information

YOUR POLITICAL MANAGEMENT CAPABILITIES

Armed with this information about your project and the political and cultural environment, work with your project leadership team to assess your individual and collective political capabilities as project leaders including how well you do the following:

➤ Enlist the help of an executive sponsor

➤ Organize and chair your project steering committee

➤ Demonstrate your expertise and encourage other project leaders to do the same

➤ Promote yourselves and your project

➤ Manage project benefits (return on investment)

➤ Manage virtual alliances

➤ Facilitate, negotiate, and build consensus

➤ Manage conflict

➤ Foster and communicate creativity and innovation effectively

➤ Develop a political management strategy for your project.

Capture this information in a simple tabular template (see Figure 11-5).

THE LANDMINES AND RISKS

Using the information you have collected, assess the political risks. Determine strategies to lessen the impact of the risks that may negatively influence the project, and leverage those that are positive to promote innovation. Work with your team to devise strategies to:

➤ Gain high-level support

Political Capabilities—How Well Does He or She Do the Following	Work with Sponsor?	Facilitate Steering Committee and Management Decision Process?	Foster Creativity and Innovation?	Promote Self and Project?	Manage Business Benefits?	Facilitate, Negotiate, Manage Conflict, Build Consensus?	Control Critical Resources?
Project Manager							
Business Analyst							
Product Owner							

FIGURE 11-5. Political Capabilities

➤ Build alliances and coalitions

➤ Control critical resources (money, people, information, expertise)

➤ Control the decision process

➤ Control the steering committee process.

Capture your political management strategies in a simple tabular template (see Figure 11-6).

Next, for each strategy, identify what success will look like. Focus on outcomes: how will you evaluate the effectiveness of the plan? Continually refine your strategy. Capture your success strategies in a simple tabular template (see Figure 11-7).

CRAFTING STRATEGIC MESSAGES

Armed with the business intelligence you have captured and your political management plan, you are now ready to begin to craft customized messages for your key stakeholders and customers.

REALLY GETTING HEARD

When presenting information to overworked executives, managers, employees, and distracted customers, you have only a few short minutes to get your message across. You need to become expert in constructing memorable messages, customizing your message for the audience, really getting your message heard, and getting decisions made quickly so that forward progress is not stalled.

Political Strategies to...	Gain Executive Support	Build Alliances and Coalitions	Control Critical Resources	Foster Creativity and Innovation	Control the Decision-Making Process	Communicate Strategically	Manage Cultural Change
You							
Key Team Member #1							
Key Team Member #2							

FIGURE 11-6. Political Management Plan

	Gain Executive Support	Build Alliances and Coalitions	Control Critical Resources	Foster Creativity and Innovation	Control the Decision-Making Process	Communicate Strategically	Manage Cultural Change
Success Criteria							
Desired Outcomes							
Validation Techniques							

FIGURE 11-7. What Will Political Success Look Like?

THE MESSAGE

Compose a customized message for each key stakeholder. First, determine the purpose of the message. Is it simply to create awareness about your project objectives? Is it to enlist support for your project? Is it to dispel negative feelings about your project? Is it to make a decision about your project approach? Is it to gain support to resolve an issue? Once the core purpose of the communication is understood, draft the message, composing it from the stakeholder's perspective. Be sure to determine what's in it for the stakeholder and tailor the message accordingly.

The Catchphrase

A catchphrase is a short phrase or sentence that deftly captures the essence of what you are trying to say. In the media world, catchphrases are referred to as *sound bites*, very short pieces of a message. The goal is for the catchphrase to capture the heart of the message in a snippet, to clearly and cleverly make a point, and to stand out in the audience's memory. One might say, in the words of Mark Twain, that a catchphrase is "a minimum of sound to a maximum of sense." Examples of catchphrases include "I have a dream," "The buck stops here," "Just do it," and "Joe the Plumber."

The Slogan

Often used effectively in advertising, a slogan is a short phrase used as a rallying cry, and like a catchphrase, it is designed to make the message memorable. It is intended to be motivational—to be a call to action. Examples of slogans include "Don't leave home without it," "Yes we can," and "We're the dot in .com."

The Delivery

Once you have determined the message you want to deliver to each stakeholder, you are ready to develop your pitch, sometimes called an elevator speech. A pitch should be about 100–150 words in length and should take no more than 30 seconds to deliver. Use a compelling "hook" that motivates people to further engage, and include catchphrases and slogans when possible. Capture the content of your pitch to each stakeholder in a simple tabular template (see Figure 11-8).

STEER YOUR STEERING COMMITTEE

Many projects are challenged—or even fail—because the project leadership team does not perform the critical analysis that is needed to determine the best path forward, both at the start of the project and all along the way as more is learned and issues arise. These project leaders do not take the time to analyze all possible solutions to the business problem or assess varying managerial approaches before marching ahead. They are not asking and answering questions such as, "Once we have defined the business problem or opportunity, should we build the solution in house?" "Do we have the appropriately skilled and talented resources? Are they available? Do we need outside expertise?" "How fast do we need the solution?" "What are our competitors doing?" The list goes on and on.

When proposing a new product innovation, escalating project issues, proposing a course correction, securing the best resources for requirements sessions, or advocating acceptance of scope changes that add business value, you are essentially in a sales role, seeking approval from upper management. There are many pitfalls: management is impatient; you must not only be brief, you must also demonstrate the wisdom of the recommendation you're making. To do so, you must facilitate an expert team to identify all potential

Stakeholder	Role in Project	What's in It For Me?	Influence Strategies	Message	Catchphrases	Slogan	Pitch
Stakeholder #1							
Stakeholder #2							
Stakeholder #3							

FIGURE 11-8. Pitch to Stakeholders

options, fostering creativity and out-of-the-building thinking, and then ask upper management to make a decision on the option you recommend.

How can you make sure management's decision goes the way you want? You need to guide your project leadership team, augmenting it with additional SMEs if needed, to analyze the issue, identify all potential options, and propose the most feasible solution as discussed in chapter 7. Use the results of your alternative analysis as decision-support information when presenting your recommended approach. Include the names of those who participated in the analysis, all the options considered, and the feasibility of each option: the economic feasibility, the time-to-market feasibility, the cultural feasibility, the technical feasibility, the success feasibility, the business process feasibility, and the feasibility of achieving an innovative solution. After this analysis is complete, it is usually very clear which option is the most feasible. Capture your feasibility analysis in a simple tabular template (see Figure 11-9) and use it as decision-support information when meeting with management.

Problem, Opportunity, or Issue							
Expert Team Members Involved in Analysis							
Option	**Cost**	**Benefits**	**Innovation (H, M, L)**	**Probability of Success**	**Process Complexity**	**Technical Complexity**	**Risks**
Option #1							
Option #2							
Option #3							
Option #4							
Option #5							

FIGURE 11-9. Feasibility Analysis Worksheet

PUTTING IT ALL TOGETHER: WHAT DOES THIS MEAN FOR THE BUSINESS ANALYST?

Don't let the political environment steer your project in the wrong direction. Establish political management and strategic communication plans to negotiate environmental land mines, manage stakeholders' influence, develop your political skills, respond to political risks, and seek approval for recommendations that are supported by rigorous alternative and feasibility analysis. Your project team will respect you, and your management team will notice your logical and disciplined approach.

PART IV

Innovation-Driven Business Practices

In this part, we explore the critical elements of innovation-driven business practices.

➤ In Chapter 12, we offer business analysts guidance in preparing an approach to their own professional development, which will help them grow as enterprise and innovation-driven leaders.

➤ In Chapter 13, we describe the elements needed to build a mature BA practice focused on innovation. Within such a practice, business requirements are managed, business needs are met, strategy is executed, and business and technology are optimized, allowing technology to provide competitive advantage.

➤ Chapter 14 examines the elements of an innovation-driven portfolio management practice that leads to competitive advantage.

➤ In Chapter 15, we discuss the purpose, structure, and implementation of an innovation-driven center of excellence, an organization within a company that works collaboratively to leverage the best practices of both business analysis and complex project management disciplines.

CHAPTER 12

How Capable Do Business Analysts Need to Be to Ignite Creativity?

The value of business analysis lies in the absolute necessity of driving innovation through projects. Organizations are beginning to acknowledge this value, but as they do, they are struggling to figure out three things:

1. What are the characteristics of our current BA workforce, and how capable does the BA team need to be?

2. What is needed to build a mature BA practice?

3. How are we going to get there?

This chapter focuses on the first question: What are the characteristics of our current BA workforce, and how capable does our BA team need to be? Looking once again to our framework (Figure 12-1), a BA workforce needs to be capable enough to perform BA work successfully on projects that are increasingly complex and innovative.

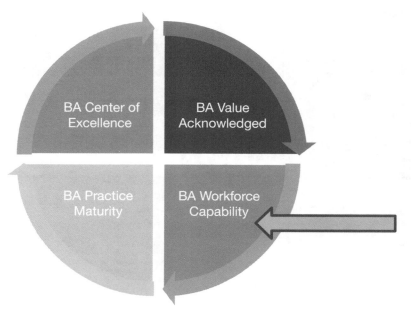

FIGURE 12-1. The Framework of a Mature BA Practice

© 2011 by Kathleen B. Hass and Associates, Inc.

THE CHALLENGE: CLOSING THE GAP IN BA CAPABILITIES

Your challenge is to close the gap in your organization's BA workforce capabilities, to meet the needs of your organization's complex innovation projects. What will it take? Are BAs up to the task? According to a recent study, most organizations' BA workforce fall into the categories listed in Figure 12-2.[1]

As a BA, you need to start grooming yourself right now to be prepared to meet your organization's needs. According to Carey Schwaber and Rob Karel of Forrester Research, Inc., "Future business/technology analysts will be the most valuable business analysts, because they can single-handedly turn business-requested IT-delivered applications into tomorrow's dynamic business applications."[2]

- **Titles**
  - 56% are BAs or senior BAs
  - 13% are SAs or senior SAs
  - 7% are consultants
- **Reporting**
  - 65% report to IT
  - 43% to applications development
  - 36% to BA team or PMO
  - 71% to business/ops units, PMO, or strategy/business dev. group
- **Education**
  - 47% have Bachelor's degree
  - 31% have Master's degree
  - 18% have professional certifications
  - 10% CBAPs; 10% PMPs
- **Length of Service**
  - ▸ 55% have been BAs for > 5 years
  - ▸ 25% for > 10 years
  - ▸ 19% for > 15 years

- ▸ **Roles**
  - 56% generalists
  - 29% requirements specialist
  - 8% process specialists
  - 3% information specialists
  - 1% design specialists
- ▸ **Methodologies**
  - 45% Mixture
  - 34% Waterfall
  - 9% Agile (Scrum, XP)
  - 9% Iterative (RUP)
- **Projects**
  - 47% Process improvement
  - 44% Enterprise projects
  - 39% Internal websites/apps
  - 35% BPM, business rules
  - 32% External websites/apps
  - 28% BACOE

FIGURE 12-2. The Current State of BAs

CREATIVE LEADERSHIP ACROSS THE BA CAPABILITY SPECTRUM

The array of BA competencies required to successfully deliver innovative products and new business solutions that meet 21st-century business needs is vast. But it's not just about competency (what you think you can do or your score on a multiple-choice knowledge assessment); it's *all* about *capability*—examining your competency level against your current and future work assignments and the performance and project outcomes you need to achieve within your organization.

To determine your own BA capabilities and those of your BA team, identify your capability gaps, and put a plan in place to close the gaps, it is helpful to use a BA capability model like the one shown in Figure 12-3, which was first presented and described in detail in Chapter 1. The model

Business Operations Enhanced	Business Objectives Met	Business Strategy Executed	New Business Strategy Forged
Operations/Support Focus	**Project Focus**	**Enterprise Focus**	**Competitive Focus**
PROJECTS Low complexity projects that continually enhance business processes, products, and/or technology	**PROJECTS** Moderately complex new development projects that improve business processes, products, and/or technology	**PROJECTS** Highly complex programs and portfolios that improve multiple business processes, products, and/or technology	**PROJECTS** Innovation projects that improve competitive advantage and translate strategy into breakthrough processes and technology
OUTCOMES Value of operational business process and systems is continually enhanced	**OUTCOMES** Business requirements and project scope are managed to ensure new solutions meet business objectives	**OUTCOMES** The enterprise is investing in the most valuable initiatives and is realizing the business benefits forecasted in the business case	**OUTCOMES** New strategies, optimized business/technology, and improved competitive position
TYPE OF LEADER Generalists, business/system specialists, product managers Entry- level and senior BAs	**TYPE OF LEADER** Business domain experts, IT system experts Entry- level and senior BAs	**TYPE OF LEADER** Enterprise change experts, business architects Senior and enterprise BAs	**TYPE OF LEADER** Strategists, business/technology optimization experts, innovation and cultural change experts, research and development Enterprise and business/technology optimization BAs

Continuous Advancement of Competence, Credibility, and Influence

FIGURE 12-3. BA Workforce Capability Model

aligns with the latest industry research, the IIBA *BABOK® Guide*, and the newly released IIBA BA Competency Model®. The BA capability model shown here is four-tiered, each tier requiring different BA competencies based on the complexity, the innovation required, and the focus of typical work assignments.

THE OPERATIONS/SUPPORT-FOCUSED BA AS INNOVATOR

Operations/support-focused business analysts, who work to continually add value to products, business processes, and their supporting IT systems, need to think about the entire business system and view their efforts as part of a larger project. They should look for opportunities to creatively change and improve the system rather than thinking that they are responsible only for fixing bugs or problems and should bundle and prioritize change requests based on business value. Once a business analyst takes a systems and business-value approach, opportunities for innovation begin to emerge. Innovation is everybody's job; it is not just up to a few superstars or senior BAs to foster creativity. And it is not just quantum-leap changes that bring about innovation; it can be done through lots of incremental improvements as well.

CAREER ADVICE
Professional Development Plan

It is important for you to take control of your career and build your own professional development plan.

A Word to the Wise

Determine which type of work you are passionate about, and then build your business analysis development plan to get you there.

THE PROJECT-FOCUSED BA AS CREATIVE LEADER

Project-focused analysts work on moderately complex projects designed to develop new or changed products, services, business processes, and IT systems. IT-oriented BAs and business-oriented BAs, who may range from entry to senior levels generally fit into this group.

It is a little more obvious how business analysts can foster innovation when working on a project to develop something new, whether it is a new product, process, or service. However, as we learned earlier, even with a project focus, it is easy to fall into inside-the-building thinking and allow the requirements SMEs to simply define requirements for rebuilding an existing system with only minor enhancements. Business analysts who allow this to happen will undoubtedly be thought of as note takers, as opposed to trailblazers.

To fulfill your role as a creative leader, it is your job to establish an environment in which creativity can surface and thrive. Once the team of SMEs has a shared vision, target, and objective, the business analyst encourages the team to create something new by imagining what could be, inspiring one another, collaborating, brainstorming, and experimenting. As you encourage team members to see themselves as unique individuals with valuable contributions to make, participants will start "getting it" and "getting with it," and you can then quietly step into the shadows and let the team do its thing.

Keep in mind that if your team members are not challenging each other and building on each other's ideas, they have not yet made it into the innovation zone. In this case, they likely need more prodding and encouragement from you in your role as expert facilitator, collaborator, and innovator. Caution the participants not to be critical or judgmental but to use conflict positively to encourage the contribution of different perspectives and new combinations of ideas. Hone your innovation-inducing facilitation skills on moderately complex projects to train yourself for the big leagues.

THE ENTERPRISE ANALYST AS CREATIVE LEADER

BAs with an enterprise or strategy-execution focus (often called enterprise analysts or business architects) are operating at the enterprise level of the organization, ensuring that business analysis activities are dedicated to the most valuable initiatives. Enterprise analysts focus on the analysis needed to prepare a solid business case for new strategic initiatives. They also work on highly complex enterprise-wide projects and programs, typically managing a team of senior BAs. BAs within this focus area are typically experienced and in high-level positions.

The need for innovation is even more critical for business analysts that are working on enterprise transformation initiatives. Here the stakes are higher, the investments bigger, the rewards greater, and the risks larger. It is at this level that business analysts most need to be on their game, familiar with and comfortable with innovative work sessions.

There is a delicate balance between instilling a culture of discipline in a team and smothering creativity. Business analysts who have mastered creativity techniques make a deliberate effort not to be too controlling; for example, they do not sit at the head of the table or get into prolonged conversations with only one or two people. They insist on full participation, summarizing and sharing their own opinion only after full discussion has taken place.

The techniques you select to encourage creativity need to be customized to your team composition: mind mapping works well for left-brain thinkers; brain-writing for right-brain thinkers. Make your team meetings fun and exciting—and yes, you may even need to "perform" a bit. Spend ample time planning how you will facilitate meetings to ensure you have lots of tools in your toolkit, experimenting with them until the team begins to gel.

THE HIGH-LEVEL LEADERSHIP OF THE COMPETITIVE/INNOVATION-FOCUSED BA

Competitive/innovation-focused business analysts are visionaries, futurists, and creative thinkers. These seasoned analysts focus outside the enterprise on what the industry is doing, formulate the future vision and strategy, and design imaginative new approaches to doing business to ensure the enterprise remains competitive or even leaps ahead of the competition. They often function as business/technology analysts, converting business opportunities into innovative business solutions and translating strategy into breakthrough processes and products. Such a business analyst is really in the major leagues—truly at the pinnacle of her career.

Interestingly, most people who are engaged in these functions are not thought of as business analysts. They often operate at the executive level, carrying the title of product manager, strategy analyst, or portfolio manager. Indisputably, however, when individuals and groups are engaged in the activities described below, they are very much carrying out business analysis pursuits.[3]

Deciding What to Build to Seize Competitive Advantage

What we build today determines our place in the market tomorrow. All of the enterprise analysis activities the business analyst leads come into play when determining the most valuable products to build, including decomposing strategic goals into measurable objectives, conducting competitive and customer analysis to determine the differentiators that will make your organization stand out, defining the business need and assessing capability gaps to meet the need, identifying the most creative and innovative solution, defining the solution scope and approach, determining when to release the new product and how to manufacture and support it, and finally capturing the opportunity in the business case to secure investment funds.

Conducting Real Portfolio Management

With so much riding on the results, companies must invest in the most valuable projects, those that will provide value to customers and revenue to the company. However, as we have seen studies show that few companies have effective portfolio management processes. The emerging role of the competitive-focused business analyst must fill this gap in organizational capabilities by acting as the vital link between opportunity and investment, converting idea to value. To do this, the business analyst brings together an expert team and facilitates discussions to:

➤ Select the most innovative solution

➤ Decide when to release it in the market to seize the greatest competitive advantage

➤ Determine how to manufacture and support the solution efficiently and quickly

➤ Figure out the solution's expected value to the company

➤ Determine the next steps to maintain the preeminent competitive position.

The business analyst then documents the opportunity in the business case.

Perhaps one of the reasons many organizations don't have effective portfolio management is that not enough business analysts are conducting these important enterprise analysis activities.[4]

Ensuring That Customer Requirements Are Met

Business analysts continually validate that an emerging solution will meet customer requirements and win the expected competitive advantage. This is the business analyst's reason for being. Specifically, the competitive focused business analyst understands the new process, product, or service as it will operate within the customer's ecosystem and describes the intent behind features, thus helping engineers develop the appropriate design.

Navigating Complexity with Modelling

Since business analysts constantly strive to make the requirements for the entire system visible, models, graphics, and rich pictures are tools of the trade. Models show the relationship between requirements statements and product capabilities. As complexity increases, models and prototypes are an absolute must.

Managing Changes

Today, we can no longer attempt to limit changes; the world is just too dynamic and systems are too complex to get everything right the first time. The goal is to welcome changes that add value and reduce the cost of changes through iterative development. It is very difficult to predict the consequences of changes to complex systems because of the interrelationships and interdependencies of solution components, but using system models and simulating the impacts of the change help build an understanding of the effects of the change. Proactively limiting the number of interrelationships among system components will go a long way toward making it easier to examine the impacts and to reduce the cost of changes.

A BUSINESS ANALYST PROFESSIONAL DEVELOPMENT PLAN

Creating a balanced professional development program will reinforce technical BA competencies for project-focused BAs, and it will also specifically target the leadership skills of enterprise BAs who work on complex innovation projects. Work with the leaders of your BA practice to implement some or all of these development strategies.

A balanced program consists of activities to increase technical, leadership, and complexity management capabilities as outlined in Figure 12-4.

A multidimensional program consists of a variety of activities, including:

➤ Coordinating self study through communities of practice

➤ Participating in local IIBA chapter events and programs

Traditional Technical Competencies	Leadership Competencies	Complex Enterprise BA Competencies
• Business analysis planning and monitoring • Elicitation • Requirements management and communication • Enterprise analysis • Requirements analysis • Solution assessment and validation • Business and technology optimization	• Leadership • Engagement • Self control • Assertiveness • Composure • Openness • Results-oriented • Efficiency • Consultation • Negotiation • Conflict resolution • Reliability • Values • Ethics	• Creativity • Innovation • Strategy • Business change • Breakthrough change • Vision • Systems leadership • Cultural change • Governance **Special Attributes:** • Influential • Credible • Action- or outcome-oriented • Focused • Courageous

FIGURE 12-4. A Balanced Approach to BA Professional Development

➤ Mentoring

➤ Attending formal training sessions

➤ Attending conferences

➤ Participating in working sessions, workshops, and seminars

➤ Conducting competency benchmarking and facilitating career planning.

COORDINATING SELF STUDY THROUGH COMMUNITIES OF PRACTICE

➤ Acquire a license to put a copy of *A Guide to the Business Analysis Body of Knowledge®* (*BABOK® Guide*) on your company's internal server and launch study groups centered on the *BABOK® Guide*.

➤ Support IIBA membership for all BAs. Membership offers your BA community access to a wealth of resources, including books in the IIBA e-library, white papers, blogs, and BA community discussions.

➤ Initiate a somewhat formal program of self study designed for each of the four BA levels in the BA Workforce Capability Model (Figure 12-3). Form communities of practice for each level, so BAs can collectively participate in free webinars and blogs, read white papers, and read books available through the IIBA website and other websites. The most senior BAs in your organization should plan and facilitate these community sessions.

PARTICIPATING IN LOCAL IIBA CHAPTER EVENTS AND PROGRAMS

➤ Provide incentives for BAs in your organization to attend local IIBA chapter meetings. Benefits include opportunities to network with other BAs, learn best practices, and develop BA capabilities.

➤ Ask your organization to reimburse BAs for the IIBA membership fees.

MENTORING

➤ Launch a mentoring program for highly capable BAs to mentor, coach, and train BAs whose skills are not commensurate with the complexity of their assignments.

➤ Design the mentoring program to achieve two objectives:

› Immediately improve BA performance on current projects

› Infuse knowledge and skills through on-the-job training and mentoring.

ATTENDING FORMAL TRAINING SESSIONS

➤ Launch a two-year training program to foster a common BA language and foundational BA practices.

➤ Design the training program to cover three areas of content:

› Technical BA competencies

› Leadership and supporting BA competencies

› Complex enterprise BA competencies.

ATTENDING CONFERENCES

➤ Provide opportunities for your senior BAs to attend conferences on business analysis (e.g., the Building Business Capability annual conference, the BusinessAnalystWorld conference, and the World Congress for Business Analysts®).

➤ Encourage attendance at relevant presentations and workshops.

PARTICIPATING IN WORKING SESSIONS, WORKSHOPS, AND SEMINARS

Schedule quarterly working sessions, workshops, and seminars for BAs, PMs, and line managers (Figure 12-5). Meeting topics could include:

➤ Diagnosing project complexity

➤ Managing project complexity

➤ Capitalizing on complexity to drive innovation

➤ Fostering a necessary collaborative partnership among the dynamic duo: project managers and business analysts

➤ Covering basic leadership topics.

CONDUCTING COMPETENCY BENCHMARKING AND FACILITATING CAREER PLANNING

➤ Conduct an individual and workforce capability assessment for your community of BAs to benchmark current competency levels based on the four BA levels in the BA Workforce Capability Model (Figure 12-3). If your organization does not support the assessment, you can at least assess yourself based on these competency levels. (See the next section for more assessment ideas.)

➤ Work with individual BAs to establish career development plans to close competency gaps.

➤ Provide assignments to individual BAs who are interested in moving to the next level; all too often, BAs are kept in maintenance and enhancement roles when they are more than ready to move on to moderately complex projects.

Project Focus	Enterprise Focus	Competitive Focus
Business Analyst	**Senior Business Analyst**	**Business Consultant**
Supporting competencies: • Decision-making • Influencing • Planning • Understanding software applications • Knowing business solutions • Problem-solving • Facilitating • Negotiating • Understanding business principles and practices • Understanding organizational concepts **These competencies are demonstrated through an ability to:** • Document and manage requirements • Structure complex requirements for reuse • Facilitate group decision-making sessions • Negotiate conflicts • Conduct complex requirement workshops • Clearly document complex requirements • Build requirements models • Organize and prioritize requirements • Communicate complex BA principles • Use modeling and requirements management tools	**Supporting competencies:** • Having leadership skills • Demonstrating systems thinking • Understanding the industry and relevant domains • Focusing on value and the customer **These competencies are demonstrated through an ability to:** • Execute strategy through projects, starting with the business case • Design the current and future state of the business • Decompose strategic and business goals • Analyze business problems and opportunities • Determine the most feasible solutions • Think strategically, systematically, and creatively • Manage and integrate requirements for complex programs and portfolios • Implement metrics and measurements programs • Manage the business benefits of project investments • Develop BA standards and communities • Apply business principles and practices • Apply industry knowledge • Apply organization knowledge • Apply solution knowledge	**Supporting competencies:** • Having vision • Innovating • Creating **These competencies are demonstrated through an ability to:** • Convert strategy into breakthrough products and services • Launch competitive products • Launch products that involve breakthrough commercial practices • Encourage creativity in others • Integrate business and IT components • Optimize business and IT components • Conduct research and development initiatives • Design breakthrough processes and technology • Design innovative products • Use technology as a competitive advantage • Innovate • Manage cultural change

FIGURE 12-5. Focusing Working Sessions, Workshops, and Seminars on Key Competencies

THE APPLIED BA CAPABILITY ASSESSMENT: A GROUNDBREAKING APPROACH

Conducting an applied BA capability assessment provides the information you need to baseline your competencies and prepare your own professional development plan, and it also can serve as input to your organization's professional development program. The results provide a basis for BA workforce adjustments and realignment, training requirements, professional development activities, and specific mentoring and coaching needs.

The applied capability assessment, which is available online at www.kathleenhass.com, collects basic demographic information about you, such as years of experience, time spent on BA activities versus project management or more technical tasks, and amount of BA education. It then compares your BA capabilities to those of other BAs in the industry as a whole.

The applied capability assessment provides an opportunity to participate in a multidimensional BA capability assessment. This assessment allows you to see where you compare against BAs at your level who are working on similar project assignments in other organizations. This tool is not your ordinary multiple-choice self-assessment. It provides an interpretive frame of reference for analyzing your responses and has high reliability and validity when you respond candidly to each question. Figure 12-6 compares the BA applied capability assessment approach to traditional competency assessments.

In addition to an integrated competency report, you receive a customized professional development plan to guide your performance-improvement and career-development efforts (see samples in Figures 12-7 and 12-8). The reports are customized to your specific work situation and provide you with

What You Receive	BA Capability Assessment	Traditional BA Competency Assessment
Competency rating for BA knowledge areas and supporting competencies	X	X
Summary competency snapshot	X	X
List of recommendations	X	X
Integrated competency report	X	
Comprehensive professional development plan	X	
Comparison against a validated BA competency model	X	
Comparison against a BA benchmark group	X	
Evaluation of your competency level against your current work assignments/ workload	X	
Analysis of BA performance outcomes and project outcomes	X	
Consultation to help you understand your results	X	

FIGURE 12-6. BA Capability Assessment Approaches

relevant, prioritized recommendations to help you focus your professional development efforts. Your customized reports arrive via email in PDF format. You may request a 15-minute telephone consultation or email consultation if you have any questions about your results or would like further recommendations for professional development.

Section 2: Improving BA Competencies	
We designed these recommendations to help you fill the gaps in competencies as needed.	
Competency Area	**Activity/Task**
Consider the following BA competency areas as candidates for professional development: • Planning BA activities • Planning BA communications • Preparing for elicitation • Communicating requirements • Prioritizing requirements	Courses: • Enlist in a formal course for these competency areas. Self study: • Download version 2.0 of the IIBA *BABOK®* and study these competency areas. Conferences: • Attend conferences on business analysis (e.g., BA World, World Congress of Business Analysis), focusing on presentations and workshops in these competency areas. Local IIBA chapter: • Attend your local IIBA chapter meetings. • Suggest that your local IIBA chapter conduct professional development events on these competency areas. Mentoring: • Seek a mentor in your group who performs well in these competency areas.
Consider the following supporting competency areas as candidates for professional development: • Business principles and practices • Industry knowledge • Organizational knowledge	Courses: • Enlist in a workshop or online courses for these competency areas. Self study: • Read books and articles on the competency areas that are published by thought leaders in the field. Conferences: • Attend conferences on business analysis (e.g., BA World, World Congress of Business Analysis), focusing on presentations and workshops in these competency areas. Local IIBA chapter: • Attend your local IIBA chapter meetings. • Suggest that your local IIBA chapter conduct professional development events on these competency areas. Mentoring: • Seek a mentor in your group who performs well in these competency areas.

FIGURE 12-7. Individual Professional Development Plan Sample

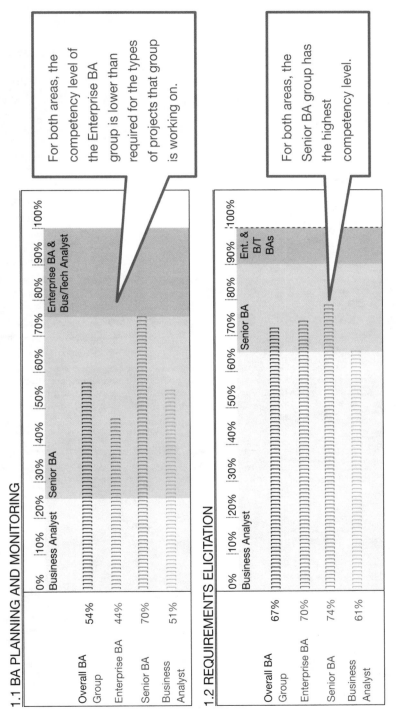

FIGURE 12-8. Overall BA Workforce Report Sample

PUTTING IT ALL TOGETHER: WHAT DOES THIS MEAN FOR THE BUSINESS ANALYST?

Don't wait any longer before putting your personal professional development plan together. You can conduct an assessment of your BA capabilities today. If you are interested in learning more about the Individual BA Capability Assessment, please visit our website at www.kathleenhass.com or contact the author at kittyhass@comcast.net.

NOTES

1. Mary Gerush, Mike Gilpin, Alissa Anderson, and Forrester Research, "Get To Know Your 2010 Business Analysts," *Report on the 2010 Survey Conducted by Forrester Research, Inc., and the International Institute of Business Analysis* (January 31, 2011): 1–39. Online at http://www.forrester.com/rb/Research/get_to_know_2010_business_analysts/q/id/58419/t/2 (accessed June 2011).

2. Carey Schwaber, Rob Karel, and Forrester Research, Inc., "The New Business Analyst," April 8, 2008. Online at http://www.forrester.com/rb/Research/new_business_analyst/q/id/43178/t/2 (accessed April 2011).

3. IBM Corporation, "Turning product development into competitive advantage. Best practices for developing smarter products," *IBM Executive Brief: Developing Competitive Products* (July 2009): 8–13. Online at http://www.idgconnect.com/download/5018/turning-product-development-competitive-advantage-best-practices-developing-smarter-products?source=connect (accessed April 2011).

4. Jim Brown, *The Product Portfolio Management Benchmark Report: Achieving Maximum Product Value* (Boston: Aberdeen Group, 2006): 2. Online at http://www.plm.automation.siemens.com/en_us/Images/aberdeen_portfolio_mgmt_tcm1023-5843.pdf (accessed April 2011).

CHAPTER 13
Building a Mature, Innovation-Driven Business Analysis Practice

An organization's journey to business analysis practice maturity begins when it acknowledges that business analysis is a critical business management discipline for the 21st century. It takes investment and resources to build a new business analysis practice, so our framework calls for a proven, structured approach coupled with expert change management skills. The framework involves a three-pronged approach: once the organization has acknowledged the value of business analysis, it develops a competent BA workforce, builds a mature BA practice, and establishes a business analysis center of excellence (BACOE) to plant the seeds for, and steer the course toward, business analysis maturity (see Figure 13-1). This chapter focuses on building a mature, innovation-driven BA practice.

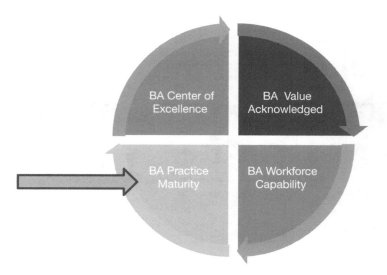

FIGURE 13-1. The Framework of a Mature BA Practice

© 2011 By Kathleen B. Hass and Associates, Inc.

To steer the course, we once again make use of a model, the BA practice maturity model shown in Figure 13-2. As you can see, the model is in strict alignment with the BA capability model introduced in Chapter 1.

THE DAUNTING ROAD AHEAD

Figure 13-3 shows that many elements need to be in place for an organization to implement a mature BA practice. So how are we ever going to get there, and how fast can we get there?

The practice maturity levels comprising the BA practice maturity model are described in Figure 13-4.

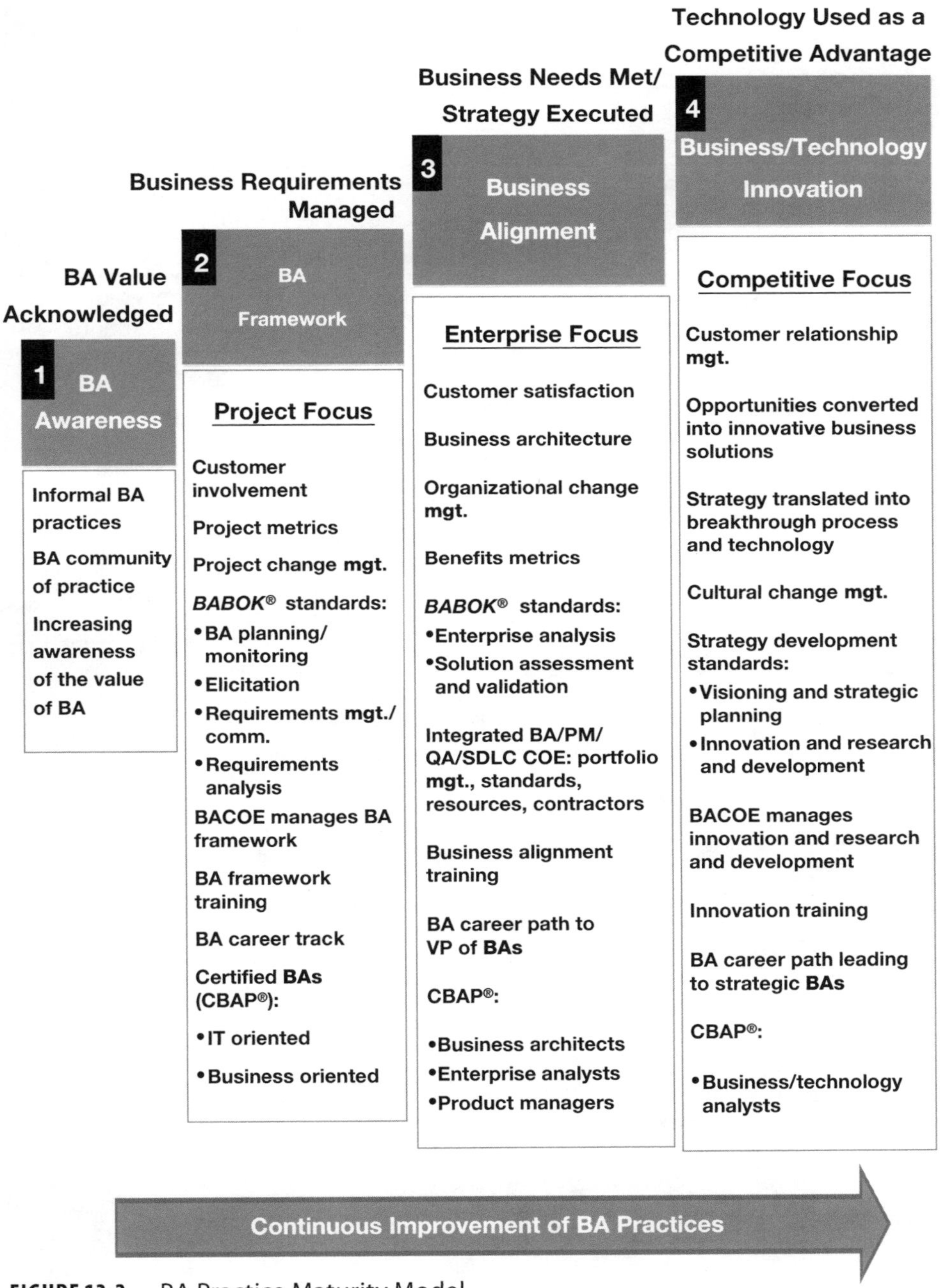

Technology Used as a Competitive Advantage

Business Needs Met/ Strategy Executed

4

Business/Technology Innovation

Business Requirements Managed

3

Business Alignment

BA Value Acknowledged

2

BA Framework

Competitive Focus

Customer relationship mgt.

Opportunities converted into innovative business solutions

1

BA Awareness

Project Focus

Enterprise Focus

Customer satisfaction

Business architecture

Organizational change mgt.

Benefits metrics

Strategy translated into breakthrough process and technology

Cultural change mgt.

Informal BA practices

BA community of practice

Increasing awareness of the value of BA

Customer involvement

Project metrics

Project change mgt.

BABOK® standards:
- BA planning/ monitoring
- Elicitation
- Requirements mgt./ comm.
- Requirements analysis

BACOE manages BA framework

BA framework training

BA career track

Certified **BAs** (CBAP®):
- IT oriented
- Business oriented

BABOK® standards:
- Enterprise analysis
- Solution assessment and validation

Integrated BA/PM/ QA/SDLC COE: portfolio mgt., standards, resources, contractors

Business alignment training

BA career path to VP of **BAs**

CBAP®:
- Business architects
- Enterprise analysts
- Product managers

Strategy development standards:
- Visioning and strategic planning
- Innovation and research and development

BACOE manages innovation and research and development

Innovation training

BA career path leading to strategic **BAs**

CBAP®:
- Business/technology analysts

Continuous Improvement of BA Practices

FIGURE 13-2. BA Practice Maturity Model

© 2011 By Kathleen B. Hass and Associates, Inc.

Mature Practices	Proactive Environment	Effective BA Workforce	Business Focus
Standards and Tools	BACOE	Competent BAs	Enterprise analysis
Metrics and Measurements	BA governance	BA role definition and career path leading to VP of BA	Customer relationships
Continuous Improvement	Periodic maturity assessments	Mentoring program	Business benefit management
Knowledge Management	Periodic BA workforce evaluations	Robust training program	Competitive and feasibility studies

FIGURE 13-3. Building Blocks of a Mature BA Practice

Level	Description
Level 4: **Business Technology Optimization**	**Business Benefit: Technology Is Used as a Competitive Advantage**
	Organizations at Level 4 recognize that they need to employ advanced business analysis practices to use technology as a competitive advantage. Level 4 organizations vest accountability for business/technology optimization in a centralized organization that is responsible for management of the entire enterprise's business/technology optimization practices. Specifically, to achieve Level 4:
	• The enterprise business analysis center of excellence (BACOE) is integrated with other centers of excellence—project management (PM), quality assurance (QA), software architecture and engineering (SE)—and manages the vision, goals, objectives, and plans to achieve business/technology optimization.
	• The following process and tools are developed, piloted, deployed, and institutionalized:
	– Innovation: converting business opportunities into innovative new business solutions
	– Strategy development and translation of strategies into breakthrough processes and technology change
	– Customer relationship management
	– Organizational readiness assessments
	– Organizational change management.
	• A quantitative BA process management program is integrated with PM, QA, and SE.
	• A business/technology optimization training program is developed and required for BAs working at this level.

Level	Description

Level 3:
 	
Business Alignment
	Business Benefit: New Business Solutions Meet Business Need; Strategy Is Executed
	
	Organizations at Level 3 recognize that business analysis is essential to ensure business alignment of project goals, objectives, and the new business solutions deployed by the project teams. Level 3 organizations vest accountability for business alignment in a centralized organization that represents the entire enterprise and is responsible for management of the business alignment practices. Specifically, to achieve Level 3:
	
	• The business analysis center of excellence's mission is the centralized management of resources, contractors, and vendors.
	• The following processes and tools for achieving business alignment are developed, piloted, deployed, and institutionalized:
	  – Enterprise analysis
	  – Portfolio management support and facilitation
	  – Strategic alignment of project investments
	  – Solution assessment and validation
	  – Benefits measurement program.
	• Business/technology architecture exists for the current and future states.
	• A business alignment training program is developed and required for BAs working at this level.

Level 2:
 	
BA Framework
	Business Benefit: Business Requirements Are Managed
	
	Organizations at Level 2 recognize that business analysis is a valuable capability by vesting accountability for it in a centralized organization that represents the entire enterprise and is responsible for the management of the BA framework. The organization, often referred to as a business analysis center of excellence, assigns roles and responsibilities and establishes plans for developing, piloting, and deploying standard requirements management practices. Specifically, to achieve Level 2:
	
	• The BACOE is established and roles and responsibilities assigned to develop and manage the BA framework.
	• The following processes and tools for managing project requirements are developed, piloted, deployed, and institutionalized:
	  – BA planning and managing
	  – Requirements elicitation
	  – Requirements management and communication
	  – Requirements analysis
	  – Requirements defect prevention.
	• A knowledge management process and system is developed and is in place to archive, manage changes, and provide appropriate access to all BA process and tool assets and actual BA artifacts.
	• A BA framework training program is developed and required for BAs working at this level.

Level 1: **BA Awareness**	**Business Benefit: Business Analysis Value Is Acknowledged** At Level 1, an organization does not have plans to implement a business analysis practice, or it has plans, but they do not yet demonstrate an understanding of the value of business analysis.

FIGURE 13-4. BA Maturity Model Description

BA PRACTICE MATURITY ASSESSMENT

What is a BA practice maturity assessment? It is an independent appraisal of organizational practices that provides a foundation for advancement. It determines where an organization is today and where it wants to be in the future. It is conducted using an appraisal process based on assessment best practices. The maturity assessment compares current capabilities are compared with a BA practice maturity model based on BA industry best practices. Specifically, a maturity assessment:

➤ Measures the ability of an organization to repeatedly deliver new business solutions that meet the business need and result in the expected benefits

➤ Provides a foundation and guidance for advancement of practices through prioritized, sequential improvements

➤ Provides an indicator of how effective an organization is in meeting business objectives and executing strategy through successful implementation of new business solutions.

A BA practice maturity assessment process and practice improvement program are needed to build a mature BA practice. Together, they provide validated, accurate information about the current state of BA practices, accompanied by recommendations for improvement and support along the way. In addition, the maturity assessment determines the readiness of the organization to accept and support the new BA practices and to form a BA center of excellence.

ASSESSMENT COMPONENTS

The scope of the assessment needs to be broad, encompassing evaluation of the following components:

➤ *BABOK*® standards, including BA planning and monitoring, elicitation, requirements management, and enterprise analysis

➤ BA metrics

➤ BA tools

➤ Knowledge management

➤ BA practice support and governance

➤ Change management

➤ BA competency and career management

➤ BA training and support

➤ Project selection and prioritization

➤ Customer relationship management

➤ BA center of excellence effectiveness.

ASSESSMENT APPROACH

The BA practice maturity model can be used as the basis for several types of maturity assessments, as described in Figure 13-5. Depending on how far your organization has come in its journey to cultivate mature BA practices, we can recommend the most appropriate evaluation of your BA practice.

The approach to conducting an organizational maturity assessment can be formal or informal. In either case, the assessment is multidimensional and includes planning meetings culminating in a kickoff session, administration of an assessment instrument, and review of project artifacts and deliverables, accompanied by a series of interviews and focus group sessions. Information is synthesized, organized, validated, and documented in a data summary

Quick Practice Evaluation	Abbreviated Assessment	Full Assessment
Questionnaire administration	Questionnaire administration	Questionnaire administration
5 interviews	5 interviews 2 focus groups 3 projects reviewed	10 interviews 4 focus groups 5 projects reviewed
Kickoff and findings presentations	Kickoff and findings presentations	Kickoff and findings presentations
Data summary report	Data summary report	Data summary report
	Findings and recommendations report	Findings and recommendations report
1 assessor	2 assessors	2 assessors
1–2 weeks	2–3 weeks	3–4 weeks

FIGURE 13-5. BA Maturity Assessment Options

report and an assessment findings and recommendations report containing a two-year road map and action plan for immediate next steps.

ASSESSMENT DELIVERABLES

There are two key assessment deliverables:

➤ The data summary report

   ❯ Overall maturity rating

   ❯ Maturity rating for each component

   ❯ Strengths

   ❯ Opportunities.

➤ The findings and recommendations report and executive presentation

  › Detailed findings

  › Detailed recommendations

  › Road map to close the gaps

  › Action plan to implement recommendations.

SAMPLE ASSESSMENT RESULTS

The graph in Figure 13-6 shows ratings for one organization's BA practice maturity by component and overall, which is part of the data summary report, while Figure 13-7 shows a portion of a detailed findings report, part of the findings and recommendations report.

PUTTING IT ALL TOGETHER: WHAT DOES THIS MEAN FOR THE BUSINESS ANALYST?

Don't wait any longer before helping your organization build a mature BA practice. If you're interested in learning more about the BA practice assessment, please visit our website at www.kathleenhass.com or contact the author at kittyhass@comcast.net.

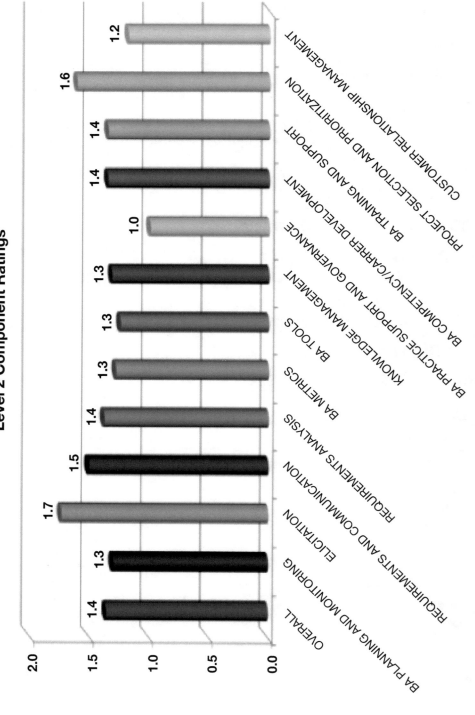

Level 2 Component Ratings

- OVERALL — 1.4
- BA PLANNING AND MONITORING — 1.3
- ELICITATION — 1.7
- REQUIREMENTS AND COMMUNICATION — 1.5
- REQUIREMENTS ANALYSIS — 1.4
- BA METRICS — 1.3
- BA TOOLS — 1.3
- KNOWLEDGE MANAGEMENT — 1.3
- BA PRACTICE SUPPORT AND GOVERNANCE — 1.0
- BA COMPETENCY/CARRER DEVELOPMENT — 1.4
- BA TRAINING AND SUPPORT — 1.4
- PROJECT SELECTION AND PRIORITIZATION — 1.6
- CUSTOMER RELATIONSHIP MANAGEMENT — 1.2

FIGURE 13-6. Ratings for BA Practice Maturity

Business Analysis Practices	Customer relationship management
Level-2 BA Capabilities	Level-2 organizations involve the customers throughout the project to continually validate and refine requirements as they learn more about the emerging solution and the customer's business needs.
Findings	Business unit representatives are involved in the early elicitation sessions, but they do not appear to continually validate and refine requirements as they learn more.
Strengths	The BAs appear strongly motivated to meet customer needs. The BAs appear to have deep business knowledge. The BAs strongly value customer satisfaction. The BAs are strong business advocates. The BAs appear to have passion in their areas of concentration.
Opportunities	Involve appropriate business unit SMEs throughout the project (29 of 40). Establish business and technology forums for collaboration: (6). • Involve the business in the changes needed to make the BA practice more mature. • Resolve issues, concerns, and misunderstandings. • Discuss the future of the business and technological needs. Assign a lead BA to projects with multiple BAs: (4).

FIGURE 13-7. Portion of Detailed Findings Report

CHAPTER 14
Innovation-Driven Portfolio Management

C hange is the norm, fierce competition is everywhere, and creative thinking is the current call to action. Portfolio management is fast becoming the critical managerial approach to drive innovation in today's business environment. Enterprise portfolio management provides the rational decision framework necessary to make the right project investment decisions—decisions that enable organizations to innovate, compete, and win in the marketplace.

To implement an innovation-driven portfolio management process and achieve organizational goals, it's necessary to move beyond strategic planning and the conventional tactical approach to project management—to *innovation management*. This entails aligning key business processes: strategic planning, strategic goal setting, portfolio management, enterprise business analysis, and complex project management.

> *Without strategy, you fail. Without strategy in a rapidly changing industry, you fail rapidly.*
>
> —Louis J. Gerstner, CEO of IBM

STRATEGIC PLANNING

In their strategic planning role, the executive management team defines the organization's future in terms of vision, mission, and strategic goals. Strategic planning focuses the executive team on the organization's reason for being and provides a foundation for selecting and prioritizing programs and projects. The strategic planning process drives portfolio management, which converts strategic goals into program initiatives and supporting projects.

In today's world, the strategic plan is considered, and should be, a living, breathing plan that changes and evolves with changes to the global economic ecosystem. However, strategy changes should be managed through a rigorous process. As the strategies change, the portfolio of programs and projects is also likely to change.

Just as the strategic plan is a living document, strategic goals are not static. Through iterative planning cycles, progress is monitored and adjustments made as needed. After selecting the right portfolio investment path, executive management must be vigilant in monitoring and adjusting the organization's project portfolio as project risk becomes too high, new opportunities arise, and change occurs in the marketplace. Today the stakes are so high that innovation is the only option, necessitating more rigorous attention to strategy, goals, and project initiatives.

PORTFOLIO MANAGEMENT BASED ON INNOVATION AND VALUE

Programs and projects must be selected and managed strategically to add value. Portfolio management is a business practice that is embedded between strategic planning and project execution. Enterprise portfolio management involves identifying innovation opportunities, assessing the business fit, preparing the business case (the business analyst's job), analyzing risks and estimating cost and schedule (the project manager's job), and selecting and prioritizing the portfolio of innovative projects (the leadership team's job). The objective of portfolio management is to create a road map that takes the organization from *strategy* to *innovation* to business *results*. Benefits include:

> ➤ ***Executive program control.*** Organizational management from the executive level down is driven by innovation; executive management balances projects like an investment portfolio.

> ➤ ***Strategic project investments.*** Portfolio management enables the leadership team to select the right investment path from a mix of potential opportunities, including research initiatives, innovative product-development activities, information technology enhancements, internal business-improvement projects, and new business endeavors.

> ➤ ***Targeted resource management.*** Through portfolio management, organizations can effectively allocate corporate assets to ensure projects have the necessary resources to meet goals and remain competitive.

> ➤ ***Achievement of strategies.*** Portfolio management allows organizations to program-manage critical initiatives to achieve key strategies and eliminate barriers to success.

Portfolio management requires a flatter, less hierarchical configuration of organizational elements to drive accountability down through the organization (see Figure 14-1). Groups within the organization each have their own responsibilities relative to portfolio management:

> ➤ The executive team is charged with defining strategy, setting priorities, and establishing strategic measures of success.

➤ Enterprise business analysts and complex project managers analyze innovation opportunities and propose creative solutions.

➤ The portfolio management team selects and prioritizes innovative programs and projects, allocates resources, and manages changes to the project portfolio.

➤ Cross-functional project teams launch and manage projects, serving as a strategic arm of the leadership team.

➤ The enterprise project management office (EPMO) or the organization's center of excellence (COE) provides services and information to all groups.

THE PORTFOLIO MANAGEMENT TEAM

As discussed in Chapter 2, for strategic goals to result in innovation and create value, they must be translated into tangible programs and projects (see Figure 14-1). The portfolio management team comprises members of the executive management team or a subset thereof. It serves as the

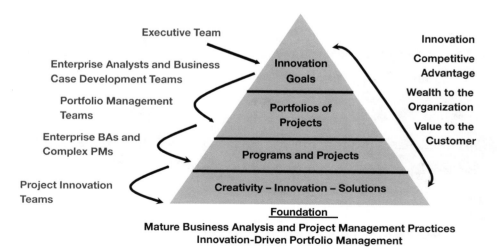

FIGURE 14-1. Innovation-Driven Portfolio Management

organization's project governance committee, selecting and prioritizing projects to maximize the value project outcomes contribute to the organization and to drive innovation.

The organization's strategic goals are translated into a portfolio of innovation projects through a process that begins with enterprise analysis—the business analyst's role—which culminates in the development of a business case to propose new projects. Decisions about project investments are no longer made within the functional silos that exist in most corporations and governmental agencies today. The portfolio management team is accountable for creating the right investment path for the enterprise. Business analysts are accountable the burden of analysis which given the senior team the information needed to make the right decisions—investing in the most innovative projects.

PORTFOLIO MANAGEMENT ACTIVITIES

The process to be followed by the portfolio planning and management team must be defined and agreed to by all team members. The process should be kept as simple and straightforward as possible. Activities include:

➤ *Development of the new idea.* The process to submit a new project idea for consideration. This should include an early filter to eliminate projects that will clearly be rejected.

➤ *Enterprise analysis/business case development.* The enterprise BA convenes a small expert team to analyze the enterprise, identify innovation opportunities, determine the most feasible solution, and build the business case to propose the new innovation project.

➤ *Project approval.* The process to review, select, and prioritize a proposed new project. This process must include making adjustments to the portfolio if a new project is approved with higher priority than current active projects. It may be necessary to reallocate resources from or even temporarily shut down an active project.

➤ *Resource allocation.* The process to allocate resources based on project priorities. Resources are finite, so management must be able to ensure these vital assets are deployed appropriately.

➤ *Project reviews.* The process to conduct control-gate reviews of ongoing projects to revalidate the business case, review current estimates of cost and time, manage risks, validate or refine the priority of a project, and make a go/no-go decision about funding the project for the next phase. Decisions are based on project status, the updated competitive analysis and business case, and the adjusted project priority. Some organizations take a two-tiered approach to project reviews, with the portfolio planning team and executive management team reviewing critical projects and a team of lower-level managers reviewing lower-risk projects.

Phase reviews and phase funding, the practice of funding only the next phase rather than the entire project, is becoming an important risk-mitigation strategy in portfolio management.

➤ *Project portfolio assessment.* The process to review, assess, and prioritize the entire portfolio of projects in terms of innovation, competitive positioning, and value. Specifically, the reviewers revisit, reaffirm, or make adjustments to the portfolio of projects based on events since the last review, new project ideas, new competitive and technology advances, and changes in business strategies. Portfolio review meetings are highly structured and typically facilitated by a member of the EPMO/COE. Ideally, this assessment is conducted on a quarterly basis.

➤ *Data management.* The process used by the EPMO/COE to store, maintain, and report information about the portfolio.

A BENEFIT OF PORTFOLIO MANAGEMENT: STRATEGICALLY ALIGNED TEAMS

As the influence of the portfolio management process permeates the organization, project team members begin to understand the alignment of their project with the strategy of the organization. Project managers are responsible for the scope, quality, risk, cost and schedule of each project, and the business analyst manages the project business case to ensure the results are on track. Project status reports directly correspond to the goals outlined on the corporate (or balanced) scorecard (see Chapter 2). The project sponsor, business analyst, and project team are accountable for business benefits. Project profitability now becomes the lowest unit of planning and control for the enterprise.

Project managers and business analysts report directly to the executive project sponsor for ongoing direction and to the portfolio planning and management team for critical milestone control-gate reviews. It is no longer necessary for information to be filtered from the project manager up through the functional chain of command.

As a result of portfolio management, cross-functional project teams become an effective strategic tool employed by management to achieve goals. Consequently, a considerable investment is made to build and sustain high-performing teams—small core project teams that are highly trained, multiskilled, highly experienced, and personally accountable. To protect this investment, management must be alert to environmental obstacles to project success. Often, management must simplify and streamline processes, eliminate outmoded policies, and remove barriers to team performance to create the optimal change-adaptive culture in which project teams can thrive.

PORTFOLIO MANAGEMENT PITFALLS

Implementation of portfolio management is not a trivial matter. Portfolio management systems continue to face ongoing challenges. Many lingering difficulties can be resolved through rigorous enterprise business analysis and disciplined, innovation-driven portfolio management practices. Some of these lingering difficulties include:

➤ Too many off-strategy projects; disconnects between spending breakdowns and priorities.

➤ Too many unfit, weak, mediocre projects; success rates at product launch inadequate.

➤ Weak go/no-go decisions.

➤ Tendency for projects to take on a life all their own; poor-performing projects are not killed.

➤ Project density: far too many projects for limited resources; cycle times and success rates suffer; project team members are over-allocated.

➤ Too many trivial projects in the new product pipeline (e.g., modifications, updates, enhancements).

➤ Not enough major-breakthrough, competitive-advantage projects (probably the result of the quest for reduced cycle time coupled with insufficient resources).

➤ Inadequate resource planning and allocation process; project team members are overcommitted. (Organizations are now using full-time, dedicated, small project teams to resolve this issue.)

DECISION-MAKING METHODOLOGY
FOR PROJECT SELECTION

Successful portfolio planning and management teams follow a structured decision-making methodology for selecting a portfolio of valuable projects. Because not all project proposals can be funded, selecting projects requires a framework consisting of a predetermined, structured, defined decision-making process.

The decision-making process is supported by tools for assessing and prioritizing projects. Portfolio planners use sophisticated data-management techniques to gather and present the information to make informed project selection decisions. Portfolio reports and graphical maps make the entire portfolio of projects visible for executive assessment. Portfolio maps are effective tools for visually demonstrating the link between projects and strategic goals. If there are no projects designed to advance progress toward a goal, it begs the question, "How do we intend to get there?" In addition, portfolio maps are created to show how projects relate (1) to the balanced scorecard dimensions, (2) to risk levels, and (3) to innovation and financial return (e.g., net present value, a project's cash value over a period of time, or economic value added, how project deliverables affect earnings).

The three overarching project selection goals that drive the process of portfolio selection are value, strategic alignment, and balance. Decision-support tools and reports are designed to support assessment of the portfolio according to these areas of business value.

> *Value:* A project should maximize the value of the entire portfolio in terms of innovation, value to the customer, and wealth to the organization.

➤ *Strategic alignment:* Project investments must be tied to business strategies.

➤ *Balance:* The organization should strive to achieve the appropriate balance of projects in the portfolio. Balance is perhaps the most difficult goal to achieve. Factors may include:

> Types of projects: research and development, IT, new product development, and product-line enhancements

> Timing: long term vs. short term; both are necessary

> Risk: some high-risk projects may provide the breakthrough that drives competitive advantage; the organization needs some "sure wins" also

> Retooling: technology or business process improvements to help the organization remain competitive.

CAREER ADVICE
The Business Case

In many organizations, portfolio management is still an immature business practice, and you may not have a business case for your current project.

A Word to the Wise

Working with other key project team members, facilitate a session to create a business case for your project. With the other project leads, present the business case information to your project sponsor for her review to ensure that you are meeting the needs of the business. Phrase the business benefits of the solution in terms of:

• Value to your customers
• Wealth to your organization
• Creativity and innovation for competitive advantage.

THE ROLE OF THE ENTERPRISE PROJECT MANAGEMENT OFFICE/CENTER OF EXCELLENCE IN PORTFOLIO MANAGEMENT

An enterprise PMO/COE is a strategic organization that serves at the direction of the executive team. The EPMO/COE is a proactive internal consulting group that provides subject-matter expertise in all aspects of innovation management. In that role, the EPMO/COE spends about 40 percent of its time facilitating and providing decision-support information to the portfolio management team. The goal is to ensure the organization is investing in the most innovative project mix. Activities include (1) metric data aggregation and balanced scorecard reporting, (2) portfolio database maintenance and reporting, (3) portfolio mapping, and (4) portfolio-planning meeting preparation and facilitation.

The EPMO/COE spends the other 60 percent of its time providing execution support to the project innovation teams. The goal is to build high-performing innovation teams that execute flawlessly, leading the earliest possible launch of the innovative product or service and helping the organization seize the opportunity to create the greatest value. Project team support activities include:

➤ Project kickoff and requirements elicitation workshop facilitation

➤ Diagnosing project complexity

➤ Coaching, mentoring, and team building

➤ Resource allocation

➤ Risk management workshop facilitation

➤ Business case review and validation

➤ Preparation for control-gate reviews

➤ Facilitation and team leadership assistance

➤ Report formatting, compilation, and publication

➤ Formal and informal training.

If your organization already has a PMO in place, it should still follow many of the steps described below when implementing or improving project portfolio management. Incorporating business analysis practices into the center will result in a project support office that encompasses both project management and BA practice maturity. Implementation of portfolio management involves an organization-wide change management effort. It does not make sense to simply train a group of project managers if the organization does not align itself in ways necessary to make project management an effective tool at all levels of the organization. Likewise, it does not make sense to conduct rigorous strategic planning without direct linkage to project delivery.

EXECUTIVE SEMINAR

Implementation of portfolio management starts at the top, with an executive seminar that introduces the concepts and elements of strategic management and explains where portfolio management fits in relation to other business management processes. The seminar is designed tenable executives to arrive at consensus on moving forward with portfolio management implementation. (This kind of seminar is also useful for conducting a review of the effectiveness of an existing portfolio management process.)

The seminar is intended to accomplish several objectives:

➤ Introducing the idea of transitioning from strategic planning to strategic management

➤ Determining the current state of strategic planning in the organization

➤ Enhancing leadership and management awareness of the importance of portfolio management, an enterprise business analysis, and complex project management

➤ Reviewing all components of innovation management

➤ Emphasizing the importance of a strategy-driven change-adaptive culture.

Topics that should be covered in the executive seminar include:

➤ The importance of a robust and dynamic strategic innovation planning process that includes the development of strategic measures

➤ The role of portfolio planning and management in ensuring initiatives are aligned with strategies

➤ An emphasis on complex program and project management enterprise and business analysis to ensure flawless execution

➤ The critical role of executive oversight through ongoing monitoring and control.

PLANNING FOR THE IMPLEMENTATION OF PORTFOLIO MANAGEMENT

Implementing project portfolio management is a significant endeavor requiring all levels of management to change their current way of selecting and managing project initiatives. The required cultural change can be painful and move slowly if the existing culture continues to determine the project selection methods. Portfolio management implementation must start at the top and trickle down to all levels of the enterprise. The change initiative must be managed as a project to avoid false starts. This can be accomplished by formally launching the initiative by means of a portfolio management kickoff workshop. The workshop brings together all key stakeholders, including the senior management team, functional managers who own project resources, senior project managers and business analysts and other formal or informal leaders within the organization. The outcome of the workshop is the charter and business case for portfolio management implementation and for establishing or expanding the role of the EPMO/COE.

PORTFOLIO ASSESSMENT AND PRIORITIZATION

After securing management commitment to implement portfolio management, the EPMO/COE conducts a current-state analysis of active projects. Serving as a resource to the portfolio management team, the EPMO/COE inventories, organizes, and makes the first attempt at prioritizing the portfolio.

PORTFOLIO ANALYSIS

The EPMO/COE determines the current state of the portfolio of projects by establishing boundaries to clearly define which projects will be subject to the portfolio management process. The portfolio planning and management team must spend its time managing only major strategic enterprise initiatives. Frequently, the organization budgets a limited amount of funding for department-specific initiatives, and those effects are managed within the business units. The projects subjected to rigorous portfolio management may include those that meet one or more of the following criteria:

➤ The project is cross-functional in nature.

➤ The initiative is designed to achieve innovation and advance one or more strategic goals.

➤ The project is high-risk, involving new, unproven technology.

PORTFOLIO DATABASE

When conducting an inventory and quick assessment of the current state of the projects in the portfolio, the EPMO/COE prepares a portfolio report describing the characteristics of each project, including:

➤ Project objective and major deliverables

➤ Phases completed and current phase

➤ Key time and cost baselines

➤ Estimated business benefits including type and level of innovation

➤ Risk rating and mitigation plans.

The EPMO/COE establishes a portfolio database to maintain an inventory of the projects in the portfolio and implements a process to keep the information current.

PROJECT PRIORITIZATION

After the current portfolio of projects is assessed, the projects can then be prioritized. The first step is to determine prioritization criteria based on strategic plans, innovation goals, and balanced scorecard performance measures. Typical prioritization criteria include organizational factors, cost/benefit analysis, customer satisfaction, stakeholder relations, risk analysis, technical uncertainty, and cultural change impact. If the organization does not have a mature strategic planning process, this might be difficult. If this is the case, a strategic planning session might need to be held to determine key strategic goals and measures.

It is imperative that the organization use a project prioritization tool to assist in making project investment decisions. Most executive teams are used to deferring to the senior team members or those members who can lobby the strongest for their pet initiatives. The EPMO/COE should develop and pilot a prototype project prioritization tool within the EPMO/COE to see if the projects appear to be prioritized appropriately. Adjustments to the prioritization tool are then made based on pilot results. The EPMO/COE then presents the prioritized list of projects and the project prioritization tool to the portfolio planning and management team for approval.

PORTFOLIO REPORTING

The EPMO/COE prepares an initial set of portfolio reports for presentation to the portfolio planning and management team. Elements of these reports include (1) projects ranked by priority, including the summary information about each project obtained during the quick assessment, (2) project dashboard reports for each project, and (3) portfolio mapping reports. The EPMO/COE determines which views will mean the most to the portfolio planning and management team and continues to refine and improve them. Remember the golden rule: keep it simple.

PUTTING IT ALL TOGETHER: WHAT DOES THIS MEAN FOR THE BUSINESS ANALYST?

Your organization may not call the individuals who conduct enterprise analysis and create business cases for proposed new projects "business analysts," but without a doubt, they are engaged in business analysis work. As organizations further develop the role of the business analyst, it will become clear that the work of converting strategic goals to valuable projects and programs is within the purview of business analysis. In the meantime, as a BA you can improve portfolio management of your current projects by:

➤ Working with your project manager and executive sponsor to make sure your projects have sound business cases.

➤ Continually validating the business case throughout the project.

➤ Working with your project leadership team to identify alternative courses of action if the business case does not remain sound.

➤ As a leadership team (the BA, project manager, business visionary, and the lead technologist), recommending a new course to the project sponsor.

As with any management practice, there are critical success factors for portfolio management—best practices that, if followed, will lead to a stable, continuously improving portfolio management process. Without understanding and following these guidelines, the implementation of a portfolio management process will be at risk.

➤ *Strategic enterprise-wide focus.* This is the foundation for selecting projects. Specific and measurable innovation goals for the entire enterprise are a prerequisite.

➤ *Simplicity.* A simple process to identify opportunities facilitates success. Most executives have an aversion to complex processes and bureaucratic paperwork. The enterprise project management office/ center of excellence does most of the work.

➤ *Early filtering criteria.* Basic requirements, often referred to as *watershed criteria*, must be met before a project is considered to be strategic and therefore a candidate for selection. Common filters include alignment with the organizational mission, business threshold minimums (e.g., return on investment, cost/benefit ratio), compliance with organizational constraints (e.g., current technology), and cross-functionality.

➤ *Standards.* If a new business idea is approved for consideration, standard templates for the business case should be used so that the decisionmakers always see consistently formatted information.

➤ *Project ranking tool.* Use standard project assessment, selection, and prioritization tools. The decision-support tool usually contains ranking criteria that are based on strategic goals and creativity and innovation levels, assigns relative weights to each criterion, determines a project's ranking based on the criteria, and calculates a score (priority rating) for each project.

➤ *Portfolio reviews.* Senior leadership holds portfolio review meetings to review the entire portfolio for balance and strategic alignment and to review new project proposals and ongoing project status at key checkpoints for go/no-go decisions.

➤ *Process support.* The EPMO/COE or a similar decision-support group will help to define and continuously improve the portfolio management process, maintain portfolio records, and prepare accurate decision-support information for the portfolio management team.

CHAPTER 15

The Business Analysis Center of Excellence: The Cornerstone of Business Transformation and Innovation

C enters of excellence are becoming invaluable to successful management of large-scale change. The business analysis center of excellence (BACOE) is emerging as an industry best practice. The BACOE is a new type of organization that serves as the single point of contact for business analysis practices. In that role, the BACOE defines the business rules, processes, knowledge, skills, competencies, and tools organizations use to perform business analysis activities throughout the business solution life cycle. It is an essential step toward implementing and maintaining a mature BA practice (see Figure 15-1).

As the discipline of business analysis becomes professionalized, it is no surprise that BACOEs are now emerging. Staffed with knowledgeable business and IT teams, who act as central points of contact and facilitate collaboration among business and IT groups, these centers are fulfilling a

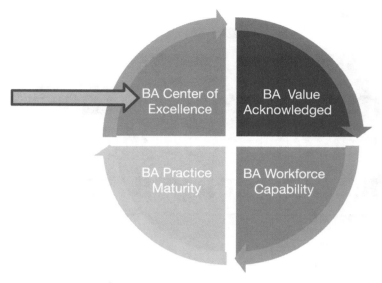

FIGURE 15-1. BA Practice Maturity Framework

vital need in organizations today by providing a business-focused home for current business analysis practices, technologies, and emerging trends.

The BACOE serves as an internal consultant and information broker to both the project teams and the executive management team. In addition, the BACOE is responsible for continuous improvement of business analysis practices. Toward that end, the BACOE continually evaluates the maturity of business analysis and implements improvements to overall business analysis capability.

HOW COMPANIES ARE USING CENTERS OF EXCELLENCE

Centers of excellence are emerging as vital strategic assets, serving as the primary vehicle for managing complex change initiatives, a business support function just as critical as accounting, marketing, finance, and human resources. A center of excellence (COE) is a team of people that is established to promote collaboration and the application of best practices.[1]

COEs exist to bring about an enterprise focus to many business issues, including data integration, project management, enterprise architecture, business and IT optimization, and enterprise-wide access to information. The concept of COEs is quickly maturing in 21st-century organizations because of the need to collaboratively determine solutions to complex business issues. The project management office (PMO), a type of COE, proliferated in the 1990s as a centralized approach to managing projects. Industry leaders are effectively using various types of COEs. Here we mention just a few.

HEWLETT-PACKARD SERVICE-ORIENTED ARCHITECTURE

Hewlett-Packard (HP) uses a service-oriented architecture (SOA) as a COE when implementing large-scale organizational change for its clients. SOA is a software design technique in which smaller services—groups of software components that perform business processes—are developed. The services are then hooked together with other services to perform larger tasks. Web services, for example, constitute an SOA. (For more on SOA, see Chapter 9.)

SOA represents a transformation in how businesses and IT develop business solutions. It is an effort to drive down the total cost of ownership of IT systems, thus freeing scarce resources to develop innovative IT applications and infrastructures. HP describes its COEs as a critical component of large-scale organizational change. It looks upon its SOA COEs as SWAT teams that are fully focused on implementing reusable service-oriented components and infrastructure.[2]

IBM CENTERS OF EXCELLENCE

IBM also is heavily invested in COEs. The IBM project management COE is dedicated to defining and executing the steps needed to strengthen IBM's project management capabilities. The IBM project management COE (PMCOE) strives to combine external industry trends with internal insight to develop project management policy, practices, methods, and tools.

IBM's PMCOE has experienced such success that in 2006 IBM announced the creation of new COEs to help customers better use information. These COEs will facilitate software and service experts in the development of six new solution portfolios: business analysis and discovery, master data management, business process innovation, risk and compliance, workforce productivity, and business performance and process management. These centers will develop products and services to better implement business analysis practices. Their goal is to help their clients transform information from utility for running their business to a competitive asset.[3]

A BACOE SUCCESS STORY

One successful BACOE is at the Bank of Montreal (BOM). According to Kathleen Barrett, former senior business consultant at BOM Financial Group and president & CEO of IIBA®, the center's formation began in early 2002. By October 2003 the center had conducted a current-state assessment; developed, piloted, and released its business analysis process standard; and received certification for its processes through the International Standards Organization (ISO). By 2005 its business analysis training and accreditation program had been rolled out.

Barrett noted that the following guidelines were critical to the successful implementation of the BMO center:

➤ Identify specific goals and deadlines (e.g., ISO certification by a certain date).

➤ Treat the COE implementation effort like a project: create a formal project team with a steering committee.

➤ Ensure senior executive support and enforcement of new practices.

➤ Link outcomes to performance pay.

➤ Adopt a formal approach to measure and evaluate compliance with standards.

➤ Involve all stakeholder areas—include everyone and overlook no one.

➤ Adopt best practices from within the organization.

➤ Provide process training to all practitioners and team members.

➤ Communicate at multiple levels, in words that mean something to each group.

Many considerations must be taken into account when establishing a new COE, including the scope in terms of disciplines and functions, organizational alignment, placement and maturity, and the implementation approach. We will now discuss these in detail.

THE SCOPE OF THE BACOE

BACOEs vary in their composition and scope. Some organizations address the entire project life cycle, whereas others focus more narrowly on requirements engineering. A center of requirements excellence, for example,

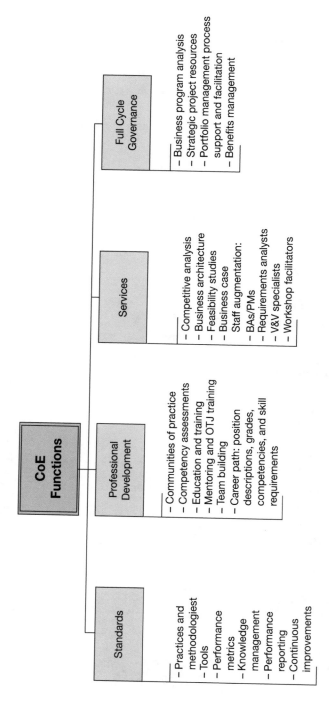

FIGURE 15-2. Typical Bacoe Functions

improves skills required for requirements elicitation, analysis, specification, and validation working to achieve maturity level 2 of the BA practice maturity model presented in Chapter 13.

A truly comprehensive BACOE, however, is broadly scoped to include the services, functions, tools, and metrics necessary to ensure that the organization invests in the most valuable projects and that those projects deliver the expected business benefits. Figure 15-2 provides a summary of typical BACOE functions.

CAREER ADVICE
Making the Most of a Center of Excellence

BACOEs are emerging all across the business landscape. However, there is a risk they will simply become one more entity imposing bureaucratic processes on already swamped project teams.

A Word to the Wise

Work with the BA pioneers and leaders in your organization to get them to understand the criticality of an innovation-driven COE. If you already have a BACOE, you are one step ahead of most. Use your influence skills to transition the center from a typical support office into an innovation-driven real-world player.

One of the critical BACOE functions is benefits management, a continuous process of identifying new opportunities, envisioning results, implementing solutions, checking intermediate results, and dynamically adjusting the path leading from investments to business results.

The role of a BACOE is multidimensional and usually includes the following components:

➤ Providing thought leadership for all initiatives to confirm that the organization's business analysis standards are innovation driven, maintained, and adhered to;

➤ Conducting feasibility studies and preparing business cases for proposed new innovation projects;

➤ Participating in the leadership of all innovation initiatives by providing expert business analysis resources; and

➤ Conducting benefits management to ensure that innovation initiatives provide the expected value to the customers and wealth to the organization.

THE INNOVATION-DRIVEN BACOE

An innovation-focused COE is capable of providing services across the gamut of the business by offering innovation and creativity training, consulting, and mentoring; providing enterprise BA resources to the project teams; facilitating the portfolio management process; and serving as the custodian of business analysis best practices.

The innovation-driven BACOE generally performs all or a subset of the following services:

➤ *Business analysis standards*

> *Methods.* The BACOE defines the methodology, metrics, and tools for use on all strategic projects within the organization.

> *Knowledge management.* The BACOE maintains the central historical database of business analysis standard tools, processes, and business architecture components.

> *Continuous improvement.* The BACOE periodically evaluates the maturity of the organization's business analysis practices and implements improvements to policies, processes, tools, and procedures.

➤ *Business analyst development*

> *Business analyst career path.* Along with the human resources department, the BACOE designs and maintains the business analyst competency model, including titles, position descriptions, and functions.

> *Coaching and mentoring.* The BACOE provides mentoring services to business analysts and project teams to help them meet the challenges of their current project.

> *Training and professional development.* The BACOE provides formal skills and knowledge assessments as well as education and training for the professional development of business analysts.

> *Team building.* The BACOE offers team-building experiences to project managers, business analysts, and team members.

➤ *Business analysis services.* Facilitators and on-the-job trainers who are skilled and accomplished business analysts provide business analysis consulting support, including:

> *Studies.* The BACOE conducts market research, benchmark, and feasibility studies.

> › *Business architecture.* The BACOE develops and maintains the business architecture.

> › *Business case.* The BACOE prepares and monitors the business case.

> ➤ **Requirements engineering.** The BACOE elicits, analyzes, specifies, documents, validates, and manages requirements.

> ➤ **User acceptance.** The BACOE manages requirements verification and validation activities, e.g., the user acceptance test.

> ➤ **Organizational readiness.** The BACOE prepares the organization for deployment of a new business solution.

> ➤ **Staff augmentation.** The BACOE provides resources to augment project teams to perform business analysis activities that are under resourced or urgent.

> ➤ **Full-cycle governance.** The BACOE promotes a full-life-cycle governance process, managing innovation investments in business solutions from research and development through deployment. It provides a home (funding and resources) for preproject business analysis and business case development. Activities include:

> › *Business program management.* The BACOE works with management and the portfolio management team to implement a 21st-century model that transitions organizations from standalone IT project management to business program management focused on innovation.

> › *Strategic project resources.* The BACOE provides senior-level business analysts to lead the business analysis effort for strategic innovation initiatives.

> › *Enterprise analysis.* The BACOE provides process coordination and meeting facilitation to the portfolio management team. It conducts

enterprise analysis activities. It also prepares the project investment decision package consisting of the business case, the results of studies, and other supporting information that provides senior management with a clear understanding of what business results are to be achieved through a major investment, including the contribution from IT to those results.

> *Benefits management.* The BACOE manages the investment throughout the project life cycle and after the solution has been delivered, measures the business benefits achieved by new solutions, and facilitates the adoption of a shared vision of the benefits realization process. It ensures that the total cost of ownership (TCO) is understood and measured. (TCO is the full-life-cycle product cost, including the cost to build or buy, deploy, support, maintain, and service the solution in both the business and IT operations.)

Although the BACOE is by definition business focused, it is of paramount importance for successful COEs to operate in an environment where business operations and IT are aligned and in sync. In addition, the disciplines of enterprise architecture, project management, software engineering, quality assurance, and business analysis must be integrated.

BACOE ORGANIZATIONAL ALIGNMENT CONSIDERATIONS

To achieve a balanced perspective, it is important to involve other groups in the design of the BACOE, including business operations, IT (e.g., enterprise architects, database managers, infrastructure support teams, service-level managers, capacity and availability managers, and application developers), PMO representatives and project managers, and representatives from the project governance group. If your organization already has one or more COEs, consider combining them into one centralized center focused on program and project excellence. The goal is for a cross-functional team of experts (business visionary, technology expert, project manager, business analyst) to address the full solution life cycle from business case development to continuous improvement and support of the solution for all major projects.

TYPES OF ORGANIZATIONAL CHANGE

One of the golden rules of organizational change management is to combine the change efforts that affect a business process under one coordinated initiative. Consider the changes your organization may have underway such as:

➤ The *executive team* might be attempting to implement or improve a portfolio management process to select, prioritize, resource, and manage critical strategic projects. In addition, management might be implementing a new corporate scorecard to measure organizational performance.

➤ For enterprise-wide projects that affect several business units, some or all of the *business units* might be implementing improvements to the same business processes that will be changed by the larger change initiative.

➤ The *IT application development and infrastructure groups* might be undergoing large-scale change, e.g. implementing a service-oriented architecture. Or the IT application group might be implementing a different software development life cycle methodology, such as the rational unified process (RUP) or agile development (SCRUM).

➤ The *IT infrastructure support team* might be implementing the Information Technology Infrastructure Library (ITIL), an internationally recognized best practice framework for the delivery of quality IT service management (ITSM). ITIL focuses on continuous improvements to IT processes to optimize service quality. It is the most comprehensive and widely used ITSM framework.

➤ The *IT enterprise architects* might be implementing a new framework to develop the business, information, technology, application, and security architectures. An architecture framework is a model that is used for developing architectures; it describes a method for designing an enterprise. The framework provides recommended standards, tools, and common language, providing order and structure to the architectural components. A number of enterprise architecture frameworks exist (e.g., the Zachman Framework, the POLDAT Framework, the Open Group Architecture Framework), but there is no accepted industry standard at this time.

➤ The *PMO* might be implementing a new project management methodology or tool.

COORDINATING AND ALIGNING CHANGE ACTIVITIES

These change initiatives must somehow be coordinated to optimize the return on the improvement efforts. COEs that support centralized full-cycle governance provide the framework for the benefits realization process from project conception to benefit harvesting. Centralized governance also provides a process of progressive resource commitment in which resources are allocated to programs in small increments through stage gates. It stands to reason, then, that a centralized COE would improve the management and coordination of strategic change initiatives.

One of the biggest challenges for the BACOE is to bridge the gap that divides business and IT. To do so, the BACOE must deliver multidimensional services to the diverse groups mentioned above. Regardless of whether there is one COE or several more narrowly focused models, the COE organization should be centralized. According to a survey on the benefits of COEs conducted by SAP America, "Organizations with centralized COEs have better consistency and coordination, leading directly to less duplication of effort. These organizations configure and develop their IT systems by business process or functional area rather than by business unit, leading to more efficient and more streamlined systems operations."[4] Best-in-class COEs evaluate the impact of proposed changes on all areas of the business and effectively allocate resources and support services according to business priorities.

BACOE ORGANIZATIONAL POSITIONING CONSIDERATIONS

Organizational positioning usually equates with organizational authority. In other words, the higher a BACOE is positioned, the more autonomy, authority, and responsibility it is likely to have. In his must-read book, *Building Project Management Centers of Excellence,* Dennis Bolles, PMP, writes that positioning the center at the highest level possible provides the "measure of autonomy necessary to extend the authority across the organization while substantiating the value and importance the function has in the eyes of executive management."[5] The success and impact of the center will likely be significantly diminished if it is not positioned at a high level. In addition, a multi-disciplined center will carry more weight and influence. Consider a model to centralize a COE integrating the project management, business analysis, and quality assurance disciplines.

Understanding the business drivers behind the establishment of the COE is of paramount importance. The motive behind establishing the center—to drive innovation—must be unambiguous because the motive will serve as the foundation to establish the purpose, objectives, scope, and functions of the center. For example, the desire to set up a BACOE might have originated in IT, because of the number of strategic, mission-critical IT projects affecting the whole organization, or in a particular business area that is experiencing a significant level of change. Whatever the genesis, strive to place the center so that it serves the entire enterprise, not just IT or a particular business area.

Regardless of the COE model or organizational positioning, the center's performance depends on the maturity of the organization's practices.

BACOE ORGANIZATIONAL MATURITY CONSIDERATIONS

The centralized COE model is important, as are the effectiveness of the strategic planning and innovation project portfolio management practices, the business performance management processes and strategies, the maturity of the IT architecture, the maturity of development and support processes, and the strength of the business focus across the enterprise.

Higher maturity levels are directly correlated to more effective procedures, higher-quality deliverables, lower project costs, higher project team morale, a better balance between cost, schedule, and scope, and ultimately added wealth for the organization. Obviously, organizations that understand the value of more mature practices achieve higher levels of value from their COEs.

BACOE IMPLEMENTATION CONSIDERATIONS

Organizations can absorb a limited amount of concurrent change while maintaining productivity at any given time. Therefore, a gradual approach to implementing a BACOE is recommended. One option is to adopt a three-phased approach moving across the BACOE maturity continuum,

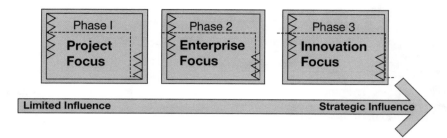

FIGURE 15-3. Typical BACOE Maturity Path

from a project-focused structure to a strategic organizational model. Figure 15-3 depicts the BACOE maturity model.

PROJECT FOCUS

BACOEs are almost always project-centric in their early, formative phase. The goals of the BACOE at this stage are to build the confidence of, and become an indispensable resource to, the innovation project teams. During this early phase, the BACOE builds trusting relationships with business analysts, project managers, functional managers, and project teams. In addition to developing business analysis practice standards, the BACOE provides services to the project teams and offers training and mentoring to develop business analysts and high-performing project teams.

ENTERPRISE FOCUS

As the BACOE begins to win confidence across the organization, it is likely that it will evolve into an enterprise-wide resource serving the entire company. At this point, the BACOE begins to facilitate the implementation of an effective innovation-driven portfolio management system. It is building the foundation to serve as a strategic business asset that provides management with decision-support information.

INNOVATION FOCUS

During the third stage of development, the BACOE is considered to be a strategic asset serving the executive team. At this point, it is well understood that business analysis has a positive effect on innovation and profitability, and that organizations achieve innovation goals through well-prioritized, well-executed projects. Emphasis at this stage is placed on achieving professionalism in enterprise business analysis through the BACOE. Strategic activities for the BACOE include conducting research and providing the executive team with accurate information on the competition, identifying and recommending viable new innovative business opportunities, and preparing business cases to facilitate project selection and prioritization.

BACOE IMPLEMENTATION BEST PRACTICES

Although there are relatively few BACOEs in existence today, best practices for developing organizational COEs to manage the business analysis function are emerging. Through a rational and defined methodology, organizations are identifying the required business analysis knowledge, skills, and abilities; assessing their current business analysis capabilities; and assembling a team to create the new entity. Best practices for establishing innovation-driven COEs combine to form a relatively standard process with four basic steps. Figure 15-4 depicts the BACOE implementation model.

STEP 1: DEFINE THE VISION AND CONCEPT

During the early study phase, it is important to create a vision for the new center. This is accomplished by researching BACOEs that have already been implemented in organizations; studying their costs, benefits, strengths, and weaknesses; and determining lessons learned.

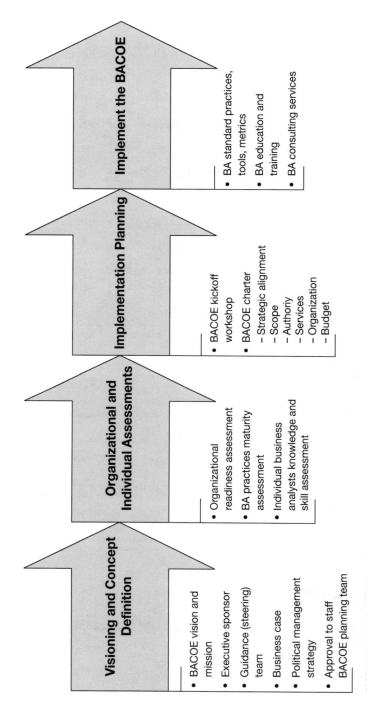

FIGURE 15-4. BACOE Implementation Model

Create a preliminary vision and mission statement for the center, and develop the concept in enough detail to prepare a business case for establishing the center. Vet the proposal with key stakeholders, and secure approval to form a small core team to conduct the assessment of business analysis practices and plan for the implementation of the BACOE. Develop a political management plan and customised manager for each key stakeholder. (See Chapter 11: Communication and Political Management Strategies to Enable Innovation).

Stakeholder Involvement

Key stakeholders include the executive enlisted as the BACOE executive sponsor, directors of existing COEs in the organization (including the PMO, if one exists), the chief information officer and IT management team, and executive directors and managers of business units undergoing significant change.

During meetings with the key stakeholders, secure buy-in and support for the concept. Large-scale organizational change of this nature typically involves restructuring, cultural transformation, new technologies, and forging new partnerships. Handling change well can mean the difference between success and failure of the effort.

Change Management

The change management techniques John Kotter and Dan Cohen describe in the book *The Heart of Change* are useful ones to consider during the early study and planning phase for a BACOE. These include:

➤ *Executive sponsorship.* A COE cannot exist successfully without an executive sponsor. Build a trusting, collaborative relationship with the sponsor, seeking mentoring and coaching at every turn.

➤ *Political management strategy.* Conduct an analysis of key stakeholders to determine who can influence the center, and whether they feel positively or negatively about the center. Identify the goals of the key stakeholders. Assess the political environment. Define problems, solutions, and action plans to take advantage of positive influences and to neutralize negative ones.

➤ *A sense of urgency.* Work with stakeholder groups to reduce complacency, fear, and anger about the change and to increase their sense of urgency.

➤ *The guiding team.* Build a team of supporters that have the credibility, skills, connections, reputations, and formal authority to provide the necessary leadership to help shape the BACOE.

➤ *The vision.* Use the guiding team to develop a clear, simple, compelling vision for the BACOE and a set of strategies to achieve the vision.

➤ *Communication for buy-in.* Execute a simple, straightforward communication plan using forceful and convincing messages sent through many channels. Use the guiding team to promote the vision whenever possible.

➤ *Empowerment for action.* Use the guiding team to remove barriers to change, including disempowering management styles, antiquated business processes, and inadequate information.

➤ *Short-term wins.* Wins create enthusiasm and momentum. Plan the implementation to achieve early successes.

➤ *Dependency management.* The success of the center is likely dependent on coordination with other groups in the organization. Assign someone from your core team as the dependency owner; she will liaise with each dependent group. A best practice is for dependency owners to attend team meetings of the dependent group to demonstrate the importance of the relationship and to solicit feedback and recommendations for improvements.[6]

STEP 2: CONDUCT ORGANIZATIONAL AND INDIVIDUAL ASSESSMENTS

It is imperative to understand the current state of the organization before building BACOE implementation plans. Once the current state is understood and documented, the vision and mission of the COE may need to be refined to ensure alignment with the cultural readiness of the organization to embrace the new COE.

Organizational Readiness Assessment

The purpose of the organizational readiness assessment is to determine organizational expectations for the BACOE and to gauge the cultural readiness for the change. The BACOE assessment team determines where the organization is on the continuum from a stovepipe, function-centric structure to an enterprise-focused organization. Additionally, it is useful to gather information about best practices already in place in the organization that might be good candidates for replication across projects.

The assessment also provides the BACOE planning team with information on key challenges, gaps, and issues that the BACOE should address immediately. The ideal assessment solution is to conduct a formal organizational maturity assessment. A less formal assessment, however, may suffice at this point.

As soon as the concept has been approved and the core BACOE implementation team is in place, conduct an assessment to understand and document the current state of business analysis practices. This assessment consists of interviews with functional managers, business analysts, project managers, and IT professionals. It is designed to determine whether the organization is ready to establish such a center and to assess the current state of the following entities:

> *Business analysts.* The individuals currently involved in business analysis practices. The assessment inquires about their knowledge, skills, experience, roles, responsibilities, organizational placement, training, professional development opportunities, and career path. The assessment also notes any other duties assigned to the business analysts, measures of their success, and performance evaluations.

> *Business analysis practices.* This part of the assessment addresses formal and informal business analysis methodologies and techniques, including feasibility study processes, business case development processes, business architecture development standards or framework, requirements elicitation, analysis, specification, validation, and change management processes, requirements prioritization and traceability methods, requirements verification (user acceptance test) methods, and any other business analysis tools, templates, and guidelines.

> *Technology.* The assessment covers requirements development and archiving tools, including powerful modeling tools, requirements repository and management systems, and team collaboration tools.

> *Governance.* Finally, the assessment looks at oversight for project selection and prioritization, ongoing reviews of BA practices, and quality assurance functions to ensure compliance with BA standards. Does the organization have a portfolio management team to select and prioritize projects? How does it manage benefits throughout the project and after solution delivery?

Organizational Maturity Assessment

If the organization is going to invest in a formal maturity assessment, we recommend conducting an assessment that determines not only the state of business analysis but also the state of project management and software engineering practices to secure a complete picture of program and project maturity. Refer to Chapter 13 for a detailed discussion of organizational BA maturity assessments.

BA Workforce Capability Assessments

It is also important to determine the skill level of existing business analysts (and project managers, if appropriate). Refer to Chapter 12 for more on BA capability assessments.

STEP 3: ESTABLISH IMPLEMENTATION PLANS

The BACOE kickoff workshop serves as the capstone event that officially launches the BACOE. All key stakeholders should attend so they can participate in the decision-making about the new BACOE.

In preparation for the workshop, develop a preliminary charter and business plan for the center describing the center's key elements. Conduct a BACOE kickoff workshop session to finalize the charter and plans and to gain consensus on an implementation approach. Refer to Figure 15-5 for a detailed list of planning considerations.

STEP 4: FINALIZE PLANNING AND FORM THE BACOE TEAM

After the workshop session, finalize the BACOE charter and staff the center (see Figure 15-6 for a typical STAFFING MODEL). Form action teams

Planning Considerations	Description
Strategic alignment, vision, and mission	Determine what we need to do
Assessment results	Include or reference the results of the assessments that were conducted: • Maturity of the business analysis practices • Summary of the skill assessments • Recommendations, including training and professional development of business analysts and improvement of business analysis practice standards.
Scope	Describe the scope of BACOE responsibilities, including: • The professional disciplines (PM/BA) guided by the center • The functions the center will perform • The processes the center will standardize, monitor, and continuously improve • The metrics that will be tracked to determine the success of the center.
Authority	COEs can be purely advisory or they can have the authority to own and direct business processes. Organizational placement should be commensurate with the authority and role of the center. When describing the authority of the COE, include the governance structure—the part of the organization to which the COE will report for guidance and approval of activities.
Services	A COE is almost always a resource center, developing and maintaining information on best practices and lessons learned and assigning business analysts to projects. Document the proposed role: • Materials (e.g., reference articles, templates, job aids, tools, procedures, methods, practices) • Services (e.g., business case development, portfolio management team support, consulting, mentoring, standards development, quality reviews, workshop facilitators, allotting resources to project teams).

Organization	Describe the BACOE team structure, management, and operations, including: • Positions and their roles, responsibilities, and knowledge and skill requirements • Reporting relationships • Linkages to other organizational entities.
Budget and staffing levels	At a high level, describe the proposed budget, including facilities, tools and technology, and staffing ramp-up plans.
Implementation approach	Document the formation of initial action teams that will begin building the foundational elements of the center. Describe the organizational placement of the center and its initial focus (e.g., project-centric, enterprise-centric, strategically focused).

FIGURE 15-5. BACOE Planning Consideration

to develop business analysis practice standards. Provide education, training, mentoring, and consulting support. Secure the needed facilities, tools, and supplies.

Then develop a BACOE business plan/operations guide, describing the implementation strategy, phases, deliverables, milestones, and a detailed budget that lists salaries and training, technology, and consulting costs. The guide should also list infrastructure requirements and plans for equipment acquisition and installation, BACOE organization formation, initial orientation and training, and communications and risk management.

PUTTING IT ALL TOGETHER: WHAT DOES THIS MEAN FOR THE BUSINESS ANALYST?

Establishing enterprise innovation-driven COEs is difficult because doing so destabilizes the sense of balance and power within the organiza-

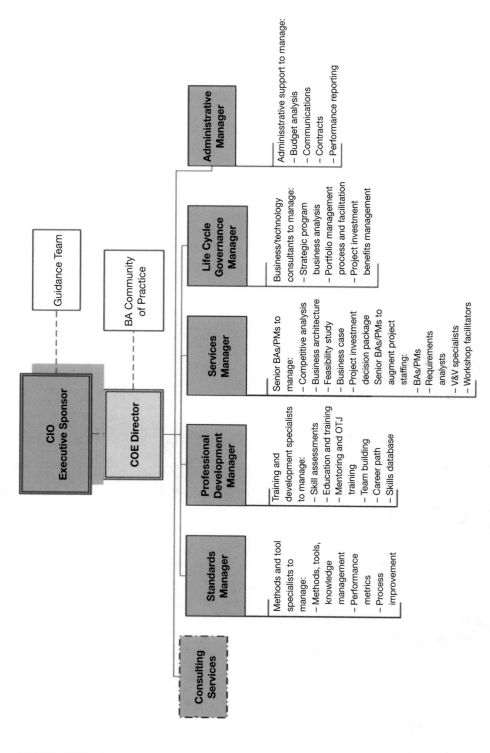

FIGURE 15-6. Typical BACOE Organization

tion. Executives are required to make decisions based on the organization's competitive position, benefits to the enterprise, and value to the customer versus their own specific functional area. Functional managers are often afraid of losing their authority and control over the resources assigned to them. In addition, project team members might be unclear about their roles and responsibilities and how they will be given assignments once the COE is established.

These ambiguities might manifest themselves as resistance to change and will pose a risk to a successful implementation. Therefore, it is imperative that robust coordination and effective communication about how the center will affect roles and responsibilities accompany center implementation. Do not underestimate the challenges you will encounter. Pay close attention to organizational change management strategies and use them liberally.

To build a BACOE that executives love and project teams trust, make the center indispensable. Provide high-quality services and support to executives, management, and project teams rather than imposing requirements and constraints. Conduct the operations of the center and design business analysis practices using lean techniques. Follow this motto: *Barely sufficient is enough to move on.*

PROVIDING VALUE TO THE ORGANIZATION

To establish a BACOE that will last, you must be able to demonstrate the value the center brings to the organization. Develop measures of success and report progress to executives. Typical measures of success include:

> ➤ *Project cost overrun reduction.* Quantify the project time and cost overruns prior to the implementation of the BACOE and for the

projects supported by the BACOE. If a baseline measurement is not available in your organization, use industry-standard benchmarks as a comparison. Other measures might be improvements in team member morale and reduction in project staff turnover; the latter may be based on the former. Be sure to include opportunity costs caused by the delayed implementation of new solutions.

➤ *Project time and cost savings.* Track the number of requirements defects discovered during testing and after the solution is in production before the implementation of the BACOE and for the projects supported by the BACOE. Quantify the value in terms of reduced rework costs and improved customer satisfaction.

➤ *Project portfolio value.* Prepare reports for the executive team that show the investment costs and expected value of the portfolio of projects; report the actual value new solutions add to the organization as compared to the expected value predicted in the business case. Be sure to use the total cost of ownership to calculate cost.

BUILDING A GREAT TEAM

When staffing the BACOE, establish a small, mighty core team dedicated full time to the center. This team should be collocated, highly trained, and multiskilled. Do not overstaff the center; the cost will seem prohibitive. Augment the core team's efforts by bringing in subject matter experts and forming subteams as needed. Select team members not only because of their knowledge and skills but also because they are passionate and love to work in a challenging, collaborative environment. Develop and use a team operating agreement. Develop team-leadership skills and dedicate efforts to transitioning your group into a high-performing team with common values, beliefs, and a cultural foundation upon which to flourish.

NOTES

1. Jonathan G. Geiger, "Establishing a Center of Excellence," *DMReview* (March 20, 2007). Online at http://www.intelsols.com/documents/2006-08%20Geiger.pdf (accessed April 2011).

2. Mark Frederick Davis, "SOA: Providing Flexibility for the Health and Life Sciences Industry," July 2006: 16. Online at http://h20247.www2.hp.com/publicsector/downloads/Technology_Davis_VB.pdf (accessed April 2011).

3. Chris Andrews, "IBM Initiative to Capture New Growth Opportunities in Information Management," February 16, 2006. Online at http://www-03.ibm.com/press/us/en/pressrelease/19249.wss (accessed January 2011).

4. SAP America Inc., *2006 USAG/SAP Best Practices Survey: Centers of Excellence: Optimize Your Business and IT Value* (February 16, 2007): 8. Online at http://www.zdnetasia.com/whitepaper/centers-of-excellence-optimize-your-business-and-it-value_wp-284768.htm (accessed January 2011).

5. Dennis Bolles, *Building Project Management Centers of Excellence* (New York: American Management Association, 2002): 11.

6. John P. Kotter and Dan S. Cohen, *The Heart of Change: Real-Life Stories of How People Change Their Organizations* (Boston: Harvard Business School Press, 2002): 7.

Suggested Reading

A wealth of resources are available to help you develop your creative leadership skills. The following suggestions include books on creativity, teams, requirements elicitation, facilitation, and portfolio management.

CREATIVITY

Kao, John. *Jamming: The Art and Discipline of Business Creativity*. New York: Harper Collins, 1996.

Kayser, Thomas. *Mining Group Gold*. El Segundo, CA: Serif Publishing, 1990.

Knowles, Malcolm. *The Adult Learner: A Neglected Species*. London: Gulf Publishing, 1990.

Rosen, Robert. *The Healthy Company*. New York: G.P. Putnam's Sons, 1991.

Senge, Peter. *The Fifth Discipline Fieldbook: Strategies and Tools for Building a Learning Organization*. New York: Doubleday Books, 1994.

TEAMS

Ancona, Deborah, and Henrik Bresman. *X-Teams: How to Build Teams that Lead, Innovate, and Succeed.* Boston: Harvard Business School Press, 2007.

Burke, Rory, and Steve Barron. *Project Management Leadership: Building Creative Teams.* London: Burke Publishing, 2007.

Guttman, Howard M. *Great Business Teams: Cracking the Code for Standout Performance.* Hoboken, NJ: John Wiley & Sons, Inc., 2008.

Hackman, J. Richard. *Leading Teams: Setting the Stage for Great Performances.* Boston: Harvard Business School Press, 2002.

Katzenback, Jon R., and Douglas K. Smith. *The Wisdom of Teams: Creating the High-Performance Organization.* New York: Harper Collins, 2003.

Mackin, Deborah. *The Teambuilding Tool Kit: Tips and Tactics for Effective Workplace Teams.* New York: AMACOM, 2007.

Scholtes, Peter R., Brian L. Joiner, and Barbara J. Streibel. *The Team Handbook, Third Edition.* Madison, WI: Oriel, Inc., 2003.

REQUIREMENTS ELICITATION

Gottesdiener, Ellen. *The Software Requirements Memory Jogger: A Pocket Guide to Help Software and Business Teams Develop and Manage Requirements.* Salem, NH: Goal/QPC, 2005.

Gottesdiener, Ellen. *Requirements by Collaboration: Workshops for Defining Needs.* Boston: Addison-Wesley Professional, 2002.

Hossenlopp, Rosemary, and Kathleen B. Hass. *Unearthing Business Requirements: Elicitation Tools and Techniques.* Vienna, VA: Management Concepts, 2008.

Wiegers, Karl E. *More About Software Requirements: Thorny Issues and Practical Advice.* Redmond, WA: Microsoft Press, 2006.

Young, Ralph R. *The Requirements Engineering Handbook.* Norwood, MA: Artech House, 2003.

FACILITATION

Andler, Nicolai. *Tools for Project Management, Workshops, and Consulting: A Compendium of Must-Have Tools and Techniques.* Hoboken, NJ: John Wiley & Sons, Inc., 2008.

Hunter, Dale, Stephen Thorpe, Hamish Brown, and Anne Bailey. *The Art of Facilitation, Revised Edition: The Essentials for Leading Great Meetings and Creating Group Synergy.* San Francisco: Jossey-Bass, 2009.

Putz, Gregory B. *Facilitation Skills: Helping Groups Make Decisions, Second Edition.* Bountiful, UT: Deep Space Technology Co., 2002.

Schwarz, Roger. *The Skilled Facilitator: A Comprehensive Resource for Consultants, Facilitators, Managers, Trainers, and Coaches.* San Francisco: Jossey-Bass, 2002.

Wilkinson, Michael. *The Secrets of Facilitation: The S.M.A.R.T. Guide to Getting Results with Groups.* San Francisco: Jossey-Bass, 2004.

Zavala, Alice, and Kathleen B. Hass. *The Art and Power of Facilitation: Running Powerful Meetings.* Vienna, VA: Management Concepts, 2008.

PORTFOLIO MANAGEMENT

Dye, Lowell D., and James S. Pennypacker. *Project Portfolio Management: Selecting and Prioritizing Projects for Competitive Advantage.* West Chester, PA: Center for Business Practices, 1999.

Goodpasture, John C. *Managing Projects for Value.* Vienna, VA: Management Concepts, 2002.

Hass, Kathleen B. "From Strategy To Action: Enterprise Portfolio Management," a white paper. Vienna, VA: Management Concepts, 2005.

Kaplan, Robert, and David Norton. *The Balanced Scorecard: Translating a Strategy into Action.* Boston: Harvard Business School Press, 1996.

The Standish Group International. *Unfinished Voyages I.* West Yarmouth, MA: The Standish Group International, 1996.

Index

The Virtual Project Management Office: Best Practices, Proven Methods
Robert L. Gordon and Wanda Curlee

Many companies are facing the challenge of addressing and implementing virtual environments. This book offers best practices for successful virtual projects and the most effective ways to create and implement a PMO in the virtual environment. For those individuals who are considering a PMO in their organization, this book provides a practical, proven implementation plan. For companies that already have a PMO, this book explains what needs to change in their environment to assist the virtual project manager and keep the company out of legal trouble.

ISBN 978-1-56726-327-5 ■ Product Code B275 ■ 250 pages

The Project Management Answer Book
Jeff Furman, PMP

In a highly accessible question-and-answer format, *The Project Management Answer Book* is a ready resource for everyone involved in project management. The book covers all aspects of project management, highlighting best practices and real-world tips and techniques, all in sync with PMI's *A Guide to the Project Body of Knowledge* (*PMBOK® Guide*). **Bonus!** Networking and social media tips for project managers as well as formulas, tips, and a quick study sheet for preparing for the PMP® certification exam.

ISBN 978-1-56726-297-1 ■ Product Code B971 ■ 416 pages

Guerrilla Project Management
Kenneth T. Hanley, M.Eng. (Project Management)

In *Guerrilla Project Management,* Ken Hanley emphasizes key project management competencies, including managing stakeholders effectively, assessing risk accurately, and getting agreement on the objective measures of project success. Focusing on these and other competencies, as well as effective tools and processes, Hanley presents an alternative approach to project management that is light, fast, and flexible... and adapts readily to the many challenges every project manager faces.

ISBN 978-1-56726-294-0 ■ Product Code B940 ■ 236 pages

Integrated Cost and Schedule Control in Project Management, Second Edition
Ursula Kuehn, PMP, EVP

This trusted project management resource, now in its second edition, includes expanded coverage of how integrated cost and schedule control works within the federal government. With the renewed emphasis on transparency in government, the processes detailed in this book are particularly relevant. The step-by-step presentation, numerous case studies, and instructive examples give practitioners relevant material they can put to use immediately.

ISBN 978-1-56726-296-4 ■ Product Code B964 ■ 319 pages

5264692R00048

Printed in Germany
by Amazon Distribution
GmbH, Leipzig